F 🌳 THE SURREY INST

Fₐ⁻⁻

Edited by
Mike Easey

4

15

D1635861

b

**Blackwell
Science**

© 1995 by
Blackwell Science Ltd
Editorial Offices:
Osney Mead, Oxford OX2 0EL
25 John Street, London WC1N 2BL
23 Ainslie Place, Edinburgh EH3 6AJ
350 Main Street, Malden
  MA 02148 5018, USA
54 University Street, Carlton
  Victoria 3053, Australia
10, rue Casimir Delavigne
  75006 Paris, France

Other Editorial Offices:

Blackwell Wissenschafts-Verlag GmbH
Kurfürstendamm 57
10707 Berlin, Germany

Blackwell Science KK
MG Kodenmacho Building
7–10 Kodenmacho Nihombashi
Chuo-ku, Tokyo 104, Japan

The right of the Author to be identified as
the Author of this Work has been asserted
in accordance with the Copyright, Designs
and Patents Act 1988.

First published 1995
Reprinted 1997, 1998, 1999

Set by Best-set Typesetter Ltd, Hong Kong
Printed and bound in Great Britain by
MPG Books Ltd, Bodmin, Cornwall

The Blackwell Science logo is a trade mark
of Blackwell Science Ltd, registered at the
United Kingdom Trade Marks Registry

DISTRIBUTORS

Marston Book Services Ltd
PO Box 269
Abingdon
Oxon OX14 4YN
(Orders: Tel: 01235 465500
          Fax: 01235 465555)

USA
Blackwell Science, Inc.
Commerce Place
350 Main Street
Malden, MA 02148 5018
(Orders: Tel: 800 759 6102
                781 388 8250
          Fax: 781 388 8255)

Canada
Login Brothers Book Company
324 Saulteaux Crescent
Winnipeg, Manitoba R3J 3T2
(Orders: Tel: 204 224 4068)

Australia
Blackwell Science Pty Ltd
54 University Street
Carlton, Victoria 3053
(Orders: Tel: 03 9347 0300
          Fax: 03 9347 5001)

A catalogue record for this title
is available from the British Library

ISBN 0–632–03459–9

Library of Congress
Cataloging-in-Publication Data

Fashion marketing/edited by Mike Easey.
    p. cm.
  Includes bibliographical references
  and index.
    ISBN 0–632–03459–9
    1. Fashion merchandising.   I. Easey,
Mike.
  HD9940.A2E37   1995
  391'.0068'8–dc20   94-36686
                                    CIP

For further information on
Blackwell Science, visit our website:
www.blackwell-science.com

Contents

List of Contributors

Mike Easey, *BA (Hons), DipM, MCIM, CertEd*, is Head of Division of Marketing in Newcastle Business School at the University of Northumbria at Newcastle. He has worked for 3 multinationals in marketing research, promotion and marketing planning positions. He is a registered DTI/CIM Marketing Consultant and has undertaken an extensive range of consultancy work including marketing for fashion manufacturers and fashion retailers. Mike Easey produced Chapters 1, 3, 7 and 10 co-wrote Chapter 5 with Christine Sorensen.

Sheila Atkinson, *MBA, PGCEd, AMCIM*, is a Researcher with the Division of Marketing in Newcastle Business School. Her working experience includes buying and merchandising for the Burton Group plc and management of design education in further education. Sheila has extensive teaching, training and consultancy experience in fashion marketing. Sheila Atkinson produced Chapter 6 on the design and marketing of fashion products.

Patricia Gray, *BSc (Hons), Dip MRS*, is a Lecturer in Marketing Research in Newcastle Business School. She has undertaken numerous marketing research consultancy tasks and has worked in publicity for the arts and for Milward Brown Market and Social Research. Patricia Gray produced Chapter 4 on fashion marketing research.

Sharon Kay, *BA (Hons)*, is Principal Lecturer in Marketing and Selling in Newcastle Business School. She has worked for Harrods and Fenwicks and has undertaken consultancy, with Mike Easey, into the UK Hosiery Market for both manufacturers and retailers. Sharon has appeared on radio discussing customer service in retail stores. Sharon Kay wrote Chapter 9 on fashion promotion.

Christine Sorensen, *BA (Hons) PGCEd, DipM*, is Senior Lecturer in Marketing in Newcastle Business School. She has worked for 3 companies in marketing positions including the print industry and franchising. Christine has considerable experience of marketing training for small business and has appeared on radio to discuss developments in promotion. Christine Sorensen produced Chapter 2 on the fashion marketing environment and co-wrote Chapter 5 with Mike Easey.

John Willans, *MSc, DipM, CertEd*, is Senior Lecturer in Fashion Marketing and Retail Distribution in Newcastle Business School. His background includes work with the Retail Sector and with textile marketing in Huddersfield. John Willans wrote Chapter 8 on fashion distribution.

Preface

If you are interested or involved in fashion you will already be aware that it is an exciting area of constant change, creativity and global commercial activity. However, skills in fashion are not enough to guarantee success, even when those skills are exceptional there is still the constant risk of failure and bankruptcy. A knowledge of marketing is essential to lessen the possibility of failure and help ensure success. To paraphrase Armani, 'Clothing that is not purchased or worn is not fashion'. A knowledge of fashion marketing can make the difference between a prototype that lingers in a dark storeroom and a garment that people really want to buy and wear.

United Kingdom fashion designers are recognized as highly skilled and the manufacturing facilities include some of the most advanced in the world. Over the last four decades our share of world markets has declined, imports have risen and many young designers have felt drawn to work in Italy, France and Hong Kong to realize their full potential. Solutions to these problems are urgently needed; fashion marketing is one of those solutions.

For the designer keen to start his or her own business, this book will offer a guide to most of the major decisions that will enable you to fulfil your creative potential and be a financial success. Established fashion businesses also need to remain competitive by asking questions such as:

- What are the major trends we should be monitoring?
- How should we set our prices?
- What is the most effective way to get our message across about the new product range?
- Which colour-wash will be the most popular with buyers?

Fashion marketing finds answers to these and many other questions.

This book has a number of special qualities that make it essential reading for anyone involved in fashion.

- It deals with contemporary issues in fashion marketing.
- It has up-to-date examples of good British practice. Over the last 20 years, all other major texts on fashion marketing have been centred on USA practice.
- This book is exclusively about fashion marketing. It is not a marketing book with a few fashion examples among the anecdotes about baked beans, industrial hoses and banking. It is all about fashion.

- There is a unique contribution on range planning which is a practical blend of sound design sense and commercial realism.
- There is a constant balance of theory and practice, with examples to illustrate key concepts. Where numerical concepts are included, there are clear worked examples to ensure the ideas are easily understood and retained.
- Each chapter contains an introduction to set the scene and a summary of key points. There are over 50 diagrams to help explain ideas and a glossary of the main fashion marketing terms is included.
- Included within each chapter is a guide to further reading. Keen fashion marketers will therefore be able to use this book as a foundation and springboard to becoming experts in specialist areas like fashion marketing research or fashion public relations.
- A coherent approach to fashion marketing is developed, based on the research, consultancy, working and teaching experiences of a team from a major centre of excellence in fashion marketing in the United Kingdom. What you will get is a systematic approach to fashion marketing, not hype or half baked ideas.

How this book is organized

Part A looks at the nature and scope of fashion marketing. In Chapter 1 the special ingredients that make for good fashion design, care for customers and commercial success are explored. All fashion enthusiasts know of some of the links between fashion and broader social change and Chapter 2 identifies those links, showing how fashion marketers are able to anticipate and participate in the process.

Part B is concerned with understanding and researching the consumer. In Chapter 3 there is a detailed look at the consumer and what he or she wants from fashion, how ideas and brands are learned and how to paint a comprehensive and sound picture of the 'muse' for the fashion designer. Chapter 4 deals with marketing research and shows how to investigate the preferences and behaviour of customers, distribution channels and competitors.

Part C looks at target marketing and the fashion marketing mix. Chapter 5 deals with choosing profitable markets to aim at and then gives an overview of possible action to meet customer requirements – the marketing mix. In Chapters 6 to 9 precise coverage is given to the design of marketing programmes to ensure the right garments (Chapter 6) are correctly priced (Chapter 7), available at the right time and place (Chapter 8) and are properly communicated (Chapter 9). The final chapter deals with planning and coordinating the whole fashion marketing process, and setting up a system that works for the consumer, offering good fashion design and delivering profits.

If, like us, you believe that consumers deserve good fashion design and that profits should flow to those who act systematically to make that happen, then join us for the challenge that is fashion marketing.

Acknowledgements

Fashion is a fascinating subject which stimulates a great many questions, an essential requirement for any academic endeavour. As mainstream marketing educators, the authors of this book brought a range of different expectations and experiences to the area of fashion. All of us have working, teaching, training or consultancy experience in the field of fashion marketing and wanted to write a book that would address real issues and would contribute, in a small way, to making the fashion industry and fashion students more aware of how marketing can enable them to be more effective in their work.

For several years the University of Northumbria has run an undergraduate course in fashion marketing. Our experiences of teaching on this course coupled with the paucity of UK texts on the subject convinced us of the need to write the book. Our research and experiences have led us to challenge the way we think about marketing and recognize the special role of design in the process. In many sectors with creative output, it has long been noted that designers need to know about marketing and marketers need to know about design. It is hoped that this book meets the needs of both groups, though in truth designers may learn more about marketing than vice versa.

Many people have helped with the production of this book with their ideas, debates and disagreements. They all have generously given time and support towards it.

Professor Mary Bromly, formerly at Newcastle Polytechnic, deserves thanks for initiating discussion about producing a book. Mary was instrumental in establishing fashion marketing education in Newcastle and always had a good understanding of the promotional dimension of fashion marketing. Professor Martin Evans, of the University of Glamorgan, deserves a similar mention for the pioneering work he undertook, along with Sheila Atkinson, in teaching marketing on the fashion marketing degree at Newcastle during the 1980s. From the Department of Design at the University of Northumbria, Barbara Rowe and Vivien Todd were most helpful in arranging visits to trade fairs and fashion firms. The late Liz Ford, also from the Department of Design, was a valuable source of inspiration and is sorely missed. Liz had a dry sense of humour and a very practical approach. Liz introduced me to the fun side of fashion as well as more complex issues like deconstructed fashion.

Geoff May, managing director of a menswear retailer, has been a constant source of ideas and information about the problems and challenges of marketing clothing. Geoff has extensive experience of buying and selling menswear and has been kind in sharing his expertise of colour, coordination and marketing of garments. From Simpson, Wright and Lowe Ltd, a number of people kindly shared their experiences and demonstrated some aspects of fashion marketing at its best. Many thanks to Jennifer Swordy, Patricia Webster and Martin Beattie. Nick Rubens, export sales manager with Westbridge International Ltd, provided his very useful views on trade fairs and the need for marketing planning in the industry.

All the contributors to this book are from the Division of Marketing in Newcastle Business School at the University of Northumbria. All the work was typed by the contributors so we cannot give thanks to secretaries, but we do thank Professor Don Cassells for providing the information technology that facilitated the exchange of ideas and production of the book. Other business school colleagues who stimulated ideas were Harry Robinson, Professor Malcolm Martin, Chris Simango and Dr Hans Christian Andersen. Dave Abson, Paul Copley, Julie Crumbley and Dr David Wesson gave considerable assistance to Sharon Kay in the production of Chapter 9.

The contributors themselves should be mentioned for their help in providing valuable ideas and data for the book and not just for their own sections. Working with others on this venture has built friendships and contributed to our critical perspectives on the subject of fashion marketing. Gratitude is felt for the efforts of Richard Miles, Publisher with Blackwell Science, who has demonstrated exceptional skills in motivation and support, to Mrs Sue Moore, also of Blackwell Science, and to Christopher Martin who edited the typescript.

Our students have constantly stimulated us to write on fashion marketing. With the absence of suitable textbooks, requests for handouts became the starting point for some of the material in this book. We have been motivated by the imaginative ways that some of our students have applied the knowledge we have imparted to particular clothing markets. The critical approach and feedback on material given by our students has enhanced the work and fired enthusiasm.

My wife, Janice, has contributed in a major way. Whenever encouragement, criticism or simply pressure to get on and do it was needed, she seemed to know just how to achieve the right result. The support given was constant and her judgments given on the first drafts were substantial and constructive.

All authors usually end these preliminaries by stating something about responsibility for errors, omissions and so on. I accept all the blame, unless, of course, I can prove otherwise!

Mike Easey

Chapter 1
An Introduction To Fashion Marketing

The fashion industry employs over 400 000 people and accounts for about one sixteenth of all consumer expenditure. The total sales of the UK fashion industry are over £8 billion a year, making fashion the fifth biggest business sector in the United Kingdom. Fashion is big business and the application of marketing plays a crucial role in achieving this. This book shows how marketing can be applied to fashion products and services.

This introduction looks at both fashion and marketing and how design and marketing work together in practice. An overview of the fashion marketing process covers the role of marketing in the fashion industry and the ethical issues raised by marketing in this context, with some practical examples of the work of fashion marketers.

1.1 What is fashion?

1.1.1 Fashion is to do with change

Fashion essentially involves change, defined as a succession of short-term trends or fads. From this standpoint there can be fashions in almost any human activity from medical treatments to popular music. For the purpose of this book though, the concept of fashion will be taken to deal with the garments and related products and services as shown in Figure 1.1.

Figure 1.1 identifies some major categories of clothing along with their main usage situations, but this list is by no means exhaustive. Fashion marketers should take a broad view of their domain – fashion is not only about clothes.

The competitive ethos of the fashion industry revolves around seasonality. The industry has a vested interest in developing new products for the customer at the expense of existing items: this process is known as planned obsolescence. Planned obsolescence is not confined to the fashion industry, it occurs in several other manufacturing sectors such as the electronics or automobile industries. While the concept of planned obsolescence can be criticized from several perspectives, many customers appreciate the continual change in fashion products and services. Unfortunately, the rate and direction of change is usually slower and less predictable than the fashion industry would like.

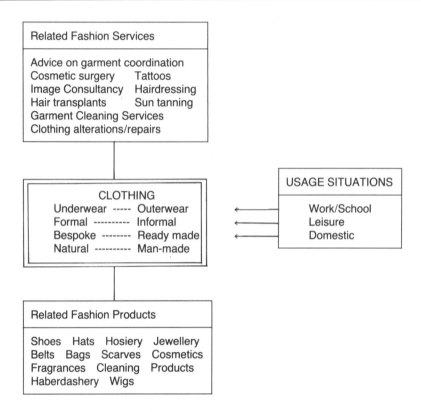

Figure 1.1 Fashion products and services.

1.1.2 Fashion is about creating

In order for the change which is intrinsic to fashion to take place, the industry must continually create new products. Used in another sense, the term fashion means to construct, mould or make. Fashion, therefore, also involves a strong creative and design component. Design skill is essential and can be seen in all products from the made-to-measure suit to the elaborate embroidery on a cardigan. The level of design can vary considerably from a basic item like a T-shirt to the artistic creations of Coco Chanel, Christian Dior, Yves St Laurent or in more recent times, Vivienne Westwood. To some the design of fashion garments can be viewed as an art in its own right, though this is a notion supported more in countries such as France and Italy than in Britain. The majority of garments sold do not come into this category, but the inspiration for the design of many of those garments may have come from works of art.

1.1.3 Fashion and marketing

The continual change that is fashion involves the exercise of creative design skills which result in products that range from the basic to the rare and elaborate. The creative design personnel provide part of the mechanism by which the industry responds to the need for change. At the same time the ability to identify products that the customer needs and will buy is also essential to the industry. Marketing can help provide this additional knowledge and the skills needed to ensure that the creative component is used to best advantage, allowing businesses to succeed and grow.

1.2 What is marketing?

Marketing is a business philosophy or way of thinking about the firm from the perspective of the customer or the potential customer. Such a view has much merit as it focuses on the acid test for all business – if we do not meet the needs of our customers we will not survive, let alone thrive. Fashion firms depend upon customers making repeat purchases and the key to such loyalty is the satisfaction of customers' needs with garments which are stylish, durable, easy to care for, comfortable, perceived value for money and all the other criteria deemed relevant by the buyer. For this reason, fashion design personnel should readily appreciate the need to understand the customer's perspective. Most designers have a mental picture of a typical customer. Fashion marketers ask how typical is that mental picture and does the 'customer' belong to a group of buyers that form a profitable prospect for the company. Notice that the notion of seeing the business from the perspective of the customer does not preclude concern for profit. Indeed, if profit is not actively sought then the firm's ability to meet customers' needs in the long term will be greatly diminished.

Marketing comprises a range of techniques and activities, some of which are highly familiar to the general public. Most people have encountered market researchers and all have seen advertisements. Other less public aspects include product development and branding, pricing, publicity, sales promotion, selling, forecasting and distribution. An overview of the range of fashion marketing activities is given later in this chapter.

Marketing is a management process concerned with anticipating, identifying and satisfying customer needs in order to meet the long-term goals of the organization. Whilst concerned with the organization's relationship with customers it is also concerned with internal organizational factors that affect the achievement of marketing goals.

1.2.1 Is marketing a solution to all business problems?

There are many views of what marketing is and what it does. To the zealots, marketing is the panacea for all business problems and can provide remedies for product failures or falling profits. Clearly, this is naive and does not recognize the interdependence of the many business and creative functions within organizations. Nor does this view fully appreciate the wider marketing environment that confronts all firms when they embark upon marketing activities.

The best marketing plans and activities can be easily and quickly undermined by changes in the economy or in competitors' actions. Such changes cannot always be anticipated. In the fashion industry, which is highly competitive and is characterized by change, the role of good fortune cannot be easily discounted. The fashion industry is well known for the high failure rate of new businesses and the regular price reductions on product lines that have not sold. Such failures are in part a reflection of the enormous risk of fashion, but some are also due to the inadequate or inappropriate application of the marketing process. It is the contention of the authors that, when properly applied, marketing will help reduce some uncertainty in the fashion industry and cut down the number of business failures.

1.3   What is fashion marketing?

Fashion marketing is the application of a range of techniques and a business philosophy that centres upon the customer and potential customer of clothing and clothing-related products and services in order to meet the long-term goals of the organization. It is a major argument of this book that fashion marketing is different from many other areas of marketing. The very nature of fashion, where change is intrinsic, gives different emphasis to marketing activities. Furthermore, the role of design in both leading and reflecting consumer demand results in a variety of approaches to fashion marketing which are explored below.

1.4   Fashion marketing in practice

Within the fashion industry there is enormous variation in the size and structure of businesses serving the needs of customers. From a small business comprising a self-employed knitwear designer to a major multinational corporation like Coates Viyella, diversity remains a key feature. With legislative changes in the European Union, the removal of trade barriers and momentous transitions in Eastern Europe, the fashion industry is increasingly an international one. This implies considerable variation in the cultural, social and economic perspective of the participants. The consequence of these variations in size, experience and perspective is that the practice of fashion marketing is not uniform at a national level let alone at an international one.

At the centre of the debate over the role of fashion marketing within firms resides a tension between design and marketing imperatives. Few fashion designers have had formal training in business or marketing, although fortunately this situation is gradually changing in the United Kingdom. Similarly, the formal training of marketing personnel can often lack an appreciation of the role of design in business. Training has tended to be separate and this, when coupled with the differing approaches of the two areas, causes divergent views. Design students were traditionally taught to approach problems as though there were no constraints on time or cost so that creativity might flourish. The assumption of much of this training was that creativity flourishes when there is freedom from

Sample statements	Fashion marketing is the same as promotion	Design should be based solely on marketing research
Assumption	Sell what we can make	Make what we can sell
Orientation	Design centred	Marketing centred
Alleged drawbacks	High failure rates Relies on intuition	Bland designs Stifles creativity

Figure 1.2 Two views of fashion marketing.

structural factors. Spontaneity, eclecticism and the willingness to take risks in challenging the *status quo* are some values central to traditional design training.

Marketing training, by contrast, embraces different values. Marketers are taught to be systematic and analytical in approaching problems. The foundation of a lot of marketing involves the setting of objectives and quantifying inputs and outputs, such as advertising expenditure and market share. Success, marketing students are taught, comes from careful research and planning, not spontaneity or ignoring market realities like competitor price levels. Due to lack of training, marketing personnel often fail to understand the aesthetic dimension of a design or many qualitative aspects of product development.

The above outlines concentrate on differences in perspective between marketing and design personnel but naturally there are areas where they share common values. Good designers and marketing personnel both recognize the need for thorough preparation and the exercise of professional skill, both understand the importance of communication, although with differing emphasis on the visual and process components and both tend to be in agreement about the functional aspects of clothing, such as whether a garment is waterproof or machine washable.

Starkly put, the designer may see the marketing person as one who constrains freedom and imagination, while the marketer may see the designer as undisciplined and oblivious to costs and profitability. Such views are stereotypes fostered by differing experiences and training and which are often held by those who do not understand the perspective of both the marketer and the designer. This difference in perspective engenders a range of views about what fashion marketing ought to be. Two views of fashion marketing are shown in Figure 1.2. These views can be labelled design-centred and marketing-centred and are detailed below.

1.4.1 Design-centred: fashion marketing as promotion

According to this view marketing is seen as synonymous with promotion. Adherents of the view state that designers are the real force, and marketers should merely help sell ideas to the public. Translated into practice this view tends to have all marketing activity carried out by either public relations or advertising departments or agencies. Customers and potential customers are seen as people to be led or inspired by creative styling that is favourably promoted. At the extreme, it is rationalized that the only people who can appreciate creative styling, in a financial sense, are the more wealthy sections of society.

Research within such a perspective is limited to monitoring the activities of others who are thought to be at the forefront of creative change i.e., film directors, musicians, artists etc. Many great fashion designers subscribe to this view and have run successful businesses based upon the above assumptions. The principal weakness of this approach is that it depends ultimately on the skill and intuition of the designer in consistently meeting genuine customer needs and consequently earning profit.

1.4.2 Marketing-centred: design as a research prescription

Here marketing is dominant and regards the designer as someone who must respond to the specifications of customer requirements as established by marketing research. Detailed cost constraints may be imposed and sample garments pretested by, for example, retail selectors who may subsequently demand changes to meet their precise needs. Several high street stores operate systems not too far removed from this, with merchandisers and selectors exerting considerable control over the designer. The result, according to many, is a certain blandness in the design content of garments available from such high street outlets.

It is argued that marketing constraints have strangled the creative aspects of design. Taking profitability as a measure of popularity, this restrictive prescription for design seems to work for many firms. Whether popular acceptance of fashion designs equates with good design is another matter.

1.4.3 The fashion marketing concept

There is another way to view the relationship between marketing and design and this is termed the fashion marketing concept. That good fashion design only requires sufficient promotion to succeed is a view applicable to a very limited number of businesses—usually those producing expensive garments for an elite market. The alternative view of fashion design as a function of marketing research fails to recognize that many people either don't know what they will like until presented with choices, or that their preferences change over time. For example, many who profess to hate a design seen on the catwalk may later come to like it when they try the garment themselves or realize others have signalled acceptance. Good fashion design can challenge conventional views. It should be recognized that consumers vary in the conservatism they have towards fashion styles and also the speed and readiness with which they change their opinions.

A simple model of the interrelationship of fashion design and marketing can be seen below:

Figure 1.3   The fashion marketing concept.

In the matrix above it can be seen that low concern for customers, profit and design leads to failure. This occurs as a consequence of over-estimating design ability whilst disregarding customers' preferences and the need for profit.

The fashion marketing concept attempts to embrace the positive aspects of high concern for design, customers and profit by recognizing the interdependence of marketing and design. If designers understand how marketing can enhance the creative process and marketing personnel appreciate that within the fashion industry design can lead as well as respond to customer requirements, progress can be made. Market researchers can establish the sizing information customers want on garments and can also analyse reactions to several provisional illustrations, but they cannot produce detailed styling specifications. Marketing as applied to the fashion industry must appreciate the role of design.

This section has discussed a number of approaches to fashion marketing. Many companies have embraced to fashion marketing concept and have demonstrated equal concern for design, customers and profits. For example, in recent years a number of winners of major fashion awards have achieved success not only in terms of design but also in terms of sales and profit. Thus the fashion marketing concept is not just a theoretical model, it does work in practice and this book sets out to develop it further.

1.5   How fashion marketing can help the fashion industry

The vast output and profits from the fashion industry come not from the designer collections seen on the catwalk but from items sold in high street stores. To put the impact of designers in perspective, one only has to note that the British Fashion Awards' Designer of the Year will often have annual earnings that amount to less than a day's sales for one large retailer in the Sears' group. Even so the designer collections are given extensive coverage in the fashion press where each season more than 150 collections are reviewed within a matter of weeks. Reporting and promotion of these collections is suffused with hyperbole, excitement and genuine enthusiasm by many who attend, the catwalk exhibitions being viewed with a range of perceptions from incredulity to sheer entertainment. However, few people see the direct link that some less experienced commentators assert exists between the garments on the catwalk and 'what we will all be wearing next season.' The influence of the designer collections on everyday apparel purchases is complex and will be considered in later chapters on the fashion consumer, product design and fashion promotion.

The main concern of fashion marketers is therefore the design and sale of garments to the majority of the public. for that reason, the techniques described in this book will concentrate on high street fashion rather than haute couture.

Many people in fashion industry have aspirations to run their own business. Indeed, the industry is characterized by many small firms and regrettably many failures. This book embraces the fashion marketing needs of people starting their own business; it does not, however, extend to all the needs of small businesses particularly the financial and legal aspects of new ventures. For the new entrepreneur the chapter on marketing research will provide a sound basis on which to start building a business plan. The marketing component of the business plan is covered in the last chapter of the book.

Medium and large businesses are also catered for. The need for cooperation and communication between the various levels of distribution in this sector is so important that manufacturer,. wholesaler, importer and exporter will all benefit from understanding the structural aspects of the marketing of clothing and related products and services. Many of the principles and techniques described in detail as applicable to the United Kingdom are transferable to other markets. For example, United Kingdom mass media data are given in the chapter on fashion promotion, but criteria for designing campaigns and selecting media are also given; these criteria are readily transferable.

1.6 What fashion marketers do: five examples

To give an overview of the sort of activities fashion marketing personnel engage in, five examples will be given. A key point to note is that job titles don't always accurately reflect what people do. In fact, few people are called fashion marketing managers, but many carry out functions that are fashion marketing, for example those with job titles such as selector, merchandiser, sales executive or public relations consultant.

1.6.1 Fashion marketing research

A fashion marketing researcher may investigate the market shares of competitors and trends in those shares. Through a group discussion with potential consumers they may discover that a possible brand name has negative connotations and needs rethinking.

1.6.2 Fashion product management

A design manager may be concerned with producing a range of shirts for a major retailer. The shirts must coordinate with other garments such as jackets, trousers and ties, all of which may be provided by other manufacturers. The design manager must collect and pass on information to ensure designers are adequately briefed. Later the manager will be required to sell the designs at a presentation to the retailer, usually in the face of fierce competition. The design manager's knowledge of the retailer's customers and an awareness of his or her own company costs will enable an effective marketing function.

1.6.3 Fashion promotion

A manufacturer of corporate workwear may have produced a range of clothes suitable for staff working in small independent restaurants. After careful research and planning the manufacturer may decide that a brochure in needed as part of the promotional effort. The brief to be given to the person preparing visual and textual material for the brochure will include an estimate of the number of brochures needed and a list of addresses – essential fashion marketing tasks.

1.6.4 Fashion distribution

An owner of a retail outlet selling her own specially designed millinery wishes to expand to needs to research a few options including franchising her business, obtaining concessions in selected department stores and linking with a leading womenswear designer to produce new complementary ranges each season. Marketing research, an analysis of the status of the business along with the preparation of a future marketing strategy, are the major fashion marketing activities needed here.

1.6.5 Fashion product positioning and pricing

A major retailer discovers that a competitor is selling imported silk lingerie similar in design and quality to its own, but at prices that are 20% lower. A fashion marketing decision must be made about the positioning and pricing of the product, taking into consideration the strategic goals of the company as well as a the price sensitivity of its customers.

1.7 Ethical issues in fashion marketing

The practice of fashion marketing is often criticized. These criticisms can be classified into two types, the micro issues and the macro issues.

Micro issues concern particular products and services where consumers may feel that they have not been fairly treated or that they have been misled. Most customers have bought clothing that has fallen below expectations by, for example coming apart at the seams or shrinking in the wash. These problems may occur due to poor quality control or at worst a callous attitude towards customers. Sadly, the view of customers as mere punters to be exploited does exist in some parts of the fashion industry but it is a short-sighted attitude as lack of repeat business, legal redress and negative word of mouth are all possible consequences. Given the number of items of clothing bought each year, however, some errors are inevitable and the issue really revolves around how the seller deals with the complaint. According to the fashion marketing concept we should be concerned about long-term consumer welfare as this is the key to building and retaining profitable custom.

The quick and fair correction of genuine errors reinforces the message to the customer that the retailer cares about long-term customer welfare. Unfortunately, some staff are placed in positions where their own interests may not coincide with those of the firm or the customer – those who work on a commission only basis, for example. Such practices should be condemned as they lead to an undermining of public confidence in the fashion industry.

Macro issues are broader and emerge not from the conscious conspiracy of individuals or groups of individuals but as unintended or unanticipated consequences of certain activities.

The most obvious example is the criticism that the bulk of the fashion industry is lacking in sensitivity to environmental issues in that it encourages a throw-away society, conspicuous consumption and unnecessary use of packaging. Though not without detractors, the Body Shop may lay claim to attempting to address some environmental concerns. Other attempts to address such concerns although on a relatively small scale include so-called 'environmentally friendly' or 'green' fibres and recycled wool. Recent German legislation requires all new clothing to by recyclable be the year 2000.

However, the charge of encouraging a throw-away society is a problem that is likely to recur with sharper and more vehement focus in the future. The public response to the various anti-fur campaigns run by Lynx and others during the 1980s in Britain, reduced the market for fur products by 90% and transformed a status symbol of the rich to an item of derision. 'Green' issues in fashion marketing are examined further in Chapter 2.

Another example of a macro issue is the use of particular models to show garments in advertising material or on the catwalk. Critics allege that this can cause damage ranging from supporting an image of women as mere sex objects to acting as a contributory factor in dietary problems of adolescent females. The over-representation of young, tall and slim female models raises many issues, not least of which is the sensitivity of some promoters to the responses of the audience. The non-response or excuse of 'We have to do it, because everyone else does it' may reveal an unwillingness to research other less potentially harmful ways of promotion. In an industry with an abundance of creative talent, it is surprising to find such conservatism.

1.8 An overview of the fashion marketing process

Fashion marketing can be viewed as a process and Figure 1.4 below illustrates that process. It also gives an indication of the structure of the book and how various parts link together.

All firms operate within a wider commercial environment that influences their activities. Changes in value added tax may inhibit demand for certain garments whereas a fall in unemployment may stimulate demand for workwear. These two simple examples illustrate how changes in the marketing environment can have significant effects on the operation of fashion firms. The marketing environment and how to analyse it are covered in Chapter 2.

Central to the concept of fashion marketing is the role of the customer and, Chapters 3 and 4, deal with understanding and researching the fashion purchaser. In Chapter 3 the behaviour of consumers will be discussed. In particular, there will be an examination of the reasons why people buy particular garments: what influences them and what criteria they use. Clothing may be an expression of how people wish others to see them, it may denote membership of a certain group or represent a particular lifestyle. To understand customers' aspirations and expectations about clothing fully, relevant psychological and sociological factors are examined in Chapter 3.

Chapter 4 takes the understanding of customers' behaviour one step further by looking at how data concerning this behaviour are obtained, namely marketing research. This research can also involve the study of competitors and analysis of the company's own marketing efforts.

In Figure 1.4 the term marketing mix is used to describe the combination of variables used by the fashion marketer to meet the needs of specific groups of customers known as target markets. The selection of target markets and the management of the marketing mix are discussed in Chapters 5 to 10 of the book.

Here is an example of how a variable may be adjusted using an example

Figure 1.4 The fashion marketing process.

concerning price. A firm may decide to charge low prices and sell large quantities making a small profit on each item, but a large profit in total. A consequence of charging low prices may be that certain outlets are selected because their image is compatible with low prices. The concept of the marketing mix and target marketing are dealt with in Chapter 5. The actual components of the marketing mix are known for the sake of simplicity as the 4 Ps i.e. Price, Product, Place and Promotion and these are covered in Chapters 6 to 9. The role of design research, integral to product design and development, is covered in Chapter 6.

Putting all aspects of the marketing mix together to achieve the goals of the organization is the most important marketing task. Activities must be planned, coordinated, implemented effectively and the results monitored. The final chapter deals with fashion marketing planning.

1.9 Summary

This chapter has introduced and defined fashion and marketing, and how fashion marketing:

- emphasizes the importance of design
- aims to meet customers' needs
- helps to achieve corporate goals.

There followed an examination of the practical side of fashion marketing:

- how fashion marketers work
- the ethical issues.

The chapter concluded by:

- examining the business environment, and the place of fashion marketing within it
- introducing the ideas of marketing research and consumer behaviour
- outlining the concepts of target marketing and the fashion marketing mix.

Further reading

Baynes, K., Brochocka, K. and Saunders, B. (1990), *Fashion and Design*, Penguin Books, Middlesex.

Drew, L. (1992), *The Business of Fashion*, Cambridge University Press, Cambridge.

Lancaster, G. and Massingham, L. (1993), *Marketing Management*, McGraw-Hill, Maidenhead.

Tomlinson, A. (1990), *Consumption, Identity and Style: Marketing, Meanings and the Packaging of Pleasure*, Routledge, London.

Chapter 2
The Fashion Market and
the Marketing Environment

2.1 Introduction

A market is a place for buying and selling, for exchanging goods and services, usually for money. The fashion market is unusual because until early this century it was almost solely the domain of kings, queens, aristocrats and other important people. As will be seen, great changes, mainly due to technology, mean that we now have a fashion marketplace open to everyone.

Fashion can be a reflection of the time from utilitarian clothing of the war years to the yuppie look of the buoyant 1980s. Fashion also can be a reflection of individuals. Clothes are often chosen to reflect among other factors our age, gender, lifestyle and personality.

Because fashion is both a reflective and yet creative discipline it is necessary for fashion marketers to be aware of the factors surrounding the market and develop a broad understanding of the issues that can affect the garments that are seen in any high street store.

2.2 The development of the fashion market

2.2.1 Origins of the modern fashion market

Until quite recently, fashion had always been élitist and was used by its adopters to show they were above the common people. Even the inventions of the eighteenth and nineteenth century; the spinning jenny, the water frame and the sewing machine have not had as great an effect on the market as have cultural changes and the explosion of the media during this century.

The end of the First World War, in 1918, really marked the start of mass fashion. Style began to be influenced by the fashion designers of Paris, Milan, New York and London. In the 1930s film personalities and later pop stars all played their part in spreading or even starting fashion trends.

Some fashion styles are more easily explained than others. The Second World War forced hemlines up because of a shortage of material. In the 1950s newer freer styles made corsets less and less necessary. However, other fashions are less easily explained and are regarded by some as merely a whim or the market just looking for a change.

Technology played its part in advancing mass production methods, so that from the 1930s onwards ordinary people could buy copies of designer fashions

Table 2.1   Some major developments in fashion.

Pre 19th Century	Fashions only for the rich and powerful
1918 onward	Start of mass fashion
1930s	Film personalities influencing popular clothing
1939–45	World War II – raised hemlimes
1950s and 60s	Freer styles, fewer control garments
1970 to 1990s	Growth of multi-nationals and mass media influence

from high street stores within weeks of the big fashion shows.

The media started to become an important influence in the late 1970s. People became more selective in what suited them, magazines and books advised them on creating their own style. Designers could no longer dictate the styles as they had until the 1960s. 'Street fashion' styles developed by young people themselves in towns and cities also affected designer clothes.

London was at the forefront of the fashion scene in the 1960s and early seventies. Mary Quant was in her heyday and her clothing was famous the world over. It was the time of Carnaby Street, and Biba was made famous by Barbara Hulkaniki.

The influence of royalty on fashion made a comeback with the Princess of Wales in the 1980s as many women copied the lace and ruffles which she wore.

While not the first to introduce lifestyle segmentation to the market, George Davies, then chief executive of the Next chain, is undoubtedly the best known. His retailing phenomenon, targeting a particular age and lifestyle group, exploded onto the marketplace and had many other high street retailers following suit.

Changes toward a healthier lifestyle advocated by the medical profession and the increase in leisure time has encouraged people to take up more sport, particularly jogging and aerobics, and so the clothing from these pursuits has moved into everyday wear.

The future for the fashion industry is mapped out, perhaps more than at any time in its history. Influences from the demographic structure, concern for the environment and further adoption of new technologies are all inevitable. These factors could stifle designers if they are not careful or could offer them greater challenges than any they have had to face so far.

2.2.2 Recent developments in the fashion market

Consumer demand for clothing is now more fragmented and discerning. Retailers are wary of carrying high levels of stock, major demographic changes are occurring, and many different styles and fabrics are available. These have all resulted in the mass market for clothing being fragmented and are eroding the advantages of long-run manufacture.

Previously the UK textile industry had a reputation for being dictatorial and short on choice. This was blamed on the nature of the relationship between retailers and manufacturers. Clothing retailing was dominated by a few large groups who exercized enormous power in the wholesale market for garments

and fabrics. Retailers emphasized basic garments with very little fashion c
and Marks and Spencer in particular set very detailed specifications for fa
making-up and quality. Manufacturers such as Courtaulds and Carrington Vi
geared their production to large volumes of basic fabrics for a few major
customers. It became uneconomic to deal with orders that were either small or
required much design detail. Competition among retail chains was over the price
and quality of garments.

Since then the market share of the multiple retailers (such as BhS and Marks
and Spencer) has been affected both by the emergence of smaller specialist
chains (Benetton, Next) and the grocery supermarkets (Asda, Tesco), many of
whom have gained market share by importing low-cost garments. To avoid
competing with the low-cost imports, the big retailers have responded by
increasing the speed with which they introduce fashion and style changes. This,
in turn, has forced suppliers to manufacture shorter runs of garments with higher
design and fashion content. In some parts of the market there has been been a
distinct shift in retail competition away from an emphasis on garment price to
non-price factors, such as design, quality and fashion.

2.3 The fashion market: size and structure

2.3.1 Structure of the fashion market

Apart from technology, another reason why fashion is now available to the
masses is that there are several levels at which fashion clothing functions as
shown in Figure 2.1 below:

- **Haute couture houses** are the major fashion houses of the world, run by
  recognised, internationally famous designers. They show their collections at
  least twice a year and sell individual garments for thousands of pounds. For
  many designers the catwalk shows are essentially a publicity exercise for the
  many goods that are sold under their name such as perfume and accessories.

Figure 2.1 Levels of fashion.

- **Designer wear** is shown at *pret à porter*. The move into ready-to-wear clothing by designers meant that they could offer their stylish designs and high quality to a wider audience. The garments are still highly priced, although in hundreds of pounds sterling rather than thousands. They are to be found in the designers' shops, independent stores and some of the more exclusive department stores. Designs are not unique, but are still produced in limited numbers and, although some garments are produced abroad, there is very strict quality control.

- **Mass market or street fashion** is the market area in which most people buy their clothes. New fashions can be in the high street stores extremely quickly and what the customers lose in exclusivity they can make up for in value for money. This is one area of the market that is undergoing many changes now and this chapter will look at how it is being affected.

This three tier view of the market is perhaps over simplistic as there are many strata and price levels between the ones mentioned. Many customers do not stick to any one level when buying their clothes.

The more affluent will buy several haute couture outfits but turn to designer wear for everyday. Women who mostly buy designer ready-to-wear may occasionally splash out on a couture dress for a very special occasion. Those who generally only buy mass market clothing may still buy designer wear occasionally if only from the discounted rail. At times it is difficult to identify the origin of our clothing and to decide who has the power in the marketplace. Is it the fibre and fabric industry who, after all, make the cloth for the garments? Is it the designers? Or perhaps the retailers are the power base in the market? Ultimately it should be the customer but traditionally the fashion market has been one where the customer was dictated to and so merely followed along almost blindly.

The fashion flow chart in Figure 2.2 illustrates the flow of goods between the various participants in the marketplace. Later it will be seen that there is even more choice in deciding where the goods will be manufactured (see the section on suppliers later in this chapter).

2.3.2 Size of the fashion market

None of the three levels of the market have shown any real growth in domestic clothing demand since 1988. Once the world's greatest cotton spinner and

Table 2.2 Consumer spending on clothes 1985–90.

Average percentage change over previous year at constant prices

1985	1986	1987	1988	1989	1990
+9.2	+9.8	+5.4	+4.4	−2.0	−0.6

Source: TMS Partnership

Figure 2.2 Fashion flow chart.

weaver, the UK now ranks only fifth in the EU behind Germany, Italy, France and Spain in the production of cotton type yarns and fabrics.

From 1978 to 1982 clothing output fell by 18%; and employment in textiles fell by 37.6% and in clothing by 30%. The output of the textile sector was at a low point in 1982 and, although it has risen every year since up to 1987 as the consumer spending figures in Table 2.2 show, it is still lower than in the early 1970s according to Cambridge Econometrics.

Despite this recent decline in the industry, clothing and textiles together are still Britain's fifth largest industrial sector with a £15 000 million turnover; £4500 million of exports and around 450 000 jobs.

Exports, up by 18% in 1990 from the late 1980s, have proved to be the saviour of many clothing producers. Overseas performance has improved, and after poor sales in the late 1980s the market has stabilized and, in some cases, boosted domestic clothing production. Consumer spending in this area is still

Table 2.3   Recent decline in employment figures (in '000s, in June each year): manufacturing, and fashion as a subset.

	1985	1986	1987	1988	1989	1990
Manufacturing Industries	5254	5122	5049	5098	5080	5046
Textile, leather, footwear, & clothing	550	555	543	546	514	491

substantial although it has shown a decline since the boom period of the seventies.

2.3.3   Employment in the fashion sector

The clothing industry has always been a major employer in the UK but two main factors have reduced this in recent years. Technology now being introduced has reduced the need for many workers, particularly in the more skilled areas of pattern cutting as much of this can be computerized. The computer systems still need to be manned by a skilled workforce, but retraining will need to be done and still there will be redundancies.

The other major problem has been the stiff level of cheap competition from abroad. With an inability to raise prices in the face of a depressed domestic market and crippled by large debts, many firms have had to make savage cuts in their labour force and investment plans as the alternative to going out of business. Table 2.3 shows the fortunes of the fashion industry in the context of the decline of manufacturing.

2.3.4   The current role of London in the fashion business

Fashion centres of the world have always included London, even before the era of Carnaby Street and Mary Quant, but recently designers have been choosing not to show in London. In 1989 over 250 designers exhibited their collections in London Fashion Week. Now this no longer has the financial backing of the French *Chambre Syndicale* (the French organization that decides which fashion houses may join the ranks of the haute couturiers) and the number of exhibition is declining.

This shift away from London is of concern to the industry, more for the knock-on effect that it will have on everything from employment to tourism. 'British designers generate relatively little income (around £185 million a year) but they contribute hugely to the overall image of British clothing.' Mark Fisher, Labour spokesperson for the arts in March 1992.

2.4   Marketing environment

Fashion is ultimately about change. Every season there are new fashions that lead to obsolescence of last year's clothes. Many of these changes are brought

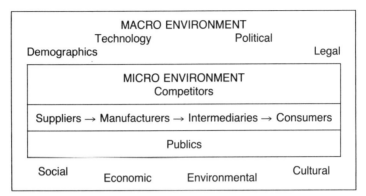

Adapted from Kotler, P. (1994), *Marketing Management*, 8th edn., Prentice Hall International, New Jersey.

Figure 2.3   The marketing environment.

about by designers trying to create something new to satisfy customers, but others are because of influences beyond the control of designers or manufacturers. These are all gathered together in what is called the marketing environment as shown in Figure 2.3. Some changes occur very slowly while others can affect the market much more quickly; some are within a company's control and others are way beyond it.

2.5 Micro marketing environment

Factors which ideally are within companies' control are their suppliers, marketing intermediaries (which help to get the goods from the factory to the consumer) and the consumers themselves. For customers the providers of fashion may seem to have a variety of sources, for instance the designer who has the idea for the style, the manufacturer who makes up the garment, or the retailer to whom the consumer goes to buy the garment.

2.5.1 Designers

While Paris is often thought of as the fashion capital of the world in fact there are five main cities supplying designs and new ideas to the international market.

Paris is historically seen as the fashion capital and has the edge on many other cities as its fashion industry is taken very seriously by government and citizens alike. The haute couture designers are protected by the French *Chambre Syndicale* which has strict codes of practice for any designer wishing to style him or herself as a haute couture house. The main French designers are Yves St Laurent, Chanel (now run by Karl Lagerfeld), Christian Dior, Pierre Cardin, Jean Paul Gaultier, and Christian Lacroix.

Milan is the other fashion capital of Europe, and Italians have always taken fashion very seriously. There are probably fewer well known designers such as

Giorgio Armani, Gianni Versace, and Emanuel Ungaro, but Italy is a country whose people and retail set-up with many more independent stores, is a successful environment for young designers.

London is no longer the focal point of fashion that it once was though it still produces many internationally influential designers. Many are quite small fish by international standards but others have their designs bought by the rich and famous from all over the world. Although London is no longer a major centre, the UK clothing industry is still significant and exports are actually growing in contrast to internal sales. The city also retains many successful designers such as Bruce Oldfield, Norman Hartnell, Emmanuels, Jasper Conran, Vivienne Westwood, Paul Smith, Katharine Hamnett, 'Joseph Ettedgui', Victor Edelstein, Alistair Blair, Rifat Ozbek, John Galliano, Body Map, and Jean Muir.

In America the major centre in New York. To a considerable extent American fashions are confined to the home market, although all the big names are known and bought internationally. American designers include Ralph Lauren, Calvin Klein, Bill Blass, Oscar de la Renta, and Donna Karan.

Tokyo, the centre of the Japanese clothing market, has a reputation for a distinct style and for almost a lack of colour. There has been considerable growth in recent years at the top end of the Japanese clothing market by designers, especially since 1981 when Comme des Garçons and Yamamoto took Paris by storm. This is a fashion city that is destined to continue to grow with such designers as Yohji Yamamoto, Comme des Garçons (Miss Rei Kawakubo), Issey Miyake, and Kenzo.

The Middle East is now considered the sixth fashion terminus of the world, not because any designs come from here but because it is where the submerged 11% of the fashion industry goes. Much clothing is bought by women either within or while on holiday from such places as Dubai, the United Arab Emirates, Kuwait, Bahrain, and Saudi Arabia.

The overall market pattern now is that designers either make for themselves or subcontract to British or overseas manufacturers. Likewise retailers either have their own designers and make them up in their own factories; subcontract their own designs to home or overseas manufacturers; or buy garments designed and made up by other companies.

2.5.2 International sourcing

The UK clothing industry is being squeezed further between the highly price sensitive volume market which gets its supplies from low-wage economies and the quality end of the market which is increasingly supplied from Europe. It is both surprising and worrying that imports from relatively high cost producers on the continent have continued to grow strongly, even during the recession.

Supplies come from 3 main sources:

- UK and Europe (Germany, France, Italy, Portugal, Eire, and Turkey) making up about one third of the market. Italy has traditionally been the major player here but German exports to the UK are increasing rapidly.

- Far East (Hong Kong, China, South Korea, Thailand, Taiwan, Malaysia, Indonesia, and Mauritius). Of this group Hong Kong is by far the largest, having increased its exports to the UK by over a third in the last five years.
- Asia (India and Pakistan).

The latter part of the 1980s showed some interesting shifts in the trading fortunes of many of our overseas suppliers. The greatest increases in supplies over the five year period from 1985 were from India, Turkey and particularly China.

The main shifts in supply are due to lower wage rates and suppliers seeking countries that are under-utilizing their quotas under the Multi Fibre Agreement, (MFA) which will be discussed shortly, although this will increasingly become less important as quotas are abandoned.

Imports from Eastern Europe are expected to rise, as these countries are given preferential access by the European Union in order to aid their economic restructuring.

While the Multi Fibre Agreement (see below) is supposed to control imports, some UK manufacturers believe that the Chinese have the economic capability to dominate every market including the rest of the Third World.

Even Marks and Spencer who used to boast that its garments were almost all produced in the UK, no longer advertises the figure but estimates put it down to 70% or less.

2.5.3 Manufacturers

Despite the apparently gloomy picture that the move to global sourcing is painting, the figures still show a healthy situation for the UK manufacturing market.

Many larger clothing companies have a network of suppliers. Marks and Spencer's supplier list includes:

- I J Dewhurst Holdings plc – 90% of whose sales go to M & S
- Coats Viyella – £300 million of sales to M & S
- Alexon Group – who supply own brand as well as M & S
- S R Gent – relies almost entirely on M & S
- J & J Fashions – largely produce for M & S.

There has undoubtedly been a reduction in the clothing manufacturing industry in the UK and many foreign companies have changed from both designing and

Table 2.4 Production of clothing in £m at 1991 prices.

	1985	1988	1989	1990	percentage change 1985–90	percentage change 1989–90
All clothing*	5612	6364	6357	6572	[+17]	[+3]

*Excludes hats, caps, millinery and gloves.
Source: BSO PQS 4531–4536, 4539, 4363

manufacturing to one of merely cut, make and trim (CMT) for other peoples' designs. Other parts of this chapter look at the way forward for the UK manufacturing industry. There is undoubtedly a role that it can play in the international sourcing market if it exploits the strengths of flexibility and quality and moves away from competing on price alone.

2.5.4 Marketing intermediaries

These are the main channels that help to get the goods from the manufacturer to the consumer. A detailed consideration of marketing intermediaries is given in Chapter 8. Their roles can be many and varied. The main ones are:

- Retailers
- Agents
- Distributors
- Wholesalers
- Advertising agencies
- Market research agencies

The intermediary having the greatest influence on the clothing market is the retailer group. British clothes retailing is unique in that 70% of garment sales come from only 17 retail chains. In 1990 the Burton Group including the menswear chain and Dorothy Perkins, Top Shop, Principles and Evans Collection turned over £1.8 billion (10.1% of UK womenswear and 13.3% of UK menswear). The largest market share is captured by Marks and Spencer, with 15.6% of the womenswear and 14.9% of menswear in 1990. In Italy, by comparison, 95% of clothes are sold by single shops.

On the whole, competition, particularly on price, has been very fierce in the 1990s. Customers are looking for value for money, not totally price driven but design, comfort and quality are important. Companies have had to rationalize and restructure to combat inflation and the recession.

Another result of the recession has been that womenswear multiples are being forced to segment markets more effectively, making the consumer much move aware of the markets they cater for. This has and will increasingly lead to a narrowing of product ranges.

The biggest change for the retailers has been the loss of the core 15–24 year old customers. Some leading multiple specialists who have been geared most to catering for the youth market are now experiencing some of the worst problems, which will affect them increasingly over the next few years. These demographic changes will force many more retailers than at present to reposition themselves in the marketplace. Targeting certain age groups in terms of age and, often as important, lifestyle will become ever more crucial. Research into market trends and close cooperation with chosen target groups will help retailers through this transition phase.

2.5.5 Fashion predictors

For the consumer it must be quite baffling to understand how each year designers, manufacturers and retailers all seem to know what styles and colours will be in fashion. The reality is that since the 1970s there have been companies who specialize in fashion prediction and act as consultants to interested parties in the fashion world.

Companies such as Peclers in France and Index in London sell their predictions on styles, colour and the market for the coming season or even further in advance for up to eighteen months. There are at least ten main organizations of this type in the world, although some specialize in specific markets such as childrenswear. Their predictions are not all identical, although there are usually many similarities between them.

These predictions help manufacturers and retail buyers alike make and stock the fashions; styles and colours that will be 'the fashion' for a coming season. However, at the end of the day the final decision rests with the customer in deciding whether to buy or not.

2.5.6 Consumers

Once fashion was dictated to consumers and there was little choice but to accept what was on offer. The tables are beginning to turn and the consumer has more power to accept or reject fashions. Recognizing this, clothing producers are researching the market more to see what will be acceptable before filling the stores with goods that just end up being discounted at sale time.

Consumers of all descriptions are more fashion-educated and consequently more fashion-conscious. They are demanding products that are designed to perform in special ways. Most want to express their personalities through their appearance and therefore their choice of clothing. The increasing numbers of working women want garments designed for their special needs. They understand fashion cycles and they know when a style has become tired. Manufacturers must constantly research and develop new fibres, fabrics and uses for these to keep up with the consumer's higher level of ability to select from the vast choices on offer.

However, there are other changes in the marketplace affecting consumers' attitudes, values and priorities. They are suffering some degree of fashion fatigue. For some the desire to acquire is more muted and rather than spending their income on fashion clothing they prefer to choose from a much wider range of products, services and leisure pursuits.

In the past, fashion styles, types of garments and advertising were all deeply influenced and directed by the interests and needs of the young consumer. Now that the increasing number of older consumers are becoming a market to be reckoned with, things must change or opportunities will be lost. The trend is towards people dressing more to please themselves. They won't be dictated to. People are more self reliant and cautious and careful for their individuality. They are putting more emphasis on self. Recognition of the new fashion consumer may mean that the fashion models of today will have the opportunity of a longer career than they first imagined.

2.5.7 Competition within the fashion market

Consumers today are presented with a bewildering array of choice, yet it is probably in the clothing market more than any other that the consumer complains that he or she cannot find what they want. The clothing producers and retailers are working hard to try to correct this but the recession of the early 1990s has slowed things down by the industry being wary of too much investment and experimentation. The high street stores have had to work much harder at tempting consumers and at times it seemed as if price cuts were their only weapon.

However, much of the major competition happens at the sourcing of goods rather than in the stores as summarized in Figure 2.4 below. It has been mentioned that globalization and sourcing from wherever cheapest, is increasingly becoming the trend, particularly among European competitors. This is enabling them to keep overall costs down, while offering merchandise of good design and quality.

Since the opening of the single European Market, competition from continental clothing producers has increased further, partly because of lower transport costs and shorter lead times. When the Multi Fibre Agreement (MFA) agreement is finalized there probably will be a single MFA quota for the European Union, which will mean the highly concentrated and accessible British clothing market will become even more of a target than it is already.

There are also concerns about increased low-cost competition from some eastern European countries whose pleas for special treatment of their exports to the EU are showing signs of success. Now that Poland, Hungary and the former

Figure 2.4 Competitive forces in fashion sourcing.

Czechoslovakian countries have been granted single association agreements with the EU, they will most probably have gained free access to this vital market by the end of the decade. By then the clothing industries in these countries will, probably is conjunction with western companies, have undergone major restructuring and re-equipping. This will enable them to present some formidable competition. In the longer run, many Far East producers have good reason to fear for their western markets.

2.5.8 Direct and indirect competition for fashion products

Marketers have to realize that with increased choice consumers have many different ways to spend their money. In the western world people rarely need to buy clothes out of pure necessity. A woman does not merely choose between one dress and another; she also may choose between a new dress or hiring one, or making one or even to spend her money on something completely different like a handbag or entertainment. A man may choose between one jacket and another, or he may choose between a jacket and some new golf clubs.

When consumers have to choose between similar goods such as one shirt or another, the garments, stores or manufacturers can be described as in direct competition. However, when the goods are different, but perhaps fulfil similar needs, like the woman choosing between buying or hiring a dress then the stores and manufacturers are deemed to be in indirect competition.

2.5.9 Publics

There are many groups of publics that can affect a company's success, notably the financial institutions, unions and pressure groups to name but a few. The concept of fashion marketing publics is developed further in Chapter 8 within the context of fashion promotion.

Perhaps one of the most powerful groups to affect the fashion market is the media. A report in the fashion press after a designer shows their collection can have disastrous results. It is for this reason that some fashion editors have been criticized for having too much power and influence on the market. Whether true or not, much time and effort is spent between fashion editor and designer to try to maintain good relations between the two. It is hoped that this courting may result in a favourable article at a critical time.

While many national newspapers have strong fashion pages the two most recognized fashion magazines in the UK are *Vogue* and *Elle*. Both are seen as essential reading for the woman or man who wants to know the important people and events in the fashion world. Powerful as these magazines are, neither have the overwhelming importance of *Women's Wear Daily*, based in the United States, whose fashion editor John Fairchild is regarded as a fashion guru.

2.6 Macro marketing environment

Factors considered within the macro environment affect not only the company, but all the other members of its micro environment, namely its suppliers, consumers etc. These generally have a much wider influence and their effects become apparent more slowly than factors within the company. Factors within the macro environment are cultural and social, political and legal, demographic, technological and environmental.

The inter-relationship of macro-environmental factors is most easily discerned in matters of world tension. Political, legal, social, and economic matters become entwined to exert a great impact upon general levels of consumption. Consumer confidence was thought to have been dented by the Gulf War in 1991, which, although now over, has influenced consumer thinking. The war and terrorist activities in London have also affected the market as tourists stayed away for fear of terrorist action, which has particularly influenced more upmarket brands and retailers such as Jaeger and Austin Reed.

2.6.1 Political and legal

Politics and law might seem a world away from fashion but both can have extensive consequences for manufacturers. With such globalized sourcing of suppliers, world political events can aid or hamper the acquisition of supplies. A new legal requirement, be it in the product or the methods of manufacture, can have a make or break effect for some companies.

The General Agreement on Tariffs and Trade and the Multi Fibre Agreement

The Arrangement Regarding International Trade in Textile popularly known as the Multi Fibre Agreement (MFA) is an international agreement that regulates imports of textile and clothing products into western industrialized countries from low-cost, mainly developing countries. Operating under the auspices of the General Agreement on Tariffs and Trade (GATT), the MFA currently has 43 signatories, the EU counting as one. Under the system most imports of textiles and clothing into developed countries are subject to detailed quantitative ceilings, implemented through a combination of import and export licences. There is,

Figure 2.5 The macro environment.

however, no regulation on exports from industrialized countries to low cost producers and no regulations between the EU and USA. The MFA is therefore unique in international regulation of trade in industrial products in that it is a formal departure from the free trade principles of GATT.

Originally signed in 1973, the MFA has been renewed on 3 occasions, most recently in December 1991 in Uruguay. Here, an agreement was made to phase out the quotas over a ten year period starting in 1993. This has since been deferred until 1994.

A regulated, gradual dismantling of the three decades of protection of western textile and clothing industries will allow them more time for adjustment before all barriers to low-cost competition are lifted. Although time to adapt to a new international order in clothing and textile trade is running out fast for Britain's clothing producers, Britain is likely to be more affected than some of its EU partners from this liberalization. Imports from developing countries, as well as exports to them would grow.

Sunday trading

In December 1993 the government finally reformed the Sunday trading laws. Most retailers and consumers have been campaigning for longer opening hours particularly for out-of-town shops that already tend to open in the evenings. Many stores have in fact opened on a Sunday and been prepared to pay the legal consequences. Sunday opening has been of much more interest to men than women and may help to boost the menswear market. The reforms that came into effect in the middle of 1994 allow small stores to be open all day, and larger stores to open for six hours per day.

Legal aspects: children's nightwear and other safety considerations

All children's nightdresses and dressing gowns, including threads and trimmings, have to comply with British Standard BS 5722. Those which do not must be labelled 'keep away from fire'. While manufacturers had two years to comply completely with this standard, some were still taken unawares.

Hoods on childrens' coats and jackets can no longer be drawn by a cord for fear of strangulation or being caught in something such as a fairground roundabout so the child is dragged along by the cord.

Copyright

Any design is the creative work of the designer – it is an original and priced as such. Imitation can be said to be the highest form of flattery, but it is unlikely that any designers who have had their creations copied would agree.

There are essentially two types of copying, either of a logo or of a design as shown in Figure 2.6 below. Both are very frustrating and often it is too late to do anything about it when, or if, it is discovered.

Logo copying might be imitations of the Lacoste crocodile, Mickey Mouse T-

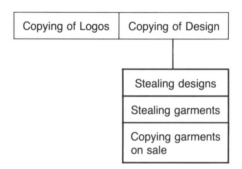

Figure 2.6   Copying of fashion.

shirts or the copy of a registered design feature such as the Levi's stitching marks. Copies of this type are an infringement of trademark and the perpetrator can be sued.

Design copying can happen in one of two ways: first, before the garment is on general release, the thief can sketch designs at a fashion show, or steal the design sketches or computer tapes or discs from the designer's place of work or even steal the actual garments. This can mean that the copies get into the shops at the same time or even before the original. Secondly, designs can be copied once they are already in the stores.

Copies are usually cheaper and of inferior quality to the original and can give the original designer many problems. Firstly, they will lose sales to the cheaper versions. At first sight the copies may not seem any different to the unsuspecting buyer who usually would go for the cheaper version. Frequently it is only after wearing the garment or more particularly washing it that the quality differences become apparent. Fabrics do not wash or clean as well and seams will not hold as well. These quality differences can lead the original designer to get an unjustly poor reputation among the consumers who think that they are buying original labels.

Copying of designs is not new. In 1975 the Fashion Design Protection Association was set up by Achilleas Constantinou of Ariella Fashion after he saw many of his designs in stores that he knew his company had not supplied. This was subsequently taken up by the British Clothing Industry Association (BCIA) who lobbied to get the Department of Trade and Industry to bring out the Copyright Designs and Patents Act in 1988. The aim of this Act is to 'to protect creativity without restricting competition'. Designers are encouraged to claim copyright of their designs by signing and dating their original drawings. However, designs are often copied and sold in other countries without the designer ever knowing although the effect might be felt in decreased sales and reputation. So these laudable efforts have not really solved the problem. Aside from the practical difficulties of time and cost in pursuing legal actions against the suppliers, there is still the problem of deciding when a fashion house is merely following a trend and when it is breaking the law.

One solution, used by Levi's, is to monitor the market outlets constantly, to make life harder for the counterfeiters. This may not be possible for a smaller company, especially when any monitoring has to be done internationally. Most of the copies are made abroad, to enable cheaper manufacture and avoid copyright laws.

The British Clothing Industries Association is currently trying to standardize legislation regarding copyright protection within the EU and advocate a new international code via GATT for dealing with counterfeiting.

2.6.2 Technological

As in all areas of industry new technology is making great inroads to improve quality of life and increase speed and quality of manufacture. In the area of fashion and clothing there have been many inventions. Some have had only minor effects on the market whereas others have or are about to revolutionize them.

Fibres and fabrics

Lycra is not a fabric. The trademark Lycra is the property of US based chemical company Du Pont and is an elastane fibre that lends itself to whichever fabric it is mixed with. Lycra is therefore an additive that gives knitted and woven textiles the quality of lasting stretch and recovery. It was first developed in 1959 and its first real use in garments was in the 1960s in ski wear and men's cord trousers. It was really not until the 1980s that it took off in knitted garments.

Lycra has become a household name associated with dancewear, swimwear, hosiery, cling-to-fit fashion separates such as leggings and vest dresses, in fact anything knitted. Lycra overcomes problems of fit and movement for body hugging designs. Manufacturers obviously benefit from associations with a consumer recognizable brand in premium, superior quality garments and fabrics.

Such is the swimwear market's reliance on Lycra that swimwear designers do not design their collections until they have received Du Pont's own fashion forecasts.

Attempts are now being made to use Lycra in woven fabrics for outerwear and tailoring to take advantage of such benefits as improved appearance, better drape and less wrinkling. There is more development into adding Lycra to other cloth to create a wide diversity of fabrics. This has resulted in all kinds of finishes for fabrics using Lycra such as bubble, cire, shiny, matt, satin finish or printed.

The development of Lycra into other clothing, notably sportswear has led to the increase of interest and sales in sportswear for professional, hobby and leisure purposes.

Computers

The dramatic increase in the use of computers has not passed by the fashion world, as shown in Figure 2.7 below. One of the main uses of computer systems

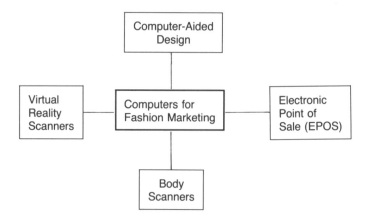

Figure 2.7   Computers in fashion marketing.

being introduced by the more innovative companies is that of Computer Aided Design (CAD). The implications that this can have on the speed of transition of goods from design to the shop floor is quite phenomenal. It also has great implications for the employment sector in this industry. It may be the saviour of the UK clothing industry if it is accepted quickly enough.

A CAD system can perform a wide variety of tasks:

- The programmer designs a motif.
- The motif can be enlarged to any size, and duplicated to cover a piece of cloth. This can then be viewed on the computer screen to see how the design will look on the draped fabric.
- The fabric can be tried in different colourways.
- The fabric can then be printed either directly onto the fabric using a bubble jet printer, or for larger lengths of fabric a printing layout can be produced.
- The operator can then design a garment, perhaps a blouse by selecting different sleeves, collar, yoke, length etc.
- The software will then print out a paper pattern to any basic measurements given.
- It can also plan a layout for the pattern pieces to get the optimum use of the fabric.

There is no reason why all these tasks cannot be performed by one skilled computer operator, however, the question today must be whether we need to train designers or computer operators. Although in 1992 only 150 out of 9000 fashion companies in the UK were using these systems to design garments, this number is increasing all the time, particularly as the systems become more flexible and prices are reduced.

These programmes can dramatically speed up the time it takes for a garment to get into the stores. It is also very cost effective both in terms of time saved but also in minimizing fabric wastage. Perhaps the biggest saving that these systems can offer is in the area of pattern making and grading.

Some high street retailers like to deal with designers using this system as they can easily ask for adjustments to be made without it delaying delivery time. So decisions are made faster and the buyer has more choice and influence.

Made-to-measure has been used as a means of producing garments since the inception of clothing. Since the industrial revolution, standardized sizing has gained prominence as it brings affordable garments to many markets. With growing populations comes diversity, the need for flexibility and the desire for better fitting clothes for all, not just those who can afford it. CAD can take a customer's measurements and reproduce designs or patterns for many different garments, quickly and accurately. It also can grade patterns for different sizes.

A further development in technology for the clothing market is for use in the made-to-measure market, where a system like a body scanner can be used to measure body size and shape within seconds to provide electronic tailoring.

For the future virtual reality could transform the fashion business. There would be no need for super-models or scrambles to get the front row at the fashion show. Designers could have the model they wanted parading around their salons, while clients could view whole couture collections in the comfort of their own homes.

Another major computerized invention for the retailer is EPoS (Electronic Point of Sale). This is very familiar in our supermarkets where bar codes are scanned to give the price. The bar codes can also tell the clothing retailer such information as size of garment, colour, and how long it has been in stock. This information can then go into a central system that controls stock, and can, if necessary, rapidly reorder.

Computerized links with suppliers are growing in importance, speeding up order processing and improving accuracy of transactions. Use of computers and EPoS are very important in retail success in the 1990s in data capture at the point of sale, management of the merchandise and links with suppliers. Those retailers who have invested in these systems will fare best in the future.

2.6.3 Demographics

This is the study of changes in the size and make-up of the population. While these changes occur slowly and can be predicted well in advance, only the foolish manufacturer ignores the effect they might have on business. The UK has begun to undergo a quite radical change in the make-up of its population and many of these changes will have strong repercussions on the fashion clothing market.

Customer size

As a nation we are changing shape and businesses are being forced to cope with the larger customer. In 1993 almost half of all men were overweight compared to 39% in 1980 and the proportion of overweight women has increased from

32% to 40%. Not only are people heavier but the average height for both men and women has increased by 10 mm. This has implications for all sorts of goods and services such as transport, furniture and clothing.

Many clothing manufacturers are offering goods in a wider range of sizes or a more generous cut, although some have pandered to their customers' vanity and disguised the increase in size. Marks and Spencer have admitted that a size 12 made in the early 1980s is not exactly the same as the equivalent size now.

Apart from offering a wider range of sizes, some stores have a special own range in store, for example BhS's range 'Extra'. There are also more retailers catering solely for the larger customer. High and Mighty, as the name suggests, is a growing chain for men. Dawn French has opened an upmarket store in South Molton Street in London for women sized 16 and upwards. If the trend continues the time may come when it is the size 10s who are complaining that they cannot find anything to wear.

Changes in the family

The much quoted statistic of the family with 2.4 children has changed. At one point it was down to 1.8 children per household althought it is expected that this will increase in the future. Couples are tending to marry later and start a family later. This gives them the opportunity to become more financially stable, to get further on in their careers and to have more disposable income to spend on their children, some of it on clothing. More exclusive children's clothing shops have, like many others, suffered during the recession of the early 1990s. However, there is still a substantial designer market for childrenswear whether the garments are bought as gifts from generous grandparents or as regular clothing by more financially indulgent parents.

With more people remarrying and starting a second family in their late thirties and early forties there is a need for maternity wear for the more mature expectant mother, who also may be working at the time. Ranges such as 'Briefcase and Bootees', a mail order company with a retail outlet in London, caters for just such women. Such mothers will also want to keep a youthful appearance consonant with their young children that will have strong design implications for other post-natal ranges. Further details about the role of the family in purchasing behaviour are given in Chapter 3.

Age changes in the population

The British population is forecast to rise by less than 3% between 1990 and the year 2000, but the change in the populating structure will have a considerable effect on the clothing market. The focus will shift further away from the highest spenders between the ages of 15 and 34 towards the opposite end of the age spectrum. Table 2.5 illustrates how different age ranges will be affected.

Table 2.5 Population trends (male and female), Great Britain '000s.

| | percentage change | |
	1990–1995	1990–2000
0–1	+4.3	+1.3
2–5	+4.6	+5.9
6–10	+5.0	+9.8
11–14	+8.3	+14.7
2–14	+5.8	+10.0
15–19	−12.1	−6.1
20–24	−13.5	−23.9
25–34	+4.4	−4.9
35–44	−1.3	+9.7
45–54	+14.1	+18.7
55–64	−0.7	+4.4
66+	+1.8	+2.5
All ages	+1.5	+2.9

Source: Government Actuary

Children

During the 1990s the number of 0–14 year olds will rise to almost 20% of the population, with the age band 10–14 growing the fastest. This high growth plus increasing trend for women to be older when they have their first children will, it is estimated, create growth of around 7% in the children's market as a whole.

As numbers of children continue to grow there will be a boom in the clothing and footwear markets for infants and childrenswear. However, many retailers have recognized this and the market is very competitive. Retailers can best compete by offering good styles and designs with good value for money. Despite the recession there is still room at the premium end of the market for some expansion.

The 10–14 age children's market remains underdeveloped in retail terms at present. Marks and Spencer have all but withdrawn their attempt to appeal to teenage boys. However, Etam have been more successful by offering Tammy for girls as an in-store department for this age group demonstrating that fashion chains rather than an extended children's chain may be the winners in this very difficult sector.

Traditional core market aged 15–34

The traditional core market for clothing suppliers, that of men and women between the ages of 15 and 34, will decline rapidly between 1990 and the year 2000. By then there will be 1.7 million fewer high spending 15–34 year olds around, with the key 15–29 year olds being reduced by 22%. Stores such as Miss Selfridge can expect to see their customer base drop by a twelfth. At present the clothing purchases of these core customers account for well over 40% of total domestic spending, but this will decline to 26% of the total population by the year 2000.

There may be some consolation in the fact that the 25–34 year old group will grow slightly, although they also have most demands on their finances with mortgages and many are starting to have families.

The mature market

Almost 54% of all inhabitants in Great Britain will be 35 years and older at the beginning of the next decade. The number of 45–54 year olds is expected to rise faster than any other age group.

Older people have traditionally been the lowest spenders on clothing. Middle aged and older people, in particular men, tend to spend considerably less on clothing than consumers in their late teens, 20s and 30s. They buy fewer garments per head and often spend less per garment than younger people. In recent years, the spending of the 55–64 year olds has risen dramatically, particularly by women. This increase is expected to continue as they benefit from inheritance money from older relatives.

Most older groups, particularly towards the higher end of the age bracket, are not as interested in fashion as in comfort and quality of clothes. Price is becoming less significant and service levels are of increasing importance. However, there are now more magazines aimed at them and a somewhat improved choice of merchandise in the shops. Such people are influenced in their fashion attitudes by their growing affluence and are more aware of different styles. This is mainly due to having been brought up in the post-war boom years. Retailers aiming to serve this older market are responding with updated classic ranges, particularly for women. There is, however, still an opportunity to stimulate more menswear sales to older consumers by updating ranges and retail presentation.

2.6.4 The social and cultural environments

These can cover a wide range of issues, but are basically the society-wide influences, values and changes that can affect the market.

Leisure activities

Changes in the amount and types of leisure activity have resulted in a move away from formal codes of dress to much more casual styling. The increased amount of leisure time that people have, due to shorter working hours, more electronic help in the home and convenience foods has led to a need for more clothing to wear in these leisure hours.

Leisure wear, particularly in the guise of sportswear has become a style to wear during the whole day for most ages and socio-economic groups. Nearly everyone wears some form of sportswear be it T-shirts, sweatshirts, jogger bottoms or polo shirts. Tracksuits and trainers are almost a social uniform, in some parts of the market, for many daily activities such as shopping, housework, looking after children, dog walking and of course sports activities themselves.

The role of work

The market for menswear and womenswear is very different in terms of occupational status of consumers. As far as the 'working wardrobe' is concerned a wearer's occupation influences both his or her garment needs as well as influencing how much they can actually spend. Changes over time in the occupations that comprise the labour market can therefore have a major effect on the overall size and composition of the domestic clothing market. The relationship between the structure of the labour market, socio-economic groups and purchasing is developed further in Chapter 3.

From a 1985 female workforce of just over 10 million, the total number of working women in the UK is expected to rise to 12 million by 1994, or almost 45% of the work force. Less free time, more disposable income, and a need for clothing for work will all have implications for the clothing market. Although many of these women will be working part time, it will still be the case that all working women will have less free time in which to shop, but more disposable income. The desire to dress smartly, along with the desire for financial status, will result in more spending on clothes for different occasions.

Women in supervisory jobs tend to spend well above the national average on their wardrobe. While there are still very few women in professional and higher managerial jobs, they do tend to spend more on their outerwear than the national average for women and are a small and highly lucrative market.

Economically inactive women spend well below average on clothing but cover a broad spectrum of ages, purchasing power and reasons for not working, for instance they may be students, pensioners, unemployed or women whose husbands have well paid jobs.

For working men there has been a long term shift from blue-collar to white-collar work, which one might think would stimulate consumption, but the steep rise in unemployment during the recession has also affected clothing sales. Indeed, the men's suit market had all but collapsed at one point. This was partly triggered off by fashion changes but pressure on the finances of many of its core customers was also a strong contributory factor.

Seasonal factors

Clothing producers and retailers have always found that demand for their goods is subject to the vagaries of the weather and the seasons. New ranges are introduced at certain times of the year in the expectation that the weather will be as normal. In the past few years the weather has been quite 'unseasonal' on many occasions. Summers have either arrived early and lasted longer than pected or even appear not to have arrived at all. Winters have been milder ad suppliers have often found themselves with the wrong stock for the weather. This has led to a loss of profits either through lost sales due to shortages of clothing or heavy discounting to get rid or leftover end-of-season stock. When viewing figures seasonally, it is necessary to look at several years together to avoid the bias of the extreme vagaries of the weather.

Clothing sales are very low in January and February with only around 6% of the total annual consumer sales. Childrenswear is particularly weak here, whereas in September, sales of school clothing make this month the second most important sales period for childrenswear. June is far more important than September for menswear and womenswear. This is the beginning of summer and the holiday season when around 9.5% of womenswear is bought, with menswear sales just slightly lower.

The largest amount of clothing is bought in December with 17% of total annual spending taking place. A large part of these sales is for gifts. This month is especially important for menswear as men very often receive clothing as gifts. On average in the last three years, 18.5% of total menswear sales were in the last five weeks of the year. Childrenswear accounted for slightly less at 18% and womenswear was 16%. Even with the high volume of sales in the January sales, they in no way match the bumper sales period before Christmas.

2.6.5 'Green' issues

As consumers are accepting the concept of conserving and recycling in other areas such as washing powders and paper, so they may soon be questioning the need for constant renewal and replacement of clothing to follow fashion. To the environmentalist an industry that advocates continual change and ensures inbuilt obsolescence in its products is far from attractive.

To satisfy the environmentally conscious consumer the pace of fashion changes must come down. The emphasis needs to shift from short-term fads to durable styles, comfort, quality and real innovations in fabrics and style that add to garments. Not only will there be consumer pressures to develop 'green fabrics' but 'green clothing' is also likely to become an increasingly important issue. There will be a need for the recycling of fibres and fabrics, and production of biodegradable clothing.

Since successful companies need not only to recognize and anticipate consumer needs and desires, research and development into these environmental issues should be happening now.

Green issues: the response of retailers

The launch of environmental clothing ranges by labels such as Esprit and Claus Steilmann reflects high profile attempts of the fashion industry to become greener. At the retail end of the business, the major chain stores are examining how they can run their stores in a more environmentally friendly way. Most of their efforts may appear minor, but in total they could be quite significant.

Environmental efforts include:

- The use of recycled paper for till rolls;
- Using recycled plastic and actually recycling garment overbags;
- Recycling hangers and not offering them to the customer, but returning them to the clothing manufacturer to use again;
- Using less packaging: Marks and Spencer now use only a recycled cardboard band around their polo shirts instead of the plastic packaging;
- Using fewer hardwoods for fittings in store design;
- Using more energy efficient transport etc.

Marks and Spencer, in particular, are taking environmental concerns into account. They are aiming to keep abreast of such issues and take them into consideration in their buying decisions and operational areas.

Second hand clothing

In some high street shopping centres charity shops seem to be almost as common as new clothing shops. The huge increase in the number of these and second hand clothing outlets can be explained in many ways. As people buy more new clothing the second hand clothing shops are an obvious place for them to dispose of their unwanted fashions from last season. Economic reasons could lead us to assume that lack of money means that the only clothing some people can afford is from the second hand market. Or it could be that more environmentally conscious people are preferring to buy second hand and so recycling clothing rather than always buying new.

Environmentally friendly fabrics

During the late 1980s, when there was a sudden focus on environmental issues, the textile industry was forced to improve its processes due to increased legislation. It had become evident that environmental damage was being caused by gaseous and liquid emissions from the industrial processes of many producers including textiles.

New legislation covers, amongst others, the wet processing activities such as dyeing and finishing. Already, many firms are spending large sums to reduce gaseous emissions from their processes and are investing in systems for recycling dyestuffs and other chemicals and even water itself.

There is much misinformation in the media that natural fibre fabrics are best, leading many people to think that natural fibres are good for the environment and synthetics are automatically bad. Most of this thinking is based on negative perceptions of the chemical industry. Although natural fibres biodegrade more easily, some give off toxic gases as they do so. Some processes for making synthetic fibres are actually more friendly to the environment than those for making natural fibres, especially when energy and water usage are taken into consideration

It is not only the manufacture of the fabrics that is of concern, but how they actually biodegrade after disposal. Germany's leading clothing producers have been working on a range of biodegradable garments.

Whilst the textile industry is usually blamed for the unfriendly emissions and wastage, it is arguable that the clothing manufacturers and fashion designers should really be blamed. They are the ones who dictate that strong dyed fabrics are required or non-crease products that need to be made from the thermo-plastic properties of synthetics. The clothing and textile industries need to integrate their efforts for the future.

'Green' fashions

Green fashion can be viewed in several different ways. On a simple level there is a growing movement against labels and conspicuous consumption. Some people are shying away from dressiness and are returning to basic clothing. Basics are usually part of traditional workwear – they have a high degree of functionality, are simply cut and built to last. Doctor Marten boots and denim jeans are items of clothing that could be considered to be following the green ethos of less consumption as they are classic items that will not date and will only need replacing when they have worn out. Some of these views are shown in Figure 2.8 below.

It is most probably for this reason that companies such as Hackett who specialize in classic quality clothing have managed to ride out the recession where other more fashionable companies have suffered.

In the late 1980s we also had the 'ecology look'. Fabrics were natural both in feel and colour. T-shirts available from the designer shop to the local chain store were adorned with environmental messages. Coming at a time when consumers had had enough of overt consumerism and the Yuppie look, the ecology look fitted in nicely as a contrast to the structured silhouettes and wide shoulders of the previous fashion.

The controversy over who is to blame for the less environmentally friendly fabrics, designer or textile manufacturer has not gone unnoticed by some

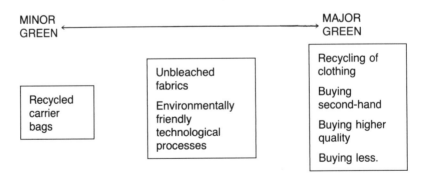

Figure 2.8 How 'green' can you be in Fashion?

designers. Most denim producers have replaced traditional chemical finishing by using pumice stone to achieve a stone washed fabric finish.

Not all designers are aloof to the environment. Many, such as Katharine Hamnett, are concerned about the fabrics they use and are developing more environmentally friendly fabrics. It will take time but these are likely to 'trickle down' to appear in the garments stocked in high street shops.

However, these new fabrics will cost the consumer more. As with many environmentally friendly products there is a conflict of interest. Consumers and retailers seem to want new, environmentally sustaining products but are reluctant to pay for the additional cost involved.

This problem is illustrated by retailers Next who produced a range of 'green'-cotton T-shirts and underwear in 1990. These were produced without the use of formaldehyde finishes, which can cause skin irritations and gaseous pollution, and they were mechanically (rather than chemically) treated to prevent shrinkage. The range was more expensive than the equivalent standard merchandise and was promoted as 'something for the quality conscious consumer'. Sales of the range were disappointing and Next did not offer a follow-up range for the following winter.

Friends of the Earth have produced ranges of 'green' fashions using un-bleached, undyed cotton. It satisfied the ecology issue but not the fashion issue and sales were limited. They were avoiding the issue by not using any processes rather than finding 'green' solutions to enable fabrics to be used for fashion items.

Consumers are also concerned about the risk of skin cancer that global warming and excessive exposure to the sun may bring about. New market opportunities for more cover-up beach wear to mix and match with swimwear is likely to lead to even more opportunities for Lycra.

2.6.6 Economy

General economic factors such as income, employment, and home ownership have just as great an effect on the clothing industry as for any other product group. There are many factors that influence the shape of the market for clothing and footwear today. Consumer spending is influenced by some economic factors mentioned above while lifestyle changes that occur such as getting married, having children, children leaving home and retirement, for example, all alter people's requirements and aspirations for clothing and footwear.

Recession

In the late 1980s and continuing into the early 1990s the UK has been in a recession that has been mirrored throughout the world. Increasing unemployment and high interest rates led consumers to be wary of spending more than was necessary. This in turn led to more frugal spending on clothing and a partial rejection of fashions that require a total new look, causing a move towards more classic styles that will last beyond the next season.

nent

cal spending power can be greatly influenced by unemployment, which
ries considerably from region to region within the UK. The retail sector
of whole towns can be devastated by the closure of a large local
employer.

Home ownership

Home ownership has been increasing steadily since the end of World War II.
However, as interest rates rose, the cost of mortgages greatly increased for a
time, putting pressure on those owner occupied households. Even as rates
began to fall again, consumer caution and the switch to saving spare cash may
not result in the anticipated increase in spending.

Credit cards

The consumer boom of the 1980s was fuelled by ready availability of credit.
Consumers were more willing to borrow when their homes rose in value and
were confident to extend their personal loans in the knowledge that their assets
were appreciating in value faster than the rate of inflation. However, as the rise
in interest rates caused depression of the housing market, and the value of
some properties fell, the banks, so willing to lend in the 1980s restricted credit.
There is also still the possibility of legislative measures being introduced to
control the amount of lending to consumers based on their ability to repay. With
or without this, consumers will not be as likely to 'buy now pay later' as has
been common in the past.

2.7 Trends in the marketing environment

Trends are relatively slow moving changes in the marketplace that can occur for
a variety of reasons, and businesses ignore them at their peril. Sometimes trends
are business-led and sometimes consumers lead the way. General fashions can
change very quickly and go from one extreme to another whereas trends in
clothing fashion tend to be slower and build upon themselves rather than ignore
what went before.

2.7.1 Styles and consumer preferences

While there probably will always be people who are interested in high fashion
there has been a noticeable move away from status and image dressing. Consumers still demand fashion, but in the 1990s they are requiring more understated
styles that combine realism, comfort and practicality.

Changing work and lifestyles, with more time for leisure pursuits, are speeding
the change from formal wear to a more casual look and sportswear. There is an
increasing blur of divisions between active wear and fashion. Sometimes the

sports store and boutique seem to be carrying almost the same merchandise. For example, are stretch leggings dance, aerobic or active sportswear, hosiery or fashion trousers?

The explosion in sportswear sales has been accompanied by a sharp rise in demand for other casual garments. Sales of conventional jumpers and cardigans have suffered a severe contraction as casual knitwear such as T-shirts and sweatshirts have grown in popularity.

Demand for womenswear is as crucial as ever to the health of the domestic clothing market. Demographic changes have already been mentioned and these will result in two major growth markets for the late 1990s. First, the upper end of the children's market should be considered. Secondly, customers in their late forties and fifties represent a great opportunity.

These changes and the long term weather pattern are encouraging lighter weight clothing and trans-seasonal clothes, where many people no longer have a winter and summer wardrobe, but use the same clothes year-round. Some of these issues concerning taste preferences and seasonal aspects are developed further in Chapter 6 in the context of product development.

2.7.2 Manufacturing

Retailers are increasingly under pressure to carry less stock in the interests of greater efficiency, and to offer the customer more choice, more often. This means that suppliers are required to deliver shorter runs of merchandise more frequently than in the past.

Too many manufacturers have also been taking a back seat and relying on retailers to keep them in touch with customers' demands. In the future the most successful manufacturers will be those who invest in market research, design and technology.

2.7.3 Trends in fibres and fabrics

Performance and versatility are becoming increasingly important. Customers are beginning to seek out specially engineered high-tech, high-performance fibres and fabrics such as Lycra and the tactile fabrics and ask for them by name. They are looking for fabrics not only to fulfil a fashion or style function, but also a clearly defined performance need.

Polyester and cotton are still the most widely used fibres, either on their own or as the dominant (50% or more) fibre in a blend, however natural fibres are still more popular, and it is expected that their use, often for reasons of cost and handling properties will rise further. Polyester is gradually losing ground and more cotton-rich blends are being used. Wool is still popular but for cost reasons it is again bought more as a blend than a pure fabric.

The main area of development in fabrics is still in blending stretch elastane yarns. They are being applied to a much wider range of fabrics either for fashion effect in body-hugging styling or for comfort and recovery in outerwear and tailoring.

Microfibres such as superfine polyesters and polyamides in new forms and applications, especially in blends with other fibres and knitwear, are likely to remain the main area of interest during the 1990s.

2.8 Summary

- This is a time of change for the clothing market. The companies who survive will be the ones who initiate change and adapt. There is not much scope for those who are slow and lag behind. In the medium term there seems little prospect of a return to the high rates of growth in clothing sales seen during much of the 1980s.

- Many companies will find that they can only survive by moving away from the price-sensitive parts of the market into segments where quality, design, variety and quick response to changes in fashion and consumer tastes matter more than price.

- There will be opportunities for producers and retailers who can meet the demand from older and more discerning customers who are looking for better quality, more comfortable styling and well informed friendly service.

- The market is not changing very much in overall size but there will be major demographic growth in certain areas. Age bands offering significant scope for sales are among older children (11–14), and 45–54 year olds.

- More garments are coming from overseas and to compete, the UK has to offer a quick response meaning low stock levels for the retailer, especially as the seasons become less distinct and retailers want to offer more frequent seasonal ranges.

- Fashion is moving into an era where marketing techniques will be more influential than ever before. Clothing producers need to be far more aware of consumer needs. To a large extent fashion still leads, but consumers are beginning to exert more leverage in the issue. No longer will they merely wear what is dictated to them. The customer is becoming king.

Further reading

Coleridge. N. (1988), *The Fashion Conspiracy*, Heinemann, London.
Drew, L. (1992), *The Business of Fashion*, Cambridge University Press, Cambridge.
Hawkins, I. (1992), *British Clothing Market Overview*, TMS Publications, London.
Herbert, H. (1986), *The Clothes They Wore: 19th and 20th Centuries*, Cambridge University Press, Cambidge.
Hirst, P. and Zeitlin, J. (eds) (1989), Markets, technology and local intervention: the case
    of clothing. In: *Reversing Industrial Decline? Industrial Structure and Policy in Britain and her Competitors*, Berg Publications, Oxford.
Kotler, P. (1994), *Marketing Management: Analysis, Planning and Control*, 8th edn., Prentice Hall International, New Jersey.

Chapter 3
The Fashion Consumer and Organizational Buyer

3.1 Introduction

This chapter is concerned with the behaviour of fashion consumers and organizations that purchase fashion products and services. The relevance of fashion buyer behaviour is examined and links with marketing research, market segmentation and the marketing mix are established.

An outline of consumers' decision making is given. The types of decisions made by consumers are described and the stages in the decision process are discussed. From the perspective of the buyer as a problem solver the chapter then focuses on the consumer as an individual. The main psychological variables relevant to fashion consumption are identified and outlined. For example, an understanding of the perceptual process allows us to comprehend more easily why some fashion promotional messages are more effective than others.

Fashion goods enable people to show identification with, or separation from, certain social groups. Clothing can be a symbol of belonging or alienation. To understand the fashion consumer, the broader social forces that help shape individual buying behaviour are assessed. These social dimensions include the family, social stratification, opinion leadership and cultural factors. Some people are more ready to adopt new fashions than others and the study of diffusion and opinion leadership helps us understand why this occurs and what may be done to facilitate the process.

Fashion firms not only sell to fashion consumers, they also sell to other firms in the industry. An obvious form of organizational buying is sales within the fashion distribution channel and this is described in Chapter 8. Another area of organizational buying of relevance is that of the corporale consumer, for instance the purchase of uniforms and distinctive clothing as part of a company's image. The nature of organizational buying will be outlined and difference and similarities with consumers will be highlighted.

3.2 Why study the fashion buyer?

A central component of the definition of fashion marketing is satisfying customers' needs profitably. To achieve that it is necessary to understand consumers, their needs and wants and how they will respond to various marketing efforts.

Everyone interested in fashion marketing brings a particular quality to their studies, i.e., their experiences as a fashion consumer. That experience is a mixed blessing. The benefits are that concepts from consumer behaviour can be understood and readily applied to one's own clothing purchases. The main drawback is the temptation to generalize and assume that all other fashion consumers behave as we do. The unfortunate fact is that the study of fashion marketing will probably change buying behaviour and make the expert fashion marketer atypical. Greater knowledge of products and promotional processes coupled with enthusiasm for fashion mean that there is a dislocation from typical consumers. Interestingly, many serious market research companies exclude marketing personnel as survey respondents because of their tendency to be atypical.

As will be seen when looking at social processes in consumer behaviour, people tend to live within fairly narrow social networks. They interact with others of similar social status and sets of interests. For fashion marketers, the danger is that these narrow social networks reinforce 'world views' of what is good about fashion and this becomes the explanation of what all consumers want. The key point is that opinions should never be accepted without question and that fashion marketing decisions should be based on evidence about the market, and not just on introspection.

Each consumer is unique and that is a good reason to trust sound marketing research rather than hunches based on the extrapolation of personal motives. As a starting point for marketing research hunches are useful when they are regarded as ideas to be tested. Therefore we can ask:

> 'Do many people share this view?'
> 'How many?'
> 'Do they have any other views that are more strongly held?'

For example, a fashion designer may be inspired by the reflection that business travel for the female executive would be enhanced by a small range of light flexible garments that do not crease. This inspiration may come from the designer or from his or her friends. The next stage is to determine via marketing research, how many women engage in business travel and of those, how many feel that the current clothing market does not meet their precise requirements. Chapter 4 provides detailed coverage of marketing research techniques used to measure the behaviour of the fashion consumer.

3.2.1 The role of consumer behaviour in marketing

Consumer behaviour provides a range of concepts to help fashion marketers think about their customers and marketing research provides the techniques to measure those concepts. Consumer behaviour is also closely integrated with all other aspects of fashion marketing, but most notably with the selection of target

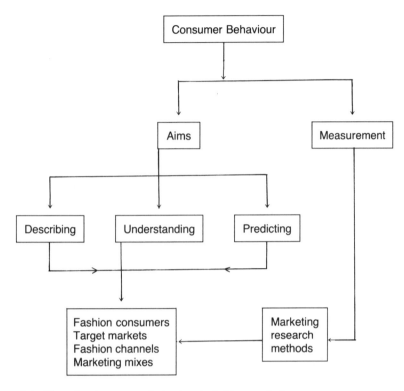

Figure 3.1   The role of consumer behaviour in fashion marketing.

markets and the development of marketing mixes. An overview is given in Figure 3.1 above.

3.2.2   Consumer behaviour and target marketing

As mentioned earlier each consumer is unique. Besides bespoke tailoring and couture items, most fashion marketing is concerned with the provision of standardized garments aimed at particular groups of consumers. All consumers are different from other consumers, but, and this is not contradictory, they are similar to some other consumers. The marketing of volume clothing demands that groups of consumers with similar needs be identified and then supplied with similar products. Chapter 5 considers the nature of target marketing further, but for the moment the links with buyer behaviour will be noted.

If the total market for clothing is considered it can easily be seen that it really comprises many smaller segments, each with specialized needs. Obvious bases for the segments include age, gender and income. Less obvious, but as important, may be segments based on psychological or social characteristics that are common to significant numbers of consumers. For example, consumers differ in their levels of aspiration and also in the relationship they see between clothing and the achievement of social mobility. Taking the example further, the 'power dressing' phase of the 1980s was immediately recognized by most people and the overt designer label almost become a badge of accomplishment for some. The 1980s also embraced some ideas that were, in part, supportive of conspicuous consumption. The recession of the late 1980s and early 1990s has been accompanied by the promulgation of other values less supportive of the more obvious forms of conspicuous consumption. However, the aspirant socially mobile person still seeks clothing to meet his or her needs. It may be the female executive wishes to say via her clothing that she is not the secretary as depicted by Melanie Griffith in the film *Working Girl*. The 1990s fashion designer meeting these needs provides garments that make the 'power dressing' statement in more subtle ways. It is the understanding of these types of consumer needs that is the essence of consumer behaviour and the subsequent identification of suitable target markets for fashion firms.

Changes in social structure, or demographics, as identified in Chapter 2, cause new market threats and opportunities and therefore different targeting imperatives. For example, the increasing interest in environmental issues has been accompanied by a whole range of views from ardent advocates to strident opponents. Research undertaken by Mintel and others shows that the vast majority of people are 'green' supporters; where differences arise is in the price people are prepared to pay for such beliefs. (Mintel Special Report, *The Green Consumer*, 1989.) Within the fashion market, consumers can be categorized according to attitudes held on environmental matters. Clearly, if significant numbers with purchasing power are active supporters of environmental issues, then they probably would be most interested in recycled or recyclable fabrics and fibres and in long lasting clothing that is manufactured and can be cared for in an environmentally friendly manner.

Investigation of consumer behaviour is sometimes designed specifically to identify particular groups of consumer with fashion interests and buying behaviour in common. The later section on lifestyles will outline one such approach to market segmentation.

3.2.3 Consumer behaviour and the marketing mix

The study of consumer behaviour not only provides a framework for identifying consumer needs and target markets, it also enables the anticipation of consumer responses to marketing action. When studying the consumer the interest lies not only in describing what is the case, but also in predicting future behaviour.

The Marketing Mix is the combination of elements that a fashion marketer offers to a target market. It comprises decisions made about products, prices, promotion, services and distribution that are assembled in a coherent manner to represent the firm's offering to the consumer. A detailed discussion of the marketing mix is given in Chapter 5. For the present a consideration of links between consumer behaviour and some elements of the marketing mix will be given.

Consumer behaviour and products

Products are bought because they meet needs. These needs may be mainly physiological such as the requirement for warmth or may include social needs such as the desire to be thought sexually attractive. A psychological need, for example, may relate to vanity and self image and be manifest in a desire to perceive oneself as smaller or larger than reality. Styling skill can create garments that emphasize or reduce the aspect size as wished, but a limited amount of 'psychological sizing' also can play a part. For example, a well known bra manufacturer produces its leading brand with labels that are one size larger. The assumption is that some consumers derive satisfaction and confidence from a size label that flatters aspirations or a particular self image. A similar situation exists with the sizing of boxer shorts where it is well known that very few men want the label small when buying or receiving underwear. Another example relates to perceptions and garment sizing where some women desire to see themselves as a smaller size and manufacturers respond accordingly by classifying what is really a size 18 dress as a 16.

It is not the contention of this book that such examples are to be advocated. Indeed we would argue that much time and effort is wasted at the retail level and that the net effect upon the consumer is probably counterproductive. When market researchers claim that the majority of British women do not accurately know their own bra size, one wonders whether this ignorance is not perpetuated by the absence of an industry standard on sizing.

Consumer behaviour and promotion

The promotion of fashion items requires an understanding of consumers' media habits so that the correct media can be chosen. Understanding consumer behaviour enables the selection of appropriate promotional messages. For example, fashion photography often seeks to reflect a particular lifestyle that the consumer can identify with and then perceive the product as a vehicle to the attainment of that lifestyle. The use of celebrities in advertisements also enables fashion firms to reach certain target audiences and influence consumers via the process of identification. A 1990 survey by Mintel identified Victoria Wood as a leading role model for many working women, whereas none of the fashion supper-models were even cited in the list of admired characters identified by the sample (Special Report, *Working Women*, Mintel, 1990.)

Consumer behaviour and price

Price for many people is a major indicator of quality. Style and design is sometimes difficult to judge, especially for the untrained. Therefore some consumers take surrogate indicators of quality and in particular price. An understanding of the perceptual process and how consumers learn about prices and value is helpful in constructing a pricing policy.

Consumer behaviour and distribution

The choice of an appropriate distribution channel and designing elements within that channel should be based on an understanding of the fashion consumer. Knowing when, where and how consumers wish to buy are fairly obvious applications. Understanding and matching self images and store images and creating of particular store amospheres to encourge certain moods need research and ideas from consumer behaviour.

3.3 Fashion consumer decision making

One main way of examining consumer behaviour is to take the view of the consumer as a problem solver. The requirement for clothing, however it is driven, is seen as a problem for the consumer to solve, usually by exchanging money with a seller. The problem-solving perspective raises many questions that will be addressed; they concern the types of decisions fashion consumers must make, the various stages of the decision process consumers progress through and major factors that influence those decisions.

3.3.1 Types of consumer decisions

It is tempting to see the purchase of a garment as just one decision, to buy or not to buy. However, it can useful to break the larger decision down into several separate decisions that collectively comprise the buy or no buy decision. For instance, consumers must decide the following matters:

- How to find out about new styles
- What style, colour, and size to buy
- Where to buy from
- How to pay
- Which bills to pay promptly
- When to buy
- How many items to buy
- Will any accessories need to be purchased?
- Whether to shop alone or accompanied
- Whether to try the garment on
- Whether to order an out of stock size or colour option
- Which sales assistant to approach for help
- What to do if the product is unsatisfactory
- What will be the reaction of significant others to the purchase?

If fashion marketers see consumer decisions as a series of smaller related problems to be solved, then the benefit comes in terms of planning activities to ensure that the consumer is helped when help is needed. For example, a consumer may not be bothered about trying a blouse on if she knows she can easily exchange it later for another size if needed.

Alternatively, another customer may dislike the whole process of shopping for clothes and appreciate speedy service with advice and nearby displays of matching accessories. Marketing research is necessary to determine which decisions are important to the particular target market of the fashion firm.

3.3.2 Consumer involvement

Another way to look at consumer decisions is the level of involvement the consumer has in the decision. Consumers differ considerably in terms of their interest in fashion. Even those people who are very interested in fashion may be more interested in some types of garment than in others. A common way consumer theorists have classified consumer decisions is into high- and low-involvement purchases. This classification, in part, reflects different theoretical paradigms, although some significant attempts at synthesis have emerged over recent years.

The level of involvement depends on the person, the purchase object and the time and place of purchase. For one consumer, the purchase of a pair of socks may involve considerable deliberation and visiting several stores to make comparisons in order to obtain a product that meets fairly precise specifications in terms of colour, size and construction. For another consumer, the purchase of socks may be relegated to a simple commodity purchase undertaken with little conscious thinking through and they may be selected along with other low-involvement purchases in a supermarket.

The implication for fashion marketers is to find out the level of involvement of the target market or markets and design the marketing mix accordingly. A central issue is the provision of marketing information to consumers who may or may not want or use it. A connection between low-level involvement and impulse buying can be shown and this has a bearing on the relative proportion of the promotional budget that goes on in-store promotions rather than on advertising. If consumers don't really pay much attention to information about some fashion products, but simply make decisions in the store, it would be more productive to concentrate promotional efforts in-store.

3.3.3 The decision process

As shown earlier, the consumer decision to buy may be seen as a series of smaller decisions. It also can be shown as consumer progression through a number of discrete stages. Most models of consumer behaviour use the stages or near equivalents as shown in Figure 3.2.

The various phases will be briefly outlined. First, problem recognition occurs when a consumer becomes aware that a need for clothing arises. This may be triggered by garments wearing out, comments from others about how unfashionable existing garments are, a change of social status prompting or facilitating purchase or a change in aspirations or taste. The extent to which fashion

Figure 3.2 The consumer decision process.

marketers are able to influence problem recognition is fiercely debated.

Whether marketers create needs is the question often asked. Engel, Blackwell and Miniard (1993) argue that marketers do not create needs, they show consumers better ways of satisfying pre-existing needs. For example, high status needs can be satisfied by any number of different purchases or activities. The fact that a fashion advertiser captures the imagination of some consumers and secures purchases probably has more to do with the understanding of those needs and careful design of a message than the creation of the needs in the first place. Many powerful social forces operate in society of which advertising is only one, and one not often held in very high regard. Advertising both reflects and influences societal values towards consumption. If it were truly able to create needs and exert such a powerful influence then it has been an outstanding failure in the world of fashion.

Having become aware of a need the consumer reflects on the situation and can decide to proceed with the purchase process and collect information, defer the purchase or conclude that the problem is insignificant or cannot be solved. In deciding to proceed the consumer reviews information already held in memory. This includes knowledge of brands and stores where solutions may be found. Inexperience or unsatisfactory prior purchases may cause external information sources to be consulted. External sources include personal sources such as friends, neutral sources such as a *Which?* report on raincoats or fashion marketing sources such a window display or a poster advertisement. These three main external types of information sources are usually regarded with different degrees of credibility by the consumer.

When sufficient information is held by the consumer about possible solutions then evaluations take place and a choice is made. The nature of the evaluations varies from individual to individual. Some consumers have extensive repertoires of buying criteria whereas others have limited and often vague mechanisms for making decisions. The process of making an evaluation may involve the mental ranking or rating of alternatives or simply eliminating items that fail to meet a certain threshold. At times consumers can suffer what is described as information overload where there are too many possibilities or too much information has been presented. An awareness of consumer information needs and the provision of information in an appropriate manner via facts and advice from sales staff or brochures can help the consumer make a choice. The decisions made by a consumer at the time of purchase have been mentioned above and the sales effort to influence purchase is covered in Chapter 9.

After a purchase consumers may engage in a process of evaluation of the product and to an extent their own efficiency as a consumer. Systematic evaluation is most unlikely except where items are bought primarily for their functional characteristics, such as safety boots where protection and durability may be closely scrutinized. The extent of evaluation seems related to how socially conspicuous the item is, how central the product is to the self image of the consumer, the particular consumer orientation and also to the purchase price. For most consumers, the evaluation can involve seeking comments from others perceived to be significant.

Fashion marketers should be interested in this post-purchase behaviour as it can relate directly to repeat purchases, the level of customer complaints and word-of-mouth communications about the firm. The law of effect in psychology states simply that behaviour that is rewarded is likely to be repeated. Satisfied customers are likely to become regular customers. The goal of fashion marketing is to move customers along the following continuum from the promiscuous to the insistent as shown in Figure 3.3.

Promiscuous – will shop around for the best deal
Occasional – will sometimes buy from us
Loyal   – will usually buy from us
Insistent   – will only buy from us

Figure 3.3 Types of customer.

Careful monitoring of customer complaints can lead to the early correction of faults and avoidance of some future complaints. Sensitive handling of genuine complaints can also help retain goodwill and avoid negative word-of-mouth communication. As research indicates that consumers are more likely to pass on negative rather than positive information about products, one dissatisfied customer may lead to many more with negative attitudes towards the store or brand.

The above discussion of the decision process has shown the need to consider factors beyond the immediate concerns of the consumer when trying to understand and predict the behaviour of the fashion consumer. The factors to be considered may be grouped under the broad headings of psychological and sociological. Psychological factors are taken from the study of individual behaviour while the sociological factors are based on the understanding that much consumer behaviour takes place as part of a group process and involves social interaction and patterns of influence. Figure 3.4 illustrates the main explanatory variables related to the decision process.

Figure 3.4 A model of consumer behaviour.

3.4 Psychological processes

3.4.1 The buyer's perceptual process

Perception is the process whereby buyers select, organize and interpret simple stimuli into a meaningful and coherent picture of the world. To explain this process further, a distinction between sensation and perception must be made. Sensation refers to the responses of our sense organs to simple stimuli, perception is the psychological consequence of sensation. An analogy would be to compare a photograph with a painting; the photograph being the 'reality' whereas the painting is a very personal view of 'reality'.

For the fashion consumer, the stimuli presented in a busy fashion store are a bewildering array of sensations that must be made sense of. The consumer goes through a number of stages in the perceptual process that can be seen as steps in filtering and distilling marketing stimuli into a unique marketing experience. The stages in this perceptual filtering and distilling process are:

- Selective exposure
- Selective attention
- Selective distortion
- Selective retention

Selective exposure

Age or income can impose some constraints on the exposure to certain stores or media as can the more deliberate choice by the consumer. This process, where there is a narrowing of the opportunities for experience of the total range of

marketing stimuli, is known as selective exposure. Examples o'
subject to selective exposure are the fashion page in a daily ne'
ments, brochures and store window displays. The task for fas'
ensure that the correct media and location for retail ou'
maximize the opportunities for selective exposure.

Selective attention

Selective attention is the next stage, and the range of possibilities is further
narrowed when the consumer only pays attention to some marketing stimuli and
not others. Consumer factors that determine consumer attention to marketing
stimuli are existing attitudes, attention span, emotional states, motives and
expectancy. The last point is illustrated by the following well known saying:

```
A stitch in time
time saves nine
```

Figure 3.5

Many people will have 'read' the above statement and not have noticed the
double use of the word 'time'; they will have perceived what they expected to
see rather than the reality. Existing attitudes and prejudice similarly influence
how we perceive marketing messages. Items which are promoted as designer
label or sale items may attract attention or may even be screened out by the
consumer depending on prior attitudes. Thus the importance of determining
consumer predispositions, via marketing research, before designing marketing
messages is underlined.

Some factors under the control of the fashion marketer can influence whether
the marketing message gains the attention of the consumer. The size and intensity
of a message (i.e. very loud) plus novelty, contrast, repetition and movement
can all enhance the chances of gaining attention. Thus advertisements in the first
10% of a magazine like *Elle* or *GQ* have a higher potential readership than the
latter part of the same magazine. Similarly, a black and white advertisement in a
glossy magazine, which is surrounded by colour advertisements stands a good
chance of gaining attention due to the contrast.

Selective distortion

Having gained the consumer's attention the next perceptual filter for the marketer
to penetrate is selective distortion. Consumers interpret stimuli in a manner that
is consistent with existing attitudes. The perceptual process operates in such a
way as to enable and maintain a coherent view of the world; too many contradic-
tions to existing views make the management of everyday life irksome. That is
not to say that changing consumers' perceptions is impossible, just that before

embarking upon change marketers need to discover the starting points and the strength with which existing views are held. An example of the distorting effect of the perceptual process is easily noted when considering the stereotypes that are brought to bear in judging garments by country of origin. To most British consumers the labels 'Made in France' or 'Designed in Italy' have connotations of higher design content and quality than an item made in a third world country. These connotations can have such an influence that they may, and often do, override the judgements that would emerge in a blind test.

Selective retention

The final perceptual filter is selective retention. This refers to the phenomenon of consumers remembering information about fashion marketers and their products in a highly subjective way. An important aspect of perception is that the consumer interprets information in terms of current priorities and concerns to such an extent that the individual in effect rewrites their personal history. The main driving force behind this selective retention is a need for consistent and, sometimes, easy explanations for our feelings and past behaviour. In this process good and bad aspects of some items may become exaggerated with, for example, nostalgia for some so-called golden age of fashion when there was 'real pride and skill in tailoring, unlike today'. The close associations that many people have between blue jeans and youth has been recognized by the jeans manufacturers in the targeting of middle aged consumers with the use of suitable music in advertisements to evoke the nostalgia.

3.4.2 Learning

The fashion consumer is not born with a knowledge of fashion brands, of criteria for judging garments, knowledge of stores or prices, preferences for certain styles or fabrics or even how to care for garments. All this information has to be learned. Consumer learning is any relatively permanent change in buying behaviour that is a result of practice or experience. Two main sources for consumer learning are the family and peer groups. However, much learning occurs through consumer experience with fashion marketers, their products and promotional methods.

Many explanations of consumer learning are given in the marketing literature, most can be classified as association learning or cognitive learning. Although the two main types of theory do compete to explain behaviour, neither category is sufficient to explain all learning that occurs. The following discussion presents aspects of both approaches.

Association learning

Association learning occurs when a marketing stimulus and the consumer response are repeatedly paired. Much low-level learning such as brand names occurs at this level. A key explanatory theory for this type of learning is known as the law of effect. When behaviour is rewarded it will tend to be repeated and when it is punished or not rewarded it will tend to diminish in frequency. Therefore we have a simple explanation for repeat buying and brand loyalty. The consumer who buys a particular brand of shirt and finds they meet his criteria in terms of being stylish, comfortable, durable and value for money will tend to buy the same brand again. The main lesson for fashion marketers is to identify the relevant buying criteria of the consumer and produce products to meet those criteria. Another consumer who finds that the skirt she purchased three weeks ago is starting to come apart at the seams will most likely avoid buying another skirt from that supplier. Yet another customer may learn to avoid certain shoe shops as the sales assistants, paid primarily by commission, all compete to serve the customer and don't allow adequate time for browsing.

An interesting aspect of association learning is the notion of shaping behaviour. This notion allows marketers the opportunity to influence consumers and help them learn more complex forms of behaviour. By selectively rewarding closer and closer approximations to the final goal sought by the marketer, consumer learning is modified. In the section in Chapter 8 on pricing the link between sales discounts and consumer behaviour is described. Some consumers learn, because of regular retailer action, to defer purchase until sale time, as they are rewarded by lower prices.

Shaping behaviour, when effectively planned, permits the fashion retailer to alter behaviour in other ways. Suppose the retailer introduces a new range of cotton underwear with Lycra and the goal is to encourage the consumer to buy several pairs. To launch the range and encourage a trial with minimum risk and maximum reward a coupon offering a discount may be offered. The consumer who buys the product receives another coupon as well, this time of lower value than the initial coupon. The second coupon should induce another purchase at reduced cost, but without coupon support. If the product performance meets expectations then the beginning of brand loyalty has been shaped. It should be stressed that the main reward should come from the product and not the coupon, otherwise the consumer learns something else, only to buy from the retailer when an incentive is offered.

Cognitive learning

Cognitive learning theories approach the problem of consumer learning by assuming consumers reason and reflect upon the relationship between marketing stimuli and consumer response. Clearly all consumers do think about some purchases in detail and may engage in mental processes to try to reach a reasoned conclusion before purchasing. Inexperience, previous dissatisfaction, expense and high involvement clothing items are most usually linked with cognitive learning. The cognitive approach concentrates on the thinking through of different courses and the identification of the decision criteria and rules used by consumers. Knowing how consumers make connections between product features and their buying criteria is obviously helpful for marketing staff in order to provide the right information at the right time. The concentration on the information processing aspect of learning will be developed further in the section on consumer attitudes below.

3.4.3 Consumer attitudes

Attitudes are a learned orientation or predisposition to a given situation, person, object or idea resulting in a tendency to respond favourably or unfavourably. There are three main components to an attitude; the congnitive, affective and conative. The cognitive dimension refers to knowledge or information possessed about the fashion product, service, image, store or prices; the knowledge possessed by the consumer may not be accurate or complete, but it is what is believed to be the truth by the consumer. The affective dimension is concerned with consumer feelings about fashion marketing offerings and is measured in terms such as like and dislike or good and bad. The conative aspect provides the behavioural aspect of attitudes and is usually expressed in terms of an intention, or not, to buy within a specified time. Thus a consumer may know of a new range of knitwear from Daniel Hechter and of the colours, prices and sizes available; the consumer may both like the new range and moreover intends to purchase a turtleneck sweater within the next seven days.

Fashion marketers are interested in consumer attitudes as they are seen to be closely linked to behaviour. A simple model of the link between attitudes and buying behaviour is shown in Figure 3.6.

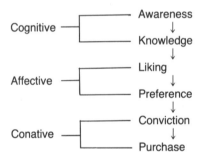

Figure 3.6 Attitude components and buying behaviour.

The above model does over-simplify matters somewhat as it is argued that sometimes attitudes emerge or become manifest after purchase. Other writers contend that liking may precede knowledge in certain circumstances. Several attitude theories offer competing explanations for the same phenomenon. It is clear that predicting behaviour from simple measurements of attitudinal components is a problematic and contentious area. Numerous studies have shown that positive attitudes towards fashion products to not always result in higher sales. The work of Fishbein and Ajzen (1980) suggests that the crucial factors to consider are the measurement of the attitude towards the act of purchase and the identification of normative beliefs. For example, a consumer may like the designs of Jean Paul Gaultier and have very positive attitudes towards the designs and cut of the garments. However, the same consumer may not buy because of negative attitudes towards the price or a belief that his or her close friends may not like the styling. Techniques for measuring attitudes are described in Chapter 4.

When considering the point that attitudes emerge and or change after purchase, it should be noted that post-purchase experience with garments can lead to attitude change both positive and negative. Festinger (1957), proposed that there is a tendency to seek consonance or harmony of thoughts, feelings and behaviour. Post-purchase doubt over a new garment or dissonance then becomes a motivating state of affairs and the consumer acts to reduce dissonance. Dissonance can be reduced in a number of ways including:

- changing behaviour (e.g. exchanging the garment for another colour);
- changing attitudes (e.g. deciding that the brand is perhaps not as good as previously thought);
- revoking the decision (e.g. asking for a refund);
- seeking extra consonant information (e.g. asking a friend for reassurance of the wisdom of the choice made); and
- avoiding dissonant information (e.g. not visiting other shops in case a lower price is seen for the same item).

A considerable amount of the early research on attitudes was conducted in the USA at the Universities of Yale and Columbia. Much of this research still provides a useful framework for the practising fashion marketer, and its findings are useful in the design of advertising efforts. Some of this work has been incorporated into Chapter 9.

3.4.4 Consumer motivation

Motivation is the inner force that drives and energizes consumers towards goals. Motivation incorporates need arousal, causing the drive that leads instrumental behaviour to reduce the drive.

Consumer motivation is a complex matter to understand for many reasons. First, motives are inferred, a consumer motive cannot be seen or observed; what is noted is behaviour and then an assumption about the underlying behaviour is made. An important distinction should be made between merely describing behaviour and explaining behaviour. Saying, for example, that a customer buys low-cut tops, becaues she is the sort of person who likes to reveal her cleavage is mere description. Whereas, for example, a particular purchaser of a Diesel jacket may be said to be satisfying status needs especially if the brand name is prominently shown on the garment.

Motivation is a complex concept as similar motives may find expression in different behaviour. Just as in the example above a status-seeking consumer bought a Diesel jacket, other people will seek different brands or may find non-fashion products or activities to satisfy status needs. Furthermore, people may buy the same product but for different motives. Another purchaser of a Diesel jacket may do so primarily for warmth and protection (a physiological motive) or for social motives, e.g. to be accepted by a particular group of friends.

Motives may change over time with, for example, a change of social status. The arrival of a child is often accompanied by a change in motivation towards clothing purchases for most women. Another consideration is that many motives may simultaneously affect purchasing behaviour. Sometimes the motives operate to make the consumer positive towards the clothing item, at other times there can be motive conflict. An example of motive conflict could be a person attracted to the purchase of a coat that will satisfy status needs, but at the same time repelled as the coat may not be warm enough to satisfy a physiological need.

There are several ways of classifying motives and these are described below. Motives can be placed along a continuum from rational to emotional. Buying a waterproof hat clearly has a strong rational element; an evening dress costing several thousand pounds that will be worn only once is obviously near the other end of the continuum. Another question to consider is whether the consumer is conscious of all the motives impelling choice. Freudian theory likens the personality to an iceberg where people are only partly aware of their motives. Many consumers may be unaware or unwilling to admit to some of the motives that cause them to buy or avoid certain garments. It is easier for many people to assert that an item was bought because it looks nice than to admit it was bought to impress others. The measurement of consumer motivation is problematic and some qualitative techniques for measuring motives are outlined in Chapter 4.

A widely cited classification system for motivation was developed by Abraham Maslow. Maslow, a psychologist, stated that motives were organised in a hierarchy and that only when lower-level needs were satisfied did higher-level needs become important.

Thus the consumer on a limited income will be concerned with perhaps the functional aspects, such as warmth, of low-cost clothing before matters of social acceptance assume importance. Social needs include the need to belong and be accepted by others. Esteem needs are the need for the consumer to think well of themselves and have others hold a high opinion of them. Self actualization, for Maslow, was the desire to grow psychologically and it embraces creativity and achievement. For one person knitting needles and some wool may enable self actualization whereas for another the participation in the design process by suggesting colours or styling aspects of a garment enable self actualization. Some clothing purchases may satisfy needs at more than one level, for example a

Figure 3.7   Maslow's Hierarchy of Needs.

Barbour waxed jacket may satisfy the need for warmth and protectioı elements as well as enabling acceptance by a group who are similarly dresseu. The translation of product features into specific benefits related to motives is a key selling task and this is described in more detail in Chapter 9.

3.4.5 Consumer personality

Personality is the particular configuration of qualities that make a person unique. Two main approaches to personality will be considered, psychographics and the self concept.

Earlier approaches to consumer behaviour concentrated on consumer personality traits and tried to discover consumer types. The hope was that having identified certain types of consumer then buyer behaviour could be predicted and fashion products could be produced and promoted accordingly. Unfortunately, the correlation between personality type and buying behaviour was very small and this approach was succeeded by one which consumers based not on traits, but on activities, intersets and opinions (AIOs). This is known as psychographics or lifestyles. Typically consumers are asked a large number of questions, usually based on a Likert scale, as described in Chapter 4, of general and specific questions relating to AIOs. Examples of such questions are 'I believe regular exercise is essential for good health' (general) and 'I go swimming at least once a week' (specific). The answers to these questions are then analysed together with demographic, purchasing and media data about consumers to derive distinct groupings, or types who have AIOs in common.

These lifestyle groups are given names and can be the basis of target marketing efforts or as a platform for advertising copy design or store design. The major drawback to lifestyle analysis is the lack of theoretical underpinning or measures of reliability or validity of much of the work undertaken. Evidence suggests that general lifestyle analysis is less useful and that research is best conducted into specific products and related areas such as health, beauty and fashion. Some labels given to the groups are plainly insulting to consumers, such as apathetics or dowdies and at worst are little more than promotional aids for advertising agencies trying to sell their services to retailers and manufacturers. When done systematically, lifestyle analysis can offer real insights into buying behaviour, but there is no consensus on methodologies and the technique is both expensive and needs to be undertaken continuously.

Analysis of the self concept is another major strand of research from the area of consumer personality studies. The dimensions of the self concept include:

- the self image, which is how the person sees him or herself;
- the ideal self image, which is how the person would like to see him or herself;
- the social self image, which is how the person thinks others see him or her; and
- the ideal social self image, which is how the person would like others to see him or her.

In addition, the self concept is influenced by situational factors such as who the 'others' are and the context of buying. Thus there seem many 'selves', although there is an enduring sense of continuity and sameness that provides coherence for the consumer and this is known as identity. It should be noted that consumers don't always accurately perceive themselves or the reactions of others towards them. The main tool for measuring the self concept is the semantic differential and that is described in Chapter 4.

For the fashion marketer, the self concept represents a promising area as clothing is a most obvious way a consumer may express him or herself and show how they would like others to judge them. Consumers buy clothes both to maintain and enhance the self, depending on the ascendency or salience of the self versus ideal-self image. Self images are affected by many factors, but most notably by age and social class. Perceived opportunities and/or the lack of opportunities can influence not only images of the self, but also the value placed upon the self, namely self esteem. For example, Mintel (1990) found that 90% of women between 55–60 wanted to be described as sensitive, understanding or warm and caring compared with 67% of women aged between 15–19. In the same survey, 42% of ABs wanted to be described as intelligent or thoughtful compared with only 21% of C2s. These classifications will be described shortly in the section on social stratification.

3.5 Sociological aspects of consumer behaviour

Consumers are social creatures, who form groups and interact in relation to goals. Consumer behaviour when viewed from a sociological perspective is more than a simple aggregation of individual acts, for the patterns and processes of both individual acts and wider social changes are profound in their impact on fashion marketing. Several social dimensions of consumer behaviour will be examined and these relate particularly to the process of influence over choice and to the basis for segmenting markets.

3.5.1 Social groups

A group may be defined as two or more people who bear a psychological relationship to one another and who interact in relation to a common purpose. People do not just form groups, they form groups for reasons such as to satisfy social needs, for mutual protection and enhancement or to check attitudes and perceptions. The price of group membership is conformity to norms, a norm being a shared expectation of behaviour. Norms are essential to groups as they enable stability and provide a framework within which identities may be expressed and common goals can be pursued.

For many aspects of life there is uncertainty and groups provide a mechanism to check that uncertainty. This checking function is apparent in clothing purchases where the advice and support of friends is sought to check, among other things, the appropriateness of styling of garments and whether the items represent good value for money. Group members do not usually dress identically, but for specific occasions there are norms, or unwritten rules about the range of garments that would be considered acceptable. The young man whose friends usually wear blue denim clothes doesn't turn up to meet his friends wearing a suit without the anticipation of a little teasing.

The mechanisms of maintaining conformity are rewards for compliance and punishments for deviance. Much of the control is exercised by non-verbal means or joking and teasing. These methods allow group members to retain dignity and comply without the great risk that would follow from blunt verbal demands. Norms for dress are most explicit for formal occasions where the expectations may be printed on invitations. Many work places have dress codes, although these vary in specificity from the rigidly prescriptive uniform to the broad list of exclusions to the vague hints about dress related to status within the organization.

The anticipation of the reactions of others can be a key factor in the choice of clothing. Consumers may not accurately anticipate those reactions or may lack confidence and rely upon friends to advise and accompany them on shopping trips. Everybody differs in their social needs and those with the highest needs will tend to conform the most. The discussion so far has concentrated on face to face groups where conformity is often greater.

Consumers also belong to many groups that are not face to face, they also may aspire to belong to certain groups and still further wish to distance themselves from others. Everyone belongs to automatic groups by virtue of age, gender, race, religion etc. and with membership come sets of expectations of how one ought to dress. Two women may both have legs that are flattered by short skirts, but if one woman is in her fifties and the other in her early twenties, the social influences and pressures to conform may be markedly different.

Groups that individuals identify with are known as reference groups and as noted they can be positive or negative or aspirational. An example of negative reference group influence may be a young man not buying a well-known brand of boot, because he thinks they are worn by skinheads and racists. Aspirational reference group influence is most apparent when people apply to join new organizations – for instance most people take care over their job interview outfit. Similarly, parents sending children to school for the first time will make an effort to dress their child in a way that will enable him or her to be accepted quickly. Reference group influence is important not only for styles of fashion products, but also for endorsements and rejections of particular brands. Teenage purchases of trainers are influenced by what brands are regarded as 'in' and what is considered 'out' by the reference group.

3.5.2 Opinion leadership

Opinion leadership refers to the degree of influence exerted where a consumer is faced with a choice. Many people discuss clothing and fashion advertising as a normal part of social interaction. The influence of others is accepted under certain circumstances. When there is little information about garments or stores

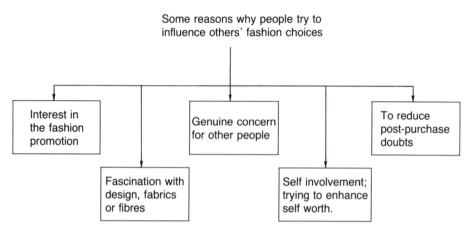

Figure 3.8 Opinion leadership.

possessed or when the information is out of date, consumers seek information from others. Where products are highly visible such as outerwear or where the garment involves risk because it may be expensive, go quickly out of fashion or simply prove unpopular with significant others.

There are many reasons why people try to influence others about fashion products and services as shown in Figure 3.8 above. There may be genuine concern for the well-being of a friend and advice is given on obtaining value for money by visiting particular stores. The influencer, or opinion leader may talk about fashion products because he or she is fascinated by the design or fabrics used. Sometimes a fashion message via advertising or public relations may prompt discussion, the controversial Benetton advertisements or the photographs of Naomi Campbell toppling over when wearing very high platform shoes on a Vivienne Westwood cat-walk show are common examples. At other times opinion leaders may talk about clothing as a way of establishing self worth by claims to superior knowledge or taste. Additionally, the opinion leader may discuss an item of clothing as a way of reducing his or her dissonance (see above).

Fashion marketers often hope to use opinion leadership as a way of encouraging the diffusion of a product range. If opinion leaders can be identified and targeted with promotional efforts, then the hope is that the message will be distributed via word-of-mouth communications. Fashion media personnel perform an important role in the word-of-mouth process and the marketing efforts directed at them will be discussed in Chapter 9, particularly with regard to public relations, trade fairs and exhibitions.

3.5.3 The family

The family is the basic social group and the main mechanism by which social values and aspirations are transmitted. The family is important to the fashion

marketer because families share finite financial resources and media exposure and they make some purchases either collectively or in anticipation of the reaction of other family members. Paying attention to the role of the family is important when it is realised that the person buying the item of clothing may not be the wearer. For example, over 50% of all pyjamas for men and a third of all knitwear for men are bought by women (TMS Partnership, 1990.)

Families, as defined by government statisticians, are persons related by blood, marriage or adoption who reside together. It is tempting to view the family as in decline when newspaper headlines about divorce rates are considered. However, the family remains a strong institution in British society, most people get married and the majority of those do not get divorced. In 1992, 74% of households in Great Britain comprised married couples, either with or without their dependant children (*Social Trends*, 1994). Over the long term, divorce is a factor that has had a major influence upon the lives of many people and is often accompanied by a reduced purchasing capacity for either or both former marriage partners.

The family lifecycle is an attempt to classify people according to the age of head of household, marital status, and the age and number of children. Early models of the family lifecycle, by Wells and Gubar, omitted the occurrence of divorce and made the assumption that everyone followed the same route from birth to old age, namely single, married without children, married with children etc. Later models of the family life cycle have recognized the role of divorce, but there is still need to account for the extent of cohabitation, the number of people who remain single all their lives and alternative lifestyles.

Modelling the progress of people through time via the family lifecyle is useful for two major reasons. People at the same stage of the lifecycle may, because of similar demands upon income, constitute target markets for companies. The fashion retailer Next grew dramatically during the early 1980s by recognizing and responding to a demographic change connected with the family lifecycle. Further, knowledge of how many people are at a certain stage in the lifecycle enables predictions for future demand. For instance, knowing the marriage rate and the fertility rate, some fairly accurate estimates can be made about the number of births over the next few years. This information is vital for manufacturers of baby clothes and stores like Adams Childrenswear.

Family decision making is important for fashion marketers, for it is important to know how decisions are made and who exerts influence over the clothing decisions made by families. Three stages of the purchasing process are relevant, they are initiation, information search and purchase decision. It may be within a family that the female notices that an item of clothing needs replacing, she also may collect information via reading magazines or clothing catalogues to narrow the choice. In the same family the male may be the sole wage earner and he may be the person sanctioning the purchase. If such a pattern of decision making was typical for the target market, then there are clear implications about which media should be used for advertising.

Family decisions can be classified according to the degree of influence husbands and wives exert for given product choices. Four types can be considered which are; husband-dominated, wife-dominated, joint and autonomic. Joint refers to equal influence and a shared decision and purchase. For example a couple may shop together to purchase a new suit for the husband. Autonomic refers to an equal number of decisions made, but those decisions are made separately. Autonomic decisions are perhaps best illustrated by gift purchases, where a female may buy some jewellery herself, but also receives other items purchased by her husband. The factors related to joint decision making are higher-priced items and where the couple are younger. Whether young couples are more egalitarian or simply less knowledgeable about one another's needs is a matter to be determined by longitudinal research.

Family decision making requires more research, in particular into the role of children in influencing clothing purchases. Changes in the level of participation in the labour market by married women and relative earnings of males and females mean continuous research is necessary in this area. Discovering the actual level of influence within families is problematic as influence is not always accurately discerned by the participants or even revealed to market researchers. The sex of the interviewer, the presence of the other party and vanity and modesty from both partners, can conspire to make this important research task very difficult to undertake.

3.5.4 Social stratification

All known human societies are stratified. Stratification refers to divisions of people according to their economic position in society, whether they are aware of that position or not. In the United Kingdom the main method of determining social stratification or social class is based on occupation. The most widely used system in the fashion market is the National Readership Survey using A, B, C1, C2, D and E. Table 3.1 gives a brief outline of this system:

The above system is not the only system nor is the basis of classification

Table 3.1 Socio-economic groups.

Class	%	Description
A	2.7	Upper middle class Higher managerial, administrative and professional
B	15.1	Middle class Intermediate managerial, administrative and professional
C1	23.9	Lower middle class Supervisory, clerical or junior managerial, administrative or professional
C2	27.8	Skilled working class Skilled manual workers
D	17.8	Working class Semi-skilled and unskilled manual workers
E	12.7	Those at the lowest level of subsistence Includes most pensioners and the unemployed.

Source: National Readership Survey 1992

uncontradicted, but it is the most widely used and can be useful in explaining some of the vagaries found in fashion purchasing. A thorough exposition and critique of theories of social class is beyond the scope of this book, however, its impact is undeniably pervasive. A simple model of the influence of social class is that a person's position in the social structure, as determined by occupation, is associated with purchasing power, sets of aspirations and constraints and membership of social groups, all of which lead to patterns of consumption. The process is not only one way, how somebody's income is spent can be relevant to some of the causal factors. Savings can be one factor in social mobility, though how particular clothing purchases, in themselves, influence social class is both less clear and less powerful.

The links between clothing purchases and social class are less clear than in the past. During the 1920s and 1930s old photographs reveal that clothing was an easy way to depict class. Hats, in particular, were markers of social status. Nowadays, because of the fragmentation of styles, the range of choice available and the change in classes themselves, clothing is no longer an unambiguous guide to class. Socio-economic groups have all changed, partly on account of the changing occupational structure of the country – while far fewer workers are employed in large scale manufacturing operations, the service sector has grown dramatically. To give one stark example, the number of coal miners has reduced from over a million in the 1940s to less than 20 000 in the 1990s. The provision of better health care, education and higher standards of living through the twentieth century have changed all social classes. Class differences during the 1990s are not the same as the class differences that prevailed during the early part of the twentieth century, but that is not to argue that a convergence of classes has occurred.

Class remains a significant discriminator of consumer behaviour. Although it is not a linear relationship, there is a link between class and income, and the prospects of increases in income. People do not wear rank overtly via their clothing as in the armed forces, but ways are found by many to indicate status. Within social classes, distinctions can be made between creative professional people like advertising copywriters and accountants in how they dress. The former may tend to favour less formal attire at work whereas the latter tend to dress more conservatively.

Many working class people may reach their earnings peak early in their career, whereas many middle class occupations have incremental salary scales. Such experiences, coupled with different entitlements to, and discretion over, holidays, pensions schemes and other 'perks' are associated with different 'world views'. The daily experience of work impacts on these views where, for example, a manager may exercise discretion and make decisions, and a manual employee may work to a rigid work schedule almost like a robot. Workplace tasks, rules or norms may place restrictions upon clothing that can be worn depending upon a person's position. Where uniforms have to be worn it is usually the lower levels that wear them – even the Japanese companies excuse their senior managers from the need to wear overalls. In consequence, clothing worn during the person's leisure time may be chosen to express a distance from, or affinity to, work identity. Class differences are evident in media use, store selection, ownership and use of credit cards and bank accounts and annual expenditure on clothing and footwear per person.

3.5.5 Geodemographics

Related to social class is a newer system of classifying consumers based upon where they live. A small number of proprietary systems exist based upon the census and categories on neighbourhoods. One such system is ACORN, which stands for A Classification of Residential Neighbourhoods and is owned by CACI, Pinpoint is another. These systems are derived from statistical analysis of census variables to discover residential areas, usually census emuneration districts comprising about 150 households and approximately 450 people, that are distinct in composition.

The census data can be linked to survey data on purchasing behaviour and information on media usage. Knowing the post code of a respondent, the market researcher can determine the geodemographic category. ACORN has six categories and 17 groups including Affluent Executives in Family Areas and Older People in Less Prosperous Areas. Pinpoint has 12 categories and some of these include Inner City Bedsits, Affluent Households, Rural and Working people with families.

Geodemographic data have been used by marketers for target marketing, media planning, setting sales targets by area, forecasting, market testing and selecting new locations for outlets. Among fashion firms, the heavy users are the mail order firms, although retailers like House of Fraser are involved.

Geodemographics presents a promising future for maketing especially when demographic data are interlaced with psychographic data. However, a number of major criticisms can made of geodemographics. First, it relies on census material that, at best, will be at least one year old when it is first used and up to 11 years old before the next census material is available. The owners of these systems claim they are able to update their databases to take account of changes in the housing mix and local economies. The systems are in competition and currently are much more expensive than data from secondary sources. Geodemographics is not equally predictive of buying behaviour across all product categories. A geodemographic category is a composite of a number of variables such as class, age, ethnic origin and housing amenities and critics assert it is either social class subdivision by another name or a statistial artifact looking for a theory.

Fashion marketers obviously need better tools for analysis and planning, and geodemographics represents a significant advance, but it is not a panacea or even a clear successor to alternative methods of analysis. To ask some obvious questions, why should the type of dwelling have any bearing on the purchase of clothing? Does the buyer of leggings live in an inner-city flat or the leafy suburbs?

3.5.6 Diffusion of innovation

An innovation can be defined in a number of ways. Innovation can be anything that is new to the company, so it could include 'copying' a method of merchandising or a new style of garment. An innovation also can be taken to mean anything that has been taken up by only a small proportion of the market, usually 10% or less, or an item that has only been on the market for a short time. For the purposes of this discussion an innovation will be taken as anything the consumer perceives to be new, thus it could include an 'old' product introduced into a new market.

Obviously different individuals will adopt new fashion products with differing degrees of enthusiasm and at different times. The process by which the acceptance of an innovation is spread by communication to members of a social system is known as diffusion. Diffusion refers to how an innovation is spread among consumers (groups) over time whereas adoption refers to individual acceptance of new products. Rogers (1983) after an extensive literature review proposed a scheme whereby consumers are classified on the basis of the time they adopt any innovation. Rogers' scheme is obviously arbitrary with regard to percentages, therefore ideal types are presented in Table 3.2. The scheme is based on the common sense notion that most users do not adopt the innovation simultaneously. Another way of looking at the issue is to conceive the process as being segmentation over time.

Instead of trying to find characteristics of the above five groups, modern research efforts have focused on the differences between innovators and non-innovators. In practice this means researchers have combined innovators and early adopters and compared them with the rest. Innovators tend to be more open-minded, inner- rather than other-directed, younger rather than older. They also tend to be higher than non-innovators in terms of income, education, social mobility and reading magazines and newspapers. Non-innovators tend to watch more television and perceive more risk in the purchase of new products than do innovators.

There is only limited, and contested, evidence of the super-innovator, that is a person who is an innovator across several unrelated product areas. As with opinion leadership, the evidence suggests there is moderate overlap depending on product interests. Therefore we may find an innovator for fashion products to be an innovator for other aspects of appearance, but not necessarily for food or electronic items.

Table 3.2 A classification of adopters of innovations.

• Innovators	2.5%
• Early adopters	13.5%
• Early majority	34%
• Late majority	34%
• Laggards	16%

Table 3.3 Comparison of opinion leaders and innovators.

	Acceptor	Rejector
Active	Opinion leader Innovator	Opinion leader
Passive	Innovator	

There is often a tendency to equate the innovator and the opinion learder. They may indeed be the same, however there are differences as shown in Table 3.3. Opinion leaders are active since they tend to communicate with others, positively and negatively, about their purchases.

Fashion marketers are interested in the factors that influence the rate of diffusion so that appropriate marketing action may be taken to overcome obstacles of speed during the process.

The main factors that influence the rate of diffusion are:

- **Relative advantage.** The more immediate and important the benefits, the faster the rate of diffusion in terms of lower cost or long product life.

- **Compatibility.** The innovation must match cultural values, beliefs and expectations. An example of a compatibility issue, when first introduced, was the *Next Directory*, one of the first major paid-for catalogues.

- **Possibility of trials.** The ability to try on garments or easily exchange those that cannot be tried on, i.e. mail order items, is a key factor.

- **Observability** or **communicability.** Ease with which information about an innovation is transmitted.

- **The complexity of the innovation.** The more complex, in terms of understanding and use, the slower the diffusion.

- **Perceived risk.** The greater the risk the slower the diffusion. Risk can be financial, physical or social. Also a perception may exist that a delay in purchasing will lead to lower prices.

- **Type of target market.** Some groups are more willing to accept change than others e.g. the young, the affluent or the highly eductated.

- **Type of decision.** Depends on whether the purchase of the innovation is an individual or collective decision.

- **Marketing effort.** The rate of diffusion is not completely beyond the control of the firm selling it. Greater promotional spending can speed the diffusion process.

Knowledge of diffusion of innovation may aid planning particularly concerning setting targets over time and forecasting. The diffusion process is directly related to the product life cycle concept discussed in Chapter 6. The key roles of the innovator and early adopter are examined from the perspective of product planning in Chapter 6 and in relation to promotion in Chapter 9.

3.6 The organizational buyer

The discussion so far has concentrated upon the retail consumer of fashion. It should be remembered that a significant amount of fashion marketing effort is directed at organizations, be they manufacturers or retailers, who buy to sell on, or companies who purchase garments for consumption by their staff. All of the concepts so far discussed have a bearing upon organizational buying, for organizational buyers are still humans with needs, attitudes, who also conform to social norms like consumers. However, there are some differences that do influence behaviour and these points will be addressed.

It is argued that because organizational buyers buy in bulk, are better trained, better informed, are accountable for their decisions and are often part of a buying team that they are more rational than consumers. Organizational buying usually involves more formality with regard to explicit buying criteria or vendor rating systems and unlike most consumer buying there is often negotiation over products and prices. Given the greater concentration in fashion retailing that has occurred in recent years (see Chapter 8), organizational buyers are subject to personal forms of promotion, more so than consumers who receive mass communications and have impersonal relations with suppliers.

The preceding arguments support the view that organizational buyers are more rational. However, there is another perspective that argues otherwise. Because organizational buyers are spending someone else's money they may be less careful than the consumer would be with his or her own money. Fashion is concerned with personal taste and the consumer needs only to be certain about his or her purchases, whereas the organizational buyer faces greater uncertainty in the anticipation of the needs of an assortment of others. This multiple responsibility for buying can, under some circumstances, lead to careless action, as personal accountability may be diffused via committees or teams. The extent of supplier loyalty displayed by retailers and manufacturers could be taken as being counter-indicative of a more rational approach to buying than that of the consumer who shows no loyalty to any brand or retailer.

Clearly the arguments about relative rationality cannot be easily resolved, but the point to note is that both types of buyer are influenced by psychological and sociological processes which are expressed in buying decisions. Key structural factors that enable fashion marketers to determine specific approaches to organizational buyers are developed further in Chapters 6 to 9, where the relationships between the organizations are explored in relation to the marketing mix.

3.7 Summary

This chapter has introduced the concept of buyer behaviour in the fashion market. It has dealt with:

- the importance of understanding buyers;
- how individual customers make decisions;
- what types of decision they must make;
- psychological influences on customer decision making;
- how fashion marketers classify customers and sociological influences; and
- a comparison of organizational and consumer buying.

Further reading

Engel, J., Blackwell, R.D. and Miniard, P.W. (1993), *Consumer Behavior*, 7th edn., The Dryden Press, Orlando, Florida.

Festinger, L. (1957), *A Theory of Cognitive Dissonance.* Stamford University Press, Connecticut.

Fishbein, M. and Ajzen, I. (1980), *Belief, Attitude, Attention and Behavior: an Introduction to Theory and Research.* Addison Wesley, Wokingham.

Goldsmith, R. and Flynn, L.R. (1992), Identifying innovators in consumer product markets. *European Journal of Marketing*, Volume 26 Number 12, pp 42–55.

Morris, M.H. (1988), *Industrial and Organisational Marketing*, Merrill, Columbus, Ohio.

Rice, C. (1993), *Consumer Behaviour: Behavioural Aspects of Marketing*, Butterworth-Heinemann, Oxford.

Rogers, E.M. (1983), *Diffusion of Innovations*, 3rd edn., Free Press, New York.

Solomon, M.R. (1994), *Consumer Behavior: Buying, Having and Being*, 2nd edn., Allyn and Bacon, Massachusetts.

Special Report (1989), *The Green Consumer.* Mintel, London.

Special Report (1990), *Working Women.* Mintel, London.

TMS Partnershop (1990), 'Buying of some men's products by women', in *The Marketing Pocket Book 1992*, NTC Publications, Hendley-on-Thames.

Chapter 4
Fashion Marketing Research

4.1 Introduction

The purpose of this chapter is to provide an introduction to some of the main concepts and decisions involved in the research process, as well as the main techniques used in survey research.

Most adults in the United Kingdom have had some experience of marketing research, usually through contact with the 'lady with the clipboard' in street surveys. As such, the main emphasis of this chapter will be on the decisions that must be made as part of survey design; from the definition of the research problem to the design of the questionnaire and data collection. The application of marketing research to the business of product development and fashion forecasting will also be considered.

4.2 The purpose of marketing research

4.2.1 What is marketing research?

Kotler (1994) defines marketing research as 'the systematic design, analysis and reporting of data and findings relevant to a specific marketing situation facing the company'.

It is often asked if there is a difference between market research and marketing research. The difference is in the scope of an investigation, as shown in Figure 4.1. Market research is used to refer to research into a specific market, investigating such aspects as market size, market trends, competitor analysis, and so on. Marketing research is a much broader concept, covering investigation into all aspects of the marketing of goods or services, such as product research and development, pricing research, advertising research, distribution research, as well as all the aspects of market analysis covered by market research.

4.2.2 Why is information necessary?

In today's fierce market economy the risks faced by businesses are great. Aggressive competitors pose serious threats for both large and small businesses in the constant fight to maintain and increase their market share. To maximize opportunities the successful business person must make the right decisions at the right time. The consequence of making the wrong decision can be financial ruin.

Figure 4.1 Comparison of market research and marketing research.

Without the gift of clairvoyance, such decisions are problematic. An under-standing of the market and the needs and wants of your consumers now, and in the future is rarely based on intuition alone. Sound market information provides the basis for marketing decisions. Marketing research, properly designed and implemented, will provide this information.

4.2.3 Marketing research as part of a marketing information system

The wealth of information flowing into a company has to be organized so that it reaches the right people. Successful companies operate marketing information systems (MIS) to gather accurate, up-to-date information, analyse it and dis-seminate the results to appropriate decision-makers in time to allow the com-pany to maximize its opportunities and to avoid potential threats. Along with other information producing departments within the company (sales, accounts, etc.), marketing research can assist management in the decision-making process across the full range of marketing activities, from description of a market segment to prediction of future trends.

4.2.4 The scope of marketing research

There is no area of marketing activity to which the techniques of marketing research cannot be applied. Marketing research can provide information on the size and structure of a specific market as well as information about current trends, consumer preferences, a competitor's activities, advertising effectiveness, distribution methods and pricing research. Marketing research also plays a vital role in the development of new products and new advertising and promotion strategies. It can also monitor performance following implementation of those strategies.

The techniques used in the collection of marketing information depend largely on the nature of the research problem, but will vary from the well known street interview carried out by the 'ladies with clipboards', to more sophisticated techniques such as projective techniques used in such areas as motivation research.

4.2.5 Types of research

Although marketing research techniques can be applied to all areas of marketing, not all techniques are appropriate to *every* situation. Broadly speaking, there are two types of research: qualitative and quantitative.

Qualitative research uses techniques such as group discussions, individual depth interviews, projectile techniques and observation. The information obtained attempts to find out the 'how' and 'why' of a situation, rather than 'how many'. Analysis may be difficult owing to the depth and complexity of the data collected and so it should be carried out by experienced and trained researchers. Qualitative research is invaluable for basic exploratory studies, new product development and creative development studies.

Quantitative research provides information to which numbers can be applied. Quantitative research is the best known face of marketing research and its main survey method is what most people recognize as marketing research.

4.3 An overview of the marketing research process

The collection of information is a process that must be planned. There are many different areas in which planning decisions need to be made, so good organization is vital.

4.3.1 Stages in the research process

Research procedures will vary depending upon the nature of the research problem, but in general, the process of marketing research can be seen to be made up of a number of stages. They are:

(1) Define the research problem and set the research objectives
(2) Design the research. This includes:
    (a) Data sources
    (b) Select the sampling method
    (c) Select the data collection method
    (d) (d) Design the data collection form (questionnaire)
(3) Test the research design (pilot)
(4) Collect the data
(5) Analyse the data and interpret the results
(6) Present the findings.

4.4 Problem definition and setting research objectives

Defining the research problem is the most critical step in the research process. Unless the problem is accurately defined, the information collected will be of limited or no use. Careful thought and discussion about the problem, the information needed to address the problem and the relative value of the information collected should take place before anything else. A structured, systematic approach to decision making will also enable management (or the commissioner of the research) to set the objectives of the research. In other words, what is the problem and what do we want to find out to try to solve it? This preliminary planning is important as it has implications for the design of the research and the quality of the information collected.

4.5 Research design

There are three types of research design; exploratory, descriptive and causal. The choice of research design will depend on the problem previously defined.

4.5.1 Exploratory research

This is most useful in the early stages of research, particularly if the researcher is not familiar with the subject area. There is no formal structure to exploratory research as the researcher needs to look at a wide range of information sources without being restricted. The aim of exploratory research is to uncover any variables that may be relevant to the reseach project as well as an investigation of the environment in which the research will take place.

4.5.2 Descriptive research

The purpose of descriptive research is to provide an accurate description of the variables uncovered by the exploratory stage. This could be used to investigate the market share of a company's products or the demographic characteristics of the target market (age, sex, income, etc.). Data is usually obtained from secondary data sources or from surveys.

4.5.3 Causal research

Causal research is used to determine the relationship between variables, e.g., the relationship between advertising and repeat purchases.

4.6 Data sources

Data come from two sources, primary and secondary. Secondary data sources consist of information that has already been collected for other purposes and primary sources of information are those used for the purpose of collecting information specifically for the current research project.

4.6.1 Secondary sources

These provide the researcher with a starting point for data collection. It may be possible to solve the research problem either wholly or in part by using secondary data. This reduces the cost of a research project as secondary data are cheaper than collecting primary data. Secondary sources of information are in the main fairly accessible, although some sources may remain confidential and others may be too expensive to acquire.

Secondary sources can be separated into the two types shown in Figure 4.2. Internal sources are those that generate information within a company or organization, e.g., sales figures, accounts information, etc. External sources are those that generate information outside the company or organization. These are by far the more numerous and some examples of external sources are listed below:

- **Government statistics:** Census data, family expenditure surveys, trade and manufacturing trends.
- **Trade Information:** Trade Press, e.g. *Fashion Weekly*, *Drapers Record*. Trade associations, e.g. CBI, trade surveys, company reports and competitors' accounts.
- **Financial Institutions:** Many major banks publish reports on regional and national industries.
- **Commercial research:** Many market research companies undertake continuous research and omnibus surveys (AGB, Millward Brown). The TMS partnership specializes in researching the fashion market. Various market reports are available, from e.g. Mintel, Keynote, Retail Intelligence.

The use of secondary data sources, also called desk research, can be very time consuming because there is such a lot of information available. Keeping

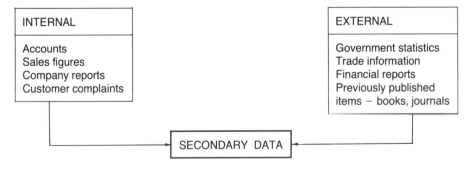

Figure 4.2   Sources of secondary data.

the objectives of the research in mind will help to ensure that time is spent efficiently.

4.6.2 Primary sources

Most marketing research projects will involve the collection of more up-to-date information than is available from secondary sources. Primary sources of information may include consumers, designers, buyers, manufacturers, retailers, and so on, depending upon the research problem.

4.7 Practical sampling methods

In designing research a major decision that the researcher must make concerns the selection of a sampling method. Sampling is a very important tool in marketing research. It involves selecting a small number of people from the larger survey population whose characteristics, attitudes and behaviour are representative of the larger group.

Before selecting the sample, however, the researcher must first define the research population from which to draw the sample. Exploratory research can help define the population to include all the players and variables that are relevant to the survey.

For some surveys, particularly if the survey population is small or concentrated in one geographic area, it may be possible to take a census, which is a useful method in some business surveys. More commonly a representative sample is interviewed as this reduces both time and cost of the research.

4.7.1 Deciding sample size

Deciding how many people to include in your sample is as important a decision as how they should be selected. Factors such as cost, time and staff availability, level of accuracy required, data collection method and location of the population all play a part in deciding sample size. In reality, cost-effectiveness is the most important factor in deciding how many should be contacted in the research, followed by time and staff availability. If it is decided to select a large number for the sample, there may be insufficient staff available to contact the respondents within the time constraints of the survey, so a smaller sample size may be accepted as a compromise.

When selecting a sample it is important that there is a high level of confidence that the sample is representative of the research population as a whole. The sample must be large enough to provide accurate results, without being so large as to increase research costs unnecessarily. It is possible to calculate confidence levels for different sample sizes and there are several texts that cover this adequately (see Further reading at the end of this chapter).

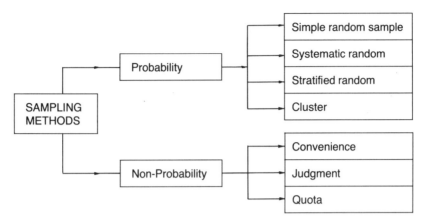

Figure 4.3 Types of sampling methods.

4.7.2 Choice of a sampling method

The two main types of sampling method – probability methods and non-probability methods are shown in Figure 4.3.

4.7.3 Probability methods

Statistically speaking, these are the best types of sampling method as each respondent has a known chance of being selected, so bias is minimized. They also allow the accuracy of the results to be estimated statistically. Sometimes probability sampling methods are referred to generically as 'random sampling' methods. In fact, this refers to a specific type of very precise probability sample. There is often some confusion over the use of the term 'random'. Selecting people in the street at random is not technically random sampling, but more often refers to selection of respondents by interviewers for quota sampling.

The main types of probability sample are simple random sampling, systematic random sampling, stratified random sampling and cluster sampling.

Simple random sampling

Items can be selected from the sampling frame by using the lottery method, e.g. taking numbers out of a hat. In the United Kingdom, ERNIE the computer selects Premium Bond winners, and does so by using simple random sampling. Random number tables are generated by computer and often used in marketing research.

Systematic random sampling

With larger samples it is more convenient to divide the population by the sample size to calculate the sampling interval (n). A random starting point is selected using random number tables and every nth item after that is selected.

Example If the sample size is 50, and the population size is 3000, then the sampling interval is calculated as:

$$n = \frac{3000}{50} = 60$$

If the random number picked from the tables was 35, for example, then the first item selected from the sampling frame would be 35. Every 60th number after that would be selected until a sample size of 50 was achieved.

As the first number was selected randomly, this method is sometimes called a 'quasi-random' method.

The advantage of these methods is that they are relatively simple to carry out and sampling error and confidence levels can be calculated statistically. The main disadvantage is that samples may be produced that do not reflect the characteristics of the survey population. For example, if a sample of students was drawn from a list of all students at a university, it is possible that all the students in the sample might be design students. This is clearly not representative of the student population as a whole.

Stratified random sampling

One way to try to overcome this type of sampling error is to use stratified random sampling. This is used when it is felt that different groups within the population have characteristics that are likely to lead to different types of answers. The population is divided into distinguishable groups (strata) who have similar characteristics. Stratification factors should be as relevant as possible to the survey (e.g., consumer surveys are often stratified by age, sex, socio-economic group, etc.). A random sample is then taken from each stratum.

There are two main methods used to stratify samples. First, with a uniform sampling fraction (proportionate sampling), or secondly, with a variable sampling fraction (disproportionate sampling).

Proportionate and disproportionate sampling

If all the strata are equally important to the survey, a proportionate sample would be taken, i.e. the same number selected from each stratum. Frequently, some strata are more important to the research than others. For example, if you were conducting a survey into the purchase of outsize garments (size 18+), it would be reasonable to assume that most of these items would be purchased by those who were larger than size 16 than those who were not. It is logical that more of these people should be included in the sample. In other words, a disproportionate sample would be taken. If a proportionate sample was taken, too few of the people who took larger sized clothes would be included in the survey and it would be difficult to extrapolate the results to the general population with any degree of accuracy.

Cluster sampling

Cluster sampling is a variation of stratified random sampling and may be used when the survey population is concentrated in a relatively small number of groups (clusters) that are considered typical of the market in question. A random sample of these clusters is then taken. A random sample of units from within these clusters is then taken. If the number of units within a cluster is small, a census may be carried out. In a national survey of specialist bridal wear retailers, for example, sales areas could be identified by geographical region and a random sample of these taken. Within each selected sales area, all or a sample of the store managers would be interviewed.

There is a problem with cluster sampling that occurs if the clusters are not sufficiently representative of the survey population. For example, in a small geographical area it is likely that it will consist of people with similar housing, incomes and lifestyle. Although cluster sampling can be more cost-effective than some other methods of probability sampling, there is a danger that sampling error will increase if the clusters are not carefully defined before the first stage of sampling.

Sampling frames

When using probability sampling methods it is necessary to use a sampling frame. This is a list of every element in the survey population. The sample is drawn from this list. A sampling frame is essential for probability-based techniques, as each element must have a known chance of selection, and so must be included in the sampling frame. According to Webb (1992), a sampling frame must have the following characteristics:

- Each element should be included only once
- No element should be excluded
- The frame should cover the whole of the population
- The information used to construct the frame should be up-to-data and accurate
- The frame should be convenient to use.

Examples of sampling frames include electoral rolls, the telephone book, the Royal Mail's lists of postcodes and other similar databases.

In practice, most sampling frames are not perfect. Not everyone with a telephone is in the phone book, for example. Finding a sampling frame that is suitable for your research can occasionally prove difficult.

4.7.4 Non-probability methods

With non-probability sampling methods, some element of judgment enters the selection process. The extent to which judgment is used, and therefore the element of bias introduced, varies in these methods. Non-probability methods do not require a sampling frame and the chance of each unit being selected is unknown. Statistical estimates of the size of the sampling error cannot therefore be made.

The methods are convenience sampling, judgment sampling and quota sampling.

Convenience sampling

Items are selected that are close or easily available. This is useful in the exploratory stage of research, giving the researcher a 'feel' for the subject. Despite being very cheap and quick to carry out, the level of error and bias with this method is likely to be very high and so it should be used with caution.

Judgment sampling

Items are selected by the researcher that are felt to be representative of the survey population. This method attempts to be more representative than convenience sampling. Experts also may be consulted for advice on which items are likely to be more appropriate for the survey. For example, in a survey of textile manufacturers, a staff specialist such as a product developer may provide useful advice on which manufacturers would be suitable for selection.

Quota sampling

This is the most likely non-probability method to produce a representative sample as items selected are based on known characteristics of the population.

Table 4.1 Quota sampling frame (A).

	16–29	30–64	65+	TOTAL
M A L E	16–29 = 27% MALE = 47% 27% of 47% of 200 = 25 Quota = 25	30–64 = 57% MALE = 47% 57% of 47% of 200 = 54 Quota = 54	65+ = 16% MALE = 47% 16% of 47% of 200 =15 Quota = 15	94
F E M A L E	16–29 = 27% FEM. = 53% 27% of 53% of 200 = 29 Quota = 29	30–64 = 57% FEM. = 53% 57% of 53% of 200 = 60 Quota = 60	65+ = 16% FEM. = 53% 16% of 53% of 200 = 17 Quota = 17	106
TOTAL	54	114	32	200

Example   Assume that your survey population has the following characteristics:

Age: 16–29 = 27%; 30–64 = 57%; 65+ = 16%
Sex: Male = 47%; Female = 53%

If we wanted to interview 200 people who were representative of the above population in terms of the two quota controls (age and sex), we would calculate the quotas as shown in Table 4.1.
     This is more conveniently represented as shown in Table 4.2.

Table 4.2   Quota sampling frame (B).

AGE	MALE	FEMALE	TOTAL
16–29	25	29	54
30–64	54	60	114
65+	15	17	32
TOTAL	94	106	200

A survey's accuracy of representation can be increased by narrowing the bands and including more characteristics e.g., social class. Interviewers are then allocated a number of interviews (quotas) with specific types of respondents.
     The advantages of quota sampling are that it is relatively quick to carry out and easy to administer from a fieldwork point of view. It is also cheaper to use than probability sampling methods. The disadvantages of quota sampling involve problems of bias and sampling errors. The responsibility for selection of respondents lies with the interviewer, which may introduce bias. There is the added problem that there is no probability mechanism with quota sampling, so the sampling error cannot easily be calculated.
     Quota samples are often used in surveys where fine degrees of accuracy are not required, for instance in product testing for preference between products.
     Although many companies who provide continuous research services use probability sampling, the majority of *ad hoc* marketing research is conducted using quota samples. If this method gave consistently biased or misleading conclusions, it would not be used.

4.8 Primary data collection methods

The researcher should not rely on the use of secondary data alone to answer the research problems. Not all secondary data are available to the researcher as some may be unavailable in e.g. confidential reports and other data may simply

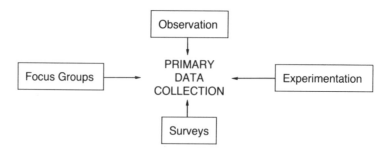

Figure 4.4 Approaches to primary data collection.

be too costly to acquire. The information that is available may be out-of-date or not sufficiently detailed to solve the research problem. Usually, primary data needs to be collected.

The four main approaches to primary data collection: observation, focus groups, experimentation and surveys are shown in Figure 4.4.

4.8.1 Observation

There are occasions when it is more useful to observe behaviour than to interview the respondent about it. Observation is usually used to complement other research methods in marketing research, rather than being used alone as this method can identify patterns of behaviour, but cannot provide information on the reasons behind that behaviour. There are a number of methods available for the observation of behaviour. They are:

Personal observation

The researcher observes behaviour and records it as it occurs. The skill and the objectivity of the researcher play a key role in the collection of unbiased data. The audit data are collected by taking an inventory of certain products or brands at the premises (at home or office) of the respondent.

Mechanical observation

Recording devices may be used either in laboratory settings or in natural settings. In the laboratory, devices such as the psychogalvanometer are used to measure the respondent's level of perspiration (and so the level of arousal) following exposure to an advertisement or other stimuli. Other devices include the eye-movement camera that detects the movement of the eye over an advertisement, identifying the visual aspects of the advertisement that gain attention. In natural settings, in-store video cameras may be used to record behaviour, with the film being used later for analysis such as researching store layout.

4.8.2 Focus groups

The focus group (also known as the group discussion) is a form of qualitative research. The group usually consists of between 6–12 respondents who discuss products, services, attitudes or other aspects of the marketing process. The discussion is led by a skilled researcher called a group moderator, who guides the discussion, following a checklist of topics. The group usually meets in an informal setting, often someone's home, and the group members are paid a small sum for attending. These discussions can take several hours to complete and are often used as a preliminary to survey research.

4.8.3 Experimentation

According to Kotler (1994), this is the most scientifically valid type of research. Here, matched groups of respondents are subjected to different treatments and the difference in the responses is observed. All variables outside the scope of the research are controlled and as such, the observed responses are taken to be as a result of the difference in treatment of the group. Experimental research seeks to identify cause-and-effect relationships that are central to marketing work.

4.8.4 Surveys

Survey research is the most well known of the research approaches and is widely used for descriptive research. Surveys collect information from a representative sample of the survey population on such topics as consumer behaviour, attitudes and beliefs as well as buying intentions. The strength of these beliefs, attitudes and intentions are measured and the results extrapolated to the population as a whole.

4.9 Data collection methods

If a survey is to be conducted, there are a number of methods available for the collection of data and each has its relative advantages and disadvantages. The three main methods are by personal interview, telephone interview and mail questionnaire.

4.9.1 Personal interview

Face-to-face interviewing is still the most widely used method of primary data collection in the United Kingdom, although telephone interviewing is becoming increasingly popular. This method is labour-intensive and costly, but is more likely to result in a satisfactorily completed questionnaire than any of the other methods. This is particularly true if the questionnaire is long, complicated or covers sensitive subjects. Respondents have the opportunity to build a rapport with the interviewer, who can elicit full and accurate answers to questions without biasing the responses.

In a personal interview there is the opportunity to show supporting material, such as examples of a product or still photographs from advertisements. Open-ended questions can also be included in the questionnaire design as the interviewer is present to record the answers verbatim.

The interviewer or fieldworker also plays a vital role in the selection of respondents for interview when using quota sampling. This however, may introduce bias into the survey.

There is another type of personal interview, the depth interview, which belongs to the realm of qualitative research. Typically, these interviews can last for over an hour. The interviewer does not have a questionnaire as such, but uses a less structured interview schedule. This may either consist of a series of open questions that must be asked as they are written, or a checklist of topics for discussion, as with the focus group. The interviewer must be very highly trained in the art of asking unbiased questions, and usually, the interviews are recorded for transcription and analysis later. This method is particularly useful and is a rich source of information if the subject of the survey is of a personal or embarrassing nature.

4.9.2 Telephone interviewing

The development of CATI (Computer Aided Telephone Interviewing) has greatly increased the extent to which telephone interviewing is undertaken. Interviewing is done from a central location, cutting the costs of fieldwork considerably, providing the sample size is large. It is not a cost-effective method for small samples. With the increased demand for immediate information, particularly for commercial omnibus surveys, CATI is ideally suited for the provision of a very fast turn-round of data as the results are recorded and processed as the questions are answered. The sample also can be drawn from a wide geographical spread, as the fieldworkers do not have to travel.

The are disadvantages to this method of data collection. It is difficult to establish a rapport with the respondent by telephone, which is partly why this method is not successful for the researching of personal or embarrassing topics. Many respondents are fearful of 'sugging', selling under the guise of marketing research, and expect the interviewer to try to sell them double glazing and the like. With a disembodied voice it is also easier for a respondent to refuse or end an interview prematurely. The telephone interview demands the use of very structured, pre-coded questionnaires that may be completed quickly without having to rely on examples of supporting material. An ideal telephone interview will last no longer than 15 minutes, on average.

4.9.3 Mail (postal) questionnaire

If the survey population is widely dispersed, it may be more useful to send the questionnaire by mail than to have an interviewer call on the respondent. Mail surveys also have the advantage of a reduction in field staff, and if there is a high response rate, the cost per questionnaire is low. A high response rate is more likely if the survey population consists of members of a special interest group (e.g., keep-fit enthusiasts) and the questionnaire relates to their area of interest. Otherwise, a response rate of between 30–40% is not uncommon. The advantage over the telephone interview with this method is that the questionnaire can be lengthy and ask for detailed information.

The disadvantages (apart from the low response rate) are several. A mail questionnaire has to compete with the increasing amounts of junk mail that pour through our letterboxes. If there is a high non-response rate then the cost per questionnaire is high, particularly if a reply-paid envelope is included. There is no guarantee that the selected respondent will actually complete the questionnaire, and in spite of careful design, the control of the question sequence is removed. If the respondent does not understand any of the questions, there is no interviewer present to clarify the problem. There also may be a long time-lag between sending out the questionnaires and receiving completed forms.

4.10 Questionnaire design

Questionnaire design is an aspect of research in which many people automatically assume expertise, even those without prior research experience. The questionnaire is a vital part of most surveys and great care must be taken with its design. To the novice, the problems inherent in designing a questionnaire tend not to become apparent until the pilot stage of the survey.

Many factors will affect the design of the questionnaire, such as the nature of the data required (qualitative or quantitative) and how the questionnaire is to be administered (by personal interview, telephone, mail or other self-completion). However, most questionnaires tend to lie between two extremes: first, the highly structured questionnaire used, for example, in telephone interviewing, where the question wording is fixed and responses are limited; and secondly, an unstructured interview schedule used in qualitative research, which consists of a list of topics to be covered, with the actual wording of the questions left to the trained interviewer.

A well designed questionnaire will provide the researcher with complete, accurate and unbiased information using the minimum number of questions and allowing the maximum number of successfully completed interviews.

4.10.1 The decision areas

Questionnaires are notoriously difficult to construct, but Tull and Hawkins (1990) suggest that a convenient way of tackling the design is by breaking up the task into a number of decision areas, namely:

● Preliminary decisions

- Question content
- Question wording
- Response format
- Question sequence
- Questionnaire layout
- Pretest and revise.

4.10.2 Preliminary decisions

These include decisions on what information is required, who will be included in the survey and how they will be contacted.

4.10.3 Question content

This section is concerned with the content of individual questions; what to include, rather than how to phrase the question. Points to consider include:

Is the question necessary?

The first decision to be made here is to decide whether or not the question is actually necessary. If the question is not necessary for the purposes of meeting the survey objectives, then leave it out.

How many questions are needed?

If the question is necessary, one must take care that the information you elicit will answer the question without ambiguity. For example, if you asked a respondent: 'Do you think woollen trousers are comfortable and warm to wear?' and the response was 'No', would that mean that woollen trousers were uncomfortable or did not keep the respondent warm? Rather than ask double-barrelled questions, it is better to use one question for each point of information required, so you would ask: 'Do you think that woollen trousers are comfortable to wear?' and 'Do you think that woollen trousers are warm to wear?'

Has the respondent the information to answer the question?

Sometimes respondents are asked questions on subjects about which they are not informed. A husband may not have the necessary information if asked how much his wife spends a month on clothing, for example. Some respondents will attempt to answer questions without being adequately informed, which will affect the validity of the results.

Is the respondent able to articulate the response?

Even if the respondent has the necessary information to answer a question, they may not always be able to articulate their responses successfully. If asked to describe the type of person who might wear a particular fragrance, many respondents would find difficulty in phrasing their answers. It is easier for the respondent if they are presented with a set of alternatives from which they can choose the response that they feel to be the most appropriate. Using aids such as descriptions, pictures, etc. makes it easier for the respondent to answer the questions, and so complete the interview.

Asking questions beyond the memory span of the respondent

Asking questions about behaviour over a long time span may not produce accurate information. For example, asking the respondent how much they spent on tights in the last year would result in an answer that was pure guesswork. Asking how much they spent on tights in the last fortnight would be more likely to provide accurate information.

Question wording

Great care must be taken with the wording of questions. Decisions about question wording include:

- Does the word mean the ssame to all respondents?
- Some words, such as 'dinner' and 'tea' mean different things in different parts of the country. Words should be chosen to mean the same to all respondents;
- The use of vague or ambiguous words also should be avoided. For example, 'Are you a regular purchaser of nylon tights?' is not specific enough. How often is 'regular'? This may mean different things to different respondents.

Are the questions loaded?

Some words or phrases should not be used in questionnaire design as they are likely to result in bias. Emotive words or phrases invite particular responses. For example, 'Are you in favour of sending money to help the poor, starving people in Africa?'

4.10.4 Response format

There are a number of types of response format that may be used. The most commonly used are dichotomous, multiple choice and open-ended formats. Most questionnaires contain a mixture of these.

Dichotomous

Only two responses are allowed; such as 'yes' or 'no', 'male' or 'female'. A neutral 'don't know' category is sometimes included. The advantages are that these questions are quick to ask and the responses easy to record and analyse.

The disadvantages are that they do not allow for any shades of meaning to be included in the responses, and many questions would have to be asked to derive information of any detail by using this format alone.

Multiple choice

Here the respondent is presented with a choice of several possible answers to the question. Frequently, the list of choices is shown to the respondent on a card. The order of the alternative answers should be rotated to avoid bias. Again, the questions are quick to ask and the responses easy to record and analyse. This format also allows for more shades of meaning and the respondent has more freedom of choice in the response. The difficulty of this format is that it is difficult to ensure that the list of possible responses is complete.

Open-ended

The respondent has complete freedom of choice in the response given with this format. This format is often used where little information exists to construct a multiple choice list, or when great detail is required. The advantage is that the information produced is extensive and is free from any bias of suggested answers. The main disadvantage is that the responses are slow to record as they must be recorded verbatim. This can lead to interviewers selecting what they think are the most important points resulting in bias. These responses are also difficult to analyse as coding frames must be constructed for each question after the fieldwork has taken place. Coding of responses at a later stage requires grouping of responses, which can lose some shades of meaning.

4.10.5 Question sequence

The questions need to be organized logically to avoid introducing error or bias. Generally, you should move from general questions that the respondent finds easy to answer, to more specific or difficult questions about attitudes or behaviour.

In some surveys it is possible to ask classification questions, which may appear personal or embarrassing, at the end of the interview. If a quota sample is being used, some of these questions will need to be asked at the start of the interview, as they may form part of the quota control. To overcome this, show-cards may be used e.g. with age or income bands:

A) 15–24	A) under £5000 p.a.
B) 25–34	B) £5000–£9999 p.a.
C) 35–44	C) £10 000–£14 999 p.a.
D) 45–54	D) £15 000–£20 000 p.a.
E) 55+	E) £20 000+ p.a.

Figure 4.5 Sample showcards.

4.10.6 Questionnaire layout

The overall aim is clarity. There are some procedures that can aid clarity. These include ensuring that all questions are numbered; filter questions (ones that may be omitted in certain situations) should be clearly marked; instructions to the interviewer should be in block capitals; arrows or visual aids may be used.

4.10.7 Pretesting (pilot) and revision

The questionnaire must be thoroughly tested, using respondents similar to those who will take part in the final survey. This is known as the pilot stage and is vitally important to the reliability and validity of your survey results. Once this has been done, any modifications needed can be made, and the questionnaire tested again.

4.11 Attitude measurement and rating scales

These are used to quantify the strength of a response. The two scales most commonly used in attitude measurement are Osgood's Semantic Differential scale and the Likert Summated Rating scale.

Attitudes are measured in scales. The main types of scale are:

4.11.1 Types of attitude scale

Nominal scales

These classify individuals into two or more groups, e.g. male/female, agree/disagree.

Ordinal scales

These rank individuals according to certain characteristics, e.g. Yves St. Laurent fragrances according to preference:

* Opium
* Paris
* Rive Gauche, etc.

Interval scales

These scales have regular calibrations, e.g.

Favourable　　　　　　　　　　　　　　　　Unfavourable

Figure 4.6 Interval scale.

The advantage of this scale is that it can be used to measure the strength of a particular attitude. It also allows the use of statistical measures such as standard deviation, correlation coefficients and significance testing.

Ratio scales

These scales have a fixed origin or zero point, which permits the use of all arithmetical functions. e.g. measurement of length or weight. Measurements of market size, market share and number of consumers are also examples of ratio scales.

As previously mentioned, the most widely used attitude scaling techniques are:

4.11.2 The Likert scale

Respondents are asked to indicate their level of agreement or disagreement to a series of statements about a subject or object. The statements used are identified as either positive or negative and scores are allocated for particular responses. The list of possible responses is usually:

- Strongly agree
- Agree
- Don't know/neutral
- Disagree
- Strongly disagree.

The Likert scale is not an interval scale, so it is not possible to infer that 'strongly agree' is twice as strong an attitude as 'agree'. The scores achieved by individual respondents are only relative to those achieved by other respondents. Likert scales are popular as they are easy to construct and give reliable information about the degree of respondents' feelings.

4.11.3 The semantic differential scale

This is another widely used technique in marketing research. A series of bipolar (opposite) adjectives of descriptive phrases are presented to the respondent at opposite ends of a five or seven point scale. Respondents are asked to indicate where on the scale best describes their feelings towards the subject or object. An example is shown in Figure 4.7 below.

Figure 4.7 An example of the semantic differential scale.

Semantic differential scales have been successfully used for such investigations as corporate image, brand image, product image, etc. It is often difficult for consumers to articulate their feelings in these areas, and the semantic differential scale offers them an easy way of expressing themselves. These scales are widely used in marketing research as they obtain information about consumer behaviour that may not be obtained with the same degree of success by direct questioning.

4.12 The role of marketing research in new product development

Marketing research has a vital role to play in ensuring that new products launched onto the market are successful ventures, rather than dismal failures. The main input that marketing research makes into the new product development process is in the areas of:

- Idea generation
- Evaluating & developing new product concepts
- Evaluating & developing new products
- Pricing new products.

These inputs are similar in the development of fashion.

Since the late 1970s, there has been an increase in the number of stores developing their own product lines. Specialists called product developers create products and test them on customers. There may be numerous reasons why a product is developed or modified to be sold in a particular market; new government legislation, changes in culture, the economy or even the climate may be responsible.

The creation of a marketing strategy for the development of a fashion product involves four stages. Each of the stages (set out below) involves marketing research with the ultimate aim of testing a product for feasibility prior to its production, and to produce a plan for its production and marketing.

4.12.1 Creation of a customer profile

By identifying potential target markets for the proposed product, it is possible to prepare a customer profile for each one. Profiling characteristics such as age, sex, occupation and geographical location are considered, together with lifestyle characteristics as used in market segmentation.

Once these target markets are identified, the attitudes and perceptions of potential consumers may be researched. Different groups of consumers have different needs, and by addressing the variables associated with buyer behaviour, it is possible to identify the product attributes that will appeal to each target group.

The information necessary to write a customer profile is available from several sources, both primary and secondary. For example, trade press, reports from fashion shows, sales staff, industry analysis and buyers can all be called upon to supply information.

The identification of specialized target markets is as important to the area of fashion retailing as it is to fashion design. Many fashion retailers for example, Next have deliberately targeted very specific niche markets, in an attempt to differentiate themselves from the competition. Emphasis has been placed on the development and acquisition of appropriate merchandise to satisfy particular market segments.

4.12.2 Preparing a profile of the competitors

Information about competitors' market size, market share, product range, consumers and marketing strategies all come under the scope of marketing research. With this information it is possible to analyse the relative strengths and weaknesses of the competition, and decide how much of a threat they pose.

4.12.3 Preparation of a market strategy report

Once the target market has been identified and a profile prepared for both the consumer and the competition, a marketing strategy must be prepared. The report will include general information about the market (size, structure, etc.) as well as particular information about the proposed target market. It also will contain information about the product, including the product's differential advantage, and pricing policy. An evaluation of potential retail outlets will also be included, and an assessment of the resources needed to produce and market the new or modified product.

4.12.4 The merchandise plan

This stage involves product testing, i.e. exposing prototypes of the product to fashion buyers. Any further developments suggested by these 'experts' will be considered, and the prototypes modified, as is the usual practice with product testing.

These are the main steps in developing and evaluating a new fashion product. The steps are slightly different from those involved in the development of more conventional consumer products, but the information necessary for a successful launch (such as an evaluation of the concept, its acceptability, consumer attitudes and preferences, information on the market in general and testing the product) is very similar.

4.13 Forecasting fashion

Estimating future demand for goods or services is extremely difficult in any market, but particularly so in fashion. Anticipating what buyers are likely to do under a given set of conditions is made more difficult due to the eclectic nature of fashions, so any predictions about the future should be flexible and open to modification as the seasons change.

There is a problem with the use of formalized techniques for prediction in that many fashion professionals mistakenly believe that their creativity will be inhibited or that their fashion acumen and flair will be trivialized by this process. This is clearly not the case, and these methods should be used to assist the decision-maker.

4.13.1 Uses of information

The basis on which forecasts can be made is one of sound information. Past and present consumer purchases are analysed for trend data. The target market for your products must be clearly identified and described by using marketing research techniques. The use of geodemographic systems such as ACORN (A Classification of Residential Neighbourhoods) can be used to identify and contact your target market, and collect information about attitudes, preferences and future buying intentions such as 'Are you likely to buy a new coat in the next three months?'.

Millers and tanners who often work years ahead of the market can be contacted for primary data on future developments, as can fashion editors and buyers, who are in the forefront of current consumer behaviour. Secondary sources such as trade magazines and newspapers provide information which is readily accessible. Range plans covering such variables as material, product type, colour and price are also an important source of data.

4.13.2 Further techniques

Information gained from the above sources will provide an analytical base for more specialized forecasting techniques. These include the use of ordinal scales to rank product alternatives as well as panels of up to eight people, who are asked to provide a consensus view of forecasts. A consensus is sought to avoid the bias introduced if the opinion of a single person regarding future sales potential was taken. Computer forecasting software has been specially developed for use in the fashion industry, which has facilitated the use of complex statistical techniques.

A form of product testing, called style testing, is used to involve the consumer in the forecasting process. A representative sample of target consumers is shown several provisional styles and ranges for future seasons. The consumers are then asked to state which they believe will be 'winners' and which are likely to be 'losers' in terms of customer appeal.

Test marketing of new styles, colours or silhouettes often takes place using a 'sample, test, re-order' system. Small quantities of garments are made up and placed in selected retail outlets. Customer reactions may be monitored without incurring the costs of full production. Similarly marketing research is used to monitor sales performance at the start of each season to identify any variations away from the forecast that may occur.

Fashion forecasting methods involve much organization and planning and are not easy to establish in the first instance. All fashion businesses are involved in forecasting to some degree, and an increasing number of companies are being set up solely to provide specialist prediction services.

Fashion buying will always rely on a high degree of intuition and gut feeling about the market. When this is combined with a structured approach to planning and the use of research, more accurate forecasting is possible.

4.14 Summary

This chapter has covered the nature and scope of marketing research, starting with the survey research process:

- definition of the research required
- decisions about the survey population
- sampling methods
- questionnaire design
- data collection.

The chapter has also covered types of research design and approach and the sources of data available to the fashion marketer. The use of marketing research in new product development and fashion prediction has also been discussed.

Further reading

Collins, M. (1986), Sampling, in Worcester, R.M. & Downham, J. (eds), *Consumer Market Research Handbook*, 3rd edn., Esomar, McGraw-Hill, Maidenhead.

Jarnow, J.A. and Judelle, B. (1974), *Inside the Fashion Business – Text and Readings*, 2nd edn., Wiley, New York.

Kent, R. (1993), *Marketing Research in Action*, Routledge, London.

Kotler, P. (1994), *Marketing Management, Analysis, Planning & Control*, 8th edn., Prentice Hall International, New Jersey.

Mouthino, L. and Evans, M. (1992), *Applied Marketing Research*, Addison-Wesley, Wokingham.

Richards, E. and Rachman, D. (eds) (1978), *Marketing Information and Research in Fashion Management*, American Marketing Association, Chicago.

Rodgers D.S. and Gamans, L.R. (1983), *Fashion: a Marketing Approach*, Holt, Rinehart & Winston, London.

Tull, D.S. and Hawkins, D.I. (1990), *Marketing Research: Measurement and Method*, (5th edn.), Macmillan Publishing Company, New York.

Webb, J.R. (ed) *Understanding and Designing Marketing Research*, Academic Press, London.

Chapter 5
Segmentation and the Marketing Mix

5.1 Introduction and overview

This chapter will discuss the nature of market segmentation and the related strategies that are open to the fashion marketer. The preceding three chapters have concentrated on customers, in the context of the marketing environment in Chapter 2, as buyers with differing needs and social characteristics in Chapter 3 and as a focus of research efforts in Chapter 4. This chapter attempts to draw together several themes to look at how to decide which market or markets to aim at, namely the target market(s).

Having determined the target market or markets, the next consideration is the positioning of the fashion marketing organization and its marketing efforts towards the target and this will be covered later.

The chapter also forms an important link with the rest of the book by introducing the concept of the marketing mix. Having shown how an organization can position itself within a market, the next task is the planning and organization of controllable variables to meet the requirements of the market profitably. The particular combination of marketing variables offered to specific markets is known as the marketing mix, and this is described shortly.

5.2 Mass marketing and market segmentation

5.2.1 What is a market?

To constitute a market a number of conditions have to be met. First there should be a genuine need, the customer(s) should be willing and able to buy the product and the aggregate demand should be sufficient to enable a supplier to operate profitably.

5.2.2 Mass marketing

Fashion marketers who assume that all customers in the market are the same are adopting a mass marketing or undifferentiated marketing approach. The assumption is based on the idea that customer needs do not vary and that the company can offer a standardized marketing mix that meets the needs of everyone. The standard marketing mix means the same product, method of distribution, prices and promotional effort aimed at everyone. The best example of this is China during the cultural revolution of the 1960s where the whole nation was offered the Mao outfit of dark blue jacket and trousers.

In Chapter 2, when considering the development of markets it was noted that the aristocracy and wealthy classes were able to obtain products that met their precise needs. Most people in the pre-industrial revolution period dressed in a variety of styles which were greatly influenced by local skills and raw materials. Mass production methods, coupled with the experience of producing clothing for large armies, led to the possibility of mass markets for clothing. Indeed the practice of mass marketing linked to the military can be illustrated by the existence of the 'demob' suit issued to servicemen upon demobilization from national service.

Where a product can be standardized, perhaps because of the predominance of function over style then it could be argued that a mass market exists. Also, when mass production methods enable considerable economies of scale, some items may be produced so efficiently that the product becomes a low-priced commodity. Certain items of underwear like white Y-Fronts or one-size tights are certainly capable of consideration as products suitable for mass marketing. The reality, however, is that although the possibility of mass marketing of clothing remains, it has never been a major feature of fashion markets in the United Kingdom or any other advanced economy.

Given choice and the diversity of suppliers, consumers have amply demonstrated the desire for individuality that clothing can give them and they have rendered elusive the idea of a mass market for clothing. This is not to argue that homogeneity is absent in the clothing market or that there is not just one mass market, but many different clothing markets.

Recognizing that the existence of many markets reflects the needs and purchasing capacity of clothing buyers leads to the idea of segmenting markets. Markets may be segmented or divided where for instance, a group of consumers has a set of homogeneous needs that is different to other groups.

5.2.3 Heterogeneous markets

The extreme form of market segmentation is where everyone has different needs and purchasing capability and this is described as market heterogeneity. An example of this would be if everyone had bespoke tailoring, which, given the economics of the prospect, is an unlikely scenario. The nearest example is the market for corporate clothing. Here large organizations may require custom-made uniforms or limited ranges of clothing for their staff to enable the achievement of corporate image and personnel goals. However, even within the corporate clothing market there will be some homogeneity, with for example smaller regional and local non-competing organizations such as restaurants who are willing to accept similar garments for their staff. Security staff and cleaning personnel from many organizations may be provided with the same garments.

5.2.4 Market segmentation

Market segmentation is where the larger market is heterogeneous and can be broken down into smaller units that are similar in character. In practice there is always the problem of balancing the similarity of needs with the desire for substantial numbers of potential buyers.

Pressure to target more closely can lead to greater fragmentation of a market so that the overheads of promotional support and information overload for consumers can become associated with lower levels of market efficiency. An acceptable balance has been found by many firms in what is known as niche marketing, where a clearly defined segment is targeted with a narrow product range. Tie Rack, Knickerbox and Sock Shop are all examples of this approach. Niche marketing is just another form of market segmentation. The extreme form of meeting customers' needs along this continuum has already been described as market heterogeneity, where each customer is treated as unique.

There are other pressures to aggregate consumers with needs that are 'similar enough', but this can lead to a situation where the resultant marketing mix is a compromise that satisfies no one. The desire for larger markets is understandable as large markets enable economies of scale in production and marketing and can command higher profits. The compromise solution of aggregating those who are 'similar enough' is vulnerable to competing businesses, who can demonstrate they are better able to satisfy more closely targeted segments. These two pressures are shown in Figure 5.1 below.

Figure 5.1 Factors influencing segmentation strategies.

5.3 Segmentation: rationale, bases and strategy

5.3.1 The advantages of market segmentation

By segmenting markets, fashion marketers gain several strategic advantages. Analysis of markets necessarily means consideration of competitors and their relative strengths and weaknesses in relation to customer needs. Such knowledge enables fashion marketers to decide whether to compete directly, if a strategic advantage is evident, or to position the company to exploit strengths and avoid retaliation from a stronger competitor.

The marketing research necessary to describe and segment a market usually leads to a deeper understanding of the customer that enables the most effective design of a marketing mix and the ability to respond to changes in the market.

Market segmentation enhances marketing planning in that it forces management to consider the relative costs, efficiency and effectiveness of the alternatives that segmentation reveals. Marketing planning is considered in detail in Chapter 10.

5.3.2 Segmentation bases

Segments have been described above as groups of customers with similar characteristics. This section deals with ways of describing and analysing those characteristics. A larger market, say the womenswear market, may be divided or segmented in many different ways. There is no standard or preferred way to divide a market, however it is important that the base(s) selected should relate to customers' needs.

Indeed it is not uncommon to find that fashion marketers use different methods for analysing the same market. What follows is an examination of some bases or dimensions that may be used to help categorize customers into meaningful, and profitable segments.

5.3.3 Segmentation based on descriptors

One approach to segmenting markets is to describe the characteristics of potential customers. Such descriptions tend to look at demographic, geographical or personality characteristics of the buyer or a combination of the three measures. This approach is termed the descriptor perspective and has the merit that it is easily understandable and less costly due to the availability of secondary data. An example would be to classify a market by age and income, thus for menswear we could show the market as in Table 5.1 below.

The next task using the table above is to quantify the various segments A to L and then analyse competitor activity within each segment. The fashion marketer can then make decisions about the positioning of the company within the market and in relation to competitors. The concept of positioning is described later in this chapter.

The prime weakness of the descriptor approach is the assumption that the dimensions selected relate directly to clothing purchase behaviour. Clearly

Table 5.1 Market Segmentation in the menswear market an example based on simple descriptors.

	Income		
Age	Low	Medium	High
16–25	A	B	C
26–35	D	E	F
36–55	G	H	I
56+	J	K	L

Table 5.2 Market segmentation descriptor variables.

Variable	Potential categorization
Sex	Male/female
Age	<2, 2–5, 6–10, 11–15, 16–25, 26–35, 36–45, 46–64, 65+
Marital Status	Single, with partner, divorced, widowed.
Occupation	A, B, C1, C2, D, E Manual or Non-Manual Full or part-time employment
Income	In decile bands, i.e. top 10%, next 10% etc.
Net wealth	In decile bands or other bands like £0–4999, £5000–14 999, etc.
Education	Terminal age of education; i.e. <15, 16, 17, 18, 19, 20, 21–23, 24+
Customer Size	In height, weight, dress/suit sizes e.g., petite, large, etc.
Religion	Atheist, Christian, Muslim, Jewish
Youth Subcultures	Rap, heavy metal, Punk, etc.
Family Lifecycle	Young single; Young couple with no children; Young couple with children; Older couple with children; etc.
Type of Neighbourhood Housing/Area	Urban/Rural or, for example, ACORN
Region/Country	e.g., North east, South west or UK, France, etc.
Climate	Hours of sunshine, rainfall, extremes of temperature.
Lifestyle	Groupings based on measurement of activities, interests and opinions. e.g. Self-aware, Green Goddesses, etc.

gender, age and income are significant variables in many clothing markets, but there is a danger in assuming that they are the only, or even the most important, variables in every market. Some of the main descriptors used in segmenting markets are shown in Table 5.2 above. Notice that some descriptors contain more than one variable. The family life cycle, for example, refers to age of head of household, marital status and the age and number of children, if any.

5.3.4 Segmentation based on benefits and customer behaviour

Another approach considers the behaviour of, and benefits for, consumers of fashion products and services as the main dimensions in segmentation. Here the concern is with monitoring how the consumer behaves and the benefits she or he seeks from the product. Then and only then are descriptors considered. An obvious example may be the categorization of customers into those who are heavy spenders, moderate spenders or low spenders. For the fashion retailer operating a store card system the data should be readily available on a database along with other demographic information about customers, i.e. region, income, marital status, age, etc.

Table 5.3   Market segmentation; behavioural and benefit variables.

Variable	Potential Categorization
Purchase Loyalty	Brand loyal to non committed.
Purchasing Mode	From comparison shopping to convenient outlets only.
Usage rates	Heavy users, medium users, light users, occasional users, non-users.
Expenditure	High spenders to low spenders in deciles.
Usage Situation	Working clothes, leisurewear, Eveningwear, formal wear e.g., weddings, etc.
Price Sensitivity	From very price aware and conscious to least price sensitive.
Benefits	Easy care garments, enviromentally friendly fabrics and/or durability, etc.

An important consideration is the number of variables that may be interlaced to provide a basis for segmentation. It would be unusual to use only one variable to divide a market, but it is wrong to assume that using more variables (multi-variable segmentation) is without difficulties. The use of more variables provides greater precision for the analyst. The cost of more variables, however, is the danger of greater market fragmentation as described above. Benefit and be-havioural bases for segmentation are rarely sufficient on their own and so they are usually combined with demographic data to display a fuller profile of the segments. Knowing that some customers want easy-care garments is one thing, knowing how many customers and how to reach them via distribution outlets and promotional efforts is another matter.

5.3.5   Criteria for selecting segments

The bases for analysing market segments have just been described. Before developing a segmentation strategy one must select a segment or segments as a focus for marketing efforts. There are four main criteria that should be taken into account to achieve this.

- The segment should be measurable and easily identifiable. Before allocating marketing resources the target should be quantified. Producing garments to appeal to 'Art Lovers' may sound a good idea, but until it is known how to identify 'Art Lovers' and work out the market size little progress can be made.

- The chosen segment or segments should be relatively stable. Within the context of fashion this factor may seem ironic. However, fashion marketers invest considerable resources in building distribution networks and marketing information systems geared to particular groups or segments of customers and there must be the assurance that investment will yield long term results. While styles may evolve over successive seasons, it is hoped that the core segment will remain loyal to the fashion marketer who leads and reflects their fashion tastes.

- The segment or segments chosen should be accessible. Accessibility refers to both distribution and promotional efforts. The role of demographic data in simplifying decisions about reaching the chosen segments has been described in the previous section.

- The segment should be large enough to be profitable for the scale of operations of the fashion marketer. Opening a boutique for women aged 35 plus in a small country town may be a sensible move for a small entrepreneur, but not for a large high street retailer. It cannot be stressed enough that the long-term goal should be profitability rather than sales or market share. It is far better to have 7% of a high margin market earning £400 000 profit per week than 15% of a low margin market earning £230 000 profit per week.

5.3.6 Segmentation strategies

Segmentation strategies can range from the choice of one target market or segment within the market to the selection of several segments in the market each with a different marketing mix. Selection of only one segment is known as concentration strategy and the selection of two or more segments is called a multi-segment strategy.

The determinants of a segmentation strategy are the company resources, the nature of the competition and the nature of demand in the particular fashion market, for instance, whether it is stable or volatile. A concentration strategy can enable the company to become expert in satisfying one segment of customers and so to acquire enough prestige and goodwill to foster loyalty among customers, Herbert Johnson (Hats) being one such example. The risk of a concentration strategy is that a downturn in one market can expose the company to considerable financial risk.

A multi-segment strategy can provide a measure of stability in times of rapid market change by spreading risk across several segments. The same firm, while offering different marketing mixes may find that the effort affords some economies of scale. For example, a company may target male and female segments via magazine advertising, and bulk purchasing of media space in magazines within the same publishing group may enable larger discounts to be earned.

Many companies have changed from a concentration segmentation strategy to a multi-segment strategy in a desire to expand or maintain growth rates. Both Jockey and Sloggi now produce underwear for males and females having expanded from single-sex segments of the market. Sometimes the expansion into new segments is problematic as with Jigsaw's recent move into menswear.

The size of the British customer is changing. Few people have the figure of a catwalk model and retailers recognizing this are offering more ranges in a wider variety of sizes. Taller consumers can buy from Long Tall Sally, a retailer who offers longer-length clothing. Evans Collection specializes in clothes for women of size 14 and over. Petite ranges for shorter women are now being offered alongside the usual ranges on many shop floors.

One leading clothing retailer, well known for floral designs, had tried to target a new market – that for boys between 8 and 11, only to realize that particular age group often places great emphasis on distance from the feminine domain. Fortunately the lesson was learned after only a limited amount of experimentation with the new market segment and at small cost. Had the same retailer chosen a more masculine name and different outlets the outcome might have been very different.

5.3.7 Multi-segment strategies in practice

The idea of segmentation has been taken on board by most of the high street retailers. Several large groups try to cover the whole market by having a variety of stores catering for different groups of customers. Table 5.4 below shows the segmentation strategy of the Burton Group. It is however significant that even within some stores listed below there may be up to seven different labels.

Retailers have to be careful that this level of segmentation and proliferation of stores and images is understood by the customer. Research carried out by the retailers has revealed that some stores are overlapping in their appeal between

Table 5.4   Burton group retail outlets 1990.

Segment	Total(*) no. of outlets	Target Customer
Menswear:		
Burton	485	Men aged 20–45, mainstream fashion
Top Man	303	Men aged 15–25, young fashion
Principles for Men	124	Men aged 20–45, updates classics
Womenswear:		
Dorothy Perkins	626	Women aged 18–40, mainstream fashion
Top Shop	275	Women aged 15–25, young fashion
Principles	214	Women aged 25–45, sophisticated fashion
Evans Collection	245	Women aged 25–60, size 14+
Department Stores:		
Debenhams	79	Mainstream fashion for individual and home
Harvey Nichols	1	Exclusive and *avant-garde* fashion for individual and home
Sport and leisure:		
Champion Sport	112	Sports clothing, footwear and goods for men, women to age 35, and children,

*includes concessions and shops
Source: Annual Reports and Accounts

different segments and so some rethinking and restructuring was required. The Sears' group is having to refocus Warehouse and Miss Selfridge to avoid saturating its own market. The aim is to move Warehouse in the market to include more classic designs rather than more of its usual high fashion styles.

5.4 Positioning and perceptual mapping

Positioning is to do with the perception of the firm and its marketing mix by the target market. Positioning is how customers see the market, although that perception may have been influenced by marketing action. The customers' perceptions include the role of the competition and may embrace some notion of an ideal offering.

The main method of determining a market position is the use of marketing research to construct a perceptual map of the market. A perceptual map is the consumers' view of the market, where consumers provide the main dimensions or criteria for making judgments. Ideally, these criteria will be the same ones identified when the firm considered behavioural and benefit bases for segmentation. Perceptual mapping involves complex statistical procedures, but is often shown as two or three dimensional diagrams. A hypothetical example of a perceptual map for positioning within the women's shoe market is shown below in Figure 5.2 below.

An important point to be made about the perceptual map is that it is hypothetical and may have only a little to do with the realities of style and pricing. If typical consumers believe things about shoe stores that are reflected in Figure 5.2 then they will behave in such a way to affirm those beliefs as described in

Perceptual map for the women's retail shoe market.

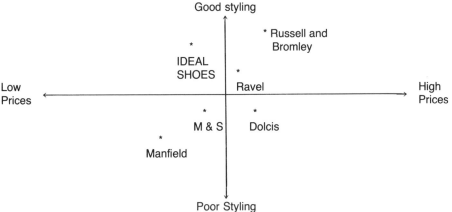

Figure 5.2   A market positioning example.

Chapter 3. Thus some customers may never even enter a Ravel store as they think it may be too expensive for them, while others do not consider M & S shoes as their perception is that they are poor on styling.

The essence of positioning is to get the product right in terms of customer needs and expectations and then to tailor the image of the firm's marketing offering to meet the aspirations of the chosen market segment. Thus in the example above, if Ravel was trying to position itself to meet aspirations then the perceptions on pricing need to be addressed. If prices are too high in reality then the purchasing policy should be reviewed. However, if the prices are in fact lower than shown by the perceptual map, then promotion efforts could emphasize, for example, the value for money aspect of Ravel shoes.

5.5 The fashion marketing mix

The marketing mix is the range of variables that can be controlled by the fashion marketer to meet the needs of buyers profitably. Simply put, the marketing mix is getting the right product to the chosen market segment at the correct time in the right place and for the right price.

Conventional descriptions of the marketing mix concentrate on what is known as the four Ps of marketing, namely Product, Price, Place and Promotion. This book does not deviate from that view but prefers the phrase Distribution decisions instead of Place decisions, as a synonym.

The last section ended with a discussion of positioning within a market and that should be the starting point for the development of a marketing mix. The positioning statement is a strategic decision taken by a company and the marketing mix is concerned with turning that decision into a reality via specific activities. To devise a combination of marketing elements, i.e. the mix, to meet customer aspirations while having a competitive advantage is the route to profitability.

5.5.1 The planning and co-ordination of the marketing mix

All fashion firms have a marketing mix whether they consciously design one or not. The mix, as seen by the customer, works in varying degrees. Over-concentration on promotion to the neglect of adequate and timely distribution is a common feature of a flawed approach as described in Chapter 1. There is little point in advertising in magazines about the new range for a new autumn season in early September if retailers do not have the product in stock. Similarly, a public relations campaign to create an upmarket quality image can be easily undermined by a policy of almost continual discount sales.

All elements of the marketing mix should be coordinated towards the positioning objective. Thus a brand image may be reinforced by the pricing policy and the sales force should be sufficient to meet the needs of the distribution channels. Chapters 6 to 9 deal in detail with the components of the marketing mix, and Chapter 10 will revisit planning and coordination, but the point should be noted now.

Table 5.5 Different marketing mixes aimed at similar markets.

	Racing Green	River Island
Segment	20–35 Male/Female Mid-market	20–35 Male/Female Mid-market
Product	Limited range Cotton garments Casual/leisure	Casual/leisure Broad range Different fibres and fabrics
Price	Mid-range	Mid-range
Distribution	Mail order	High street outlets
Promotion	Direct mail, Brochures, Press advertising	Mainly In-store Promotion

5.5.2 Alternative marketing mixes

Firms may pursue a multi-segmentation strategy and offer different marketing mixes to different market segments. Therefore a designer dress offered at a higher price in department stores to an upmarket customer may be accompanied by a diffusion range with less design content and lower quality fabrics at lower prices through chain stores to another segment by the same company. Different marketing mixes from the same company can coexist easily and are often unknown to consumers via the use of different company names and brands.

An important principle to note in relation to the marketing mix is the principle of equi-finality. This means that there may be more than one way to reach a goal, and that alternative routes or mixes may be equally effective in achieving marketing objectives. Table 5.5 above gives a brief example of alternative marketing mixes to illustrate, in part, the principle of equi-finality.

5.6 Summary

This chapter has introduced the concepts of segmentation and the marketing mix. Segmentation was discussed in terms of:

- ways of segmenting a market
- criteria for selecting target markets
- descriptor, behavioural and benefit dimension of segments
- concentrated and multi-segment strategies, and their benefits and risks examples from real fashion markets.

The chapter then went on to discuss market positioning and the relevance of the marketing mix to this, covering:

- building a strategy
- coordinating the mix elements
- alternative marketing mixes
- customer perceptions of the marketing mix.

Further reading

Lancaster, G. and Massingham, L. (1993), *Marketing Management*, McGraw-Hill Maidenhead.

Kotler, P. (1994), *Marketing Management: Analysis, Planning and Control*, 8th edn., Prentice Hall International, New Jersey.

Loudon, D.L. and Della Bitta, A.J. (1993), *Consumer Behavior: Concepts and Applications*, McGraw-Hill, New York.

Zikmund, W.G. and d'Amico, M.D. (1993), *Marketing*, 4th edn., West Publishing Company, Minneapolis.

Chapter 6
Designing and Marketing Fashion Products

6.1 Introduction

This chapter will examine the product element of the marketing mix and its pivotal role in the success or failure of businesses within the fashion industry. First it addresses the concept of fashion and its economic and social importance in the UK, followed by an analysis of the nature and attributes of fashion products. Then there is a description of how the industry is organized for the diffusion of new trends and an examination of the process of new fashion product development. Concepts are then applied by examining a retail buying sequence.

Later there is an assessment of the concept of fashion and other life cycles and the implications for marketing decision makers. Finally the relevance and use of the concept when determining seasonal product mixes and planning and controlling the introduction of new ranges is examined.

In this chapter, the definition of fashion as a current mode of consumption behaviour has been applied specifically to clothing products. However, it is acknowledged that in its broadest sense the term can be used to describe any product or service consumed as part of a particular way of living. More specifically the contents of the chapter could equally apply to other, clothing-related aspects of fashion, such as shoes, cosmetics, accessories or hairstyles, as outlined in Chapter 1.

6.2 The importance of fashion products

6.2.1 The concept of fashion

The product element of the marketing mix is fundamental to the fashion design industry. The continual process of new product development and resulting change drives the whole industry and answers the demand from consumers for a constant stream of new ideas and offerings. Indeed it could be argued that without this constant generation and introduction of new ideas into the marketplace the concept of 'fashion' would not exist.

Axiomatically, if consumers were not constantly engaged in the process of looking for new products or services to satisfy their emerging needs, (and once having consumed them, allowing a set of new and different needs to emerge), the fashion process could not function.

Thus the industry revolves around a time-based, i.e. seasonal, process in which new fashions are introduced into the marketplace, are adopted by enough consumers to warrant the description of 'fashion' in its proper context in the first place (as a current mode of consumption behaviour), only to wane eventually in terms of popularity, thus rendering them 'unfashionable'. While some product offerings will remain popular over several or even many seasons, others will fade very quickly; these differences are discussed further in the chapter. The important point to stress here, however, is that this regenerative process is intrinsic to the fashion industry and is very necessary for its continued survival.

6.2.2 The economic importance of fashion

In the early 1990s, clothing and related industries were still the fourth largest employer in the UK. Together, the clothing and textile industries employed over 400 000 people in 1991; clothing and footwear alone accounting for almost 300 000 employees. In the same year total sales of clothing and footwear amounted to over £8bn and exports were valued at around £1.8bn (rising to almost £1.95bn in 1992). Many UK designers and fashion companies have been successfully exporting their ranges for many years. The 1960s fashion explosion brought British design to the forefront of the industry and the continued wealth of new talent even today ensures that the industry continues to maintain its well-established high-profile.

Although household expenditure on clothing and footwear in the UK has slightly declined in the recent recession, it still amounts to nearly 6% of the total of all consumer expenditure at current prices. While historically not as fashion conscious as their European counterparts, UK consumers have, during the 1980s, become much more fashion aware and consequently much more discerning when it comes to appearance.

To remain competitive many UK clothing manufacturers have chosen to follow an upmarket, high-cost route embracing high quality rather than competing with manufacturers elsewhere in the world who are able to maintain very low labour costs (and therefore offer volume-produced garments at very low prices). Others, however, have developed purchasing strategies that involve subcontracting work into low-cost countries while still maintaining a high design 'edge' over competitors.

6.2.3 The social role of fashion

It has often been suggested that fashion plays an important societal role in terms of individual wellbeing. This, it is maintained, comes through enhanced self-esteem and acceptance by peers and various other social groups through the 'correct' choice of clothing and use of other image developing accessories. Thus one could argue altruistically that the primary objective in gaining greater understanding of the nature of fashion products and the process of new product development is to become more effective in targeting specific market segments and thereby satisfy some of the most basic needs within a society.

Commercially this will lead to increased customer loyalty and trust in what is being offered by the organization or designer in question, and improved sales performance and profitability will thereby result. In the UK in particular, improved marketing capabilities should lead to the maximization of design and manufacturing potential; British manufacturers cannot compete with low-cost producing countries on price and so should use their design and marketing talent as a basis to distinguish the UK in the marketplace.

6.3 The nature of fashion products

6.3.1 Product definition and classifications

Quite literally a product can be defined as anything that might satisfy a need that can be offered in the marketplace. Classifying products in terms of their characteristics and how consumers purchase them assists marketers in determining the appropriate blend of other marketing variables, i.e. promotion, pricing and distribution for the product in question.

Traditionally three categories have been used to define tangible product offerings, namely, convenience, shopping and specialty as shown in Figure 6.1.

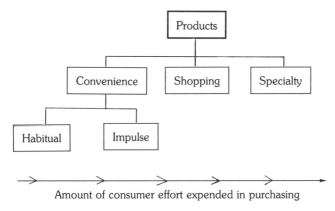

Figure 6.1 Classification of products.

Convenience goods

Convenience goods are frequently purchased with little thought, effort or attempt to undertake comparisons with similar products. Convenience goods can be further subdivided into staple goods, purchased habitually and where brand loyalty is probably very strong, and impulse goods, purchased without any pre-planning or searching. It could be advocated that certain basic items of clothing such as hosiery and underwear are often purchased as convenience goods, perhaps along with the family's regular one-stop shopping from the supermarket.

Indeed many food retailers have capitalized on this approach by stocking such ranges alongside other non-food ranges.

Shopping goods

Shopping goods are where consumers compare product attributes such as price, quality and design by shopping around. Products in this category will constitute high-volume markets similar to those of high street fashions. However, they will lack the seasonal variations intrinsic to the fashion industry and are likely to be purchased less frequently than most clothing items.

Specialty goods

Specialty goods are products with characteristics that differentiate them from the other two classifications, usually based on high quality and higher perceived value. Brand image is very important here, often customers will make the effort to seek out the exact product they require; it may be that they will also expect some degree of exclusivity in the product offering and will go out of their way to find it. More upmarket, branded fashion items obviously fall neatly into this category. However, one could argue that the material 1980s have resulted in a more educated and discerning general public in the 1990s. As a result the desire for better quality and relative exclusivity, even in many less expensive high street fashions, may result in a slightly misleading use of this category when applied to clothing.

6.3.2 Classifying products with a fashion element

Although the categories above do apply to certain items of clothing in the fashion industry, they are slightly limited in use when one is trying to analyse buying motives and methods. It is probably more accurate therefore to classify tangible fashion products slightly differently, categorizing them as classics, fashions or fads.

Classics

It is possible to use the term classic in several contexts. In terms of 'bundles of utilities', classics can usually be seen as the midpoint compromise of any style, i.e. total look or composite effect. Indeed, the term 'style' is often used to describe the classic in this context, complying with the basic laws of harmony in proportion, aesthetic sense and incorporation of balanced design features. Colour and pattern may vary but the classic customer does not seek the satisfaction of a new seasonal experience in the way that his or her fashion and fad counterparts do. However, it is likely that some satisfaction will be sought at the core of the product's tangible attributes, e.g., good quality, good fit, durability, etc.

In a product sense a classic is never out of style for its market segment and will rarely appeal to the majority. Design changes will be minimal; these changeless and always acceptable garments are found in all recognizable areas of fashion, e.g., the women's tailored suit with knee- or just above knee-length skirt or for men the City pinstripe, the double-breasted trench coat, the blazer; even denim jeans have their classic in the 5 pocket Western style.

Classic garments, sharing the quality of 'timelessness' will collectively make up the classic styles described above. At any given time, however, it will be possible to identify dominant and secondary styles. What should be added here is that although often described as timeless, classics also evolve gradually over many years according to the style of the age.

Certain designers have also been described as classic, producing fashions that are seen by many as timeless and therefore can be worn despite the season and current high fashions. Jean Muir or Ralph Lauren are examples of this.

Classic products may occasionally become fashionable, for example the recent revival of the Chanel suit, albeit in a 1990s mode. However, it is more likely that the classic will form the basis for the annual slow, continuous change that forms fashion. There is a skill in combining the appropriate variations on the appropriate classics for any given moment in time to create an appropriate contemporary style.

Fashions and fads

The distinction between a fashion and a fad is usually defined on the basis of their acceptance cycle. Fashions usually have a slower rise to popularity, reach a plateau with continuing popularity and then decline gradually; often this cycle relates to a season, whether autumn/winter or spring/summer. Mid-season modifications to the original fashions may be introduced with the specific intention of maintaining buying interest and encouraging further purchases from early as well as later adopters (see Chapter 3). Leggings and figure-hugging stirrup pants were fashionable over several seasons in the early 1990s. The influence of 1970s style revived in a contemporary 1990s way and the New Romantic revival during the 1980s both resulted in styles that were fashionable over several seasons.

Fads on the other hand will rise meteorically in popularity only to suffer an abrupt decline as they become adopted. As a fad becomes fashionable it also becomes unfashionable. The silver training shoe, popularized by youth magazines such as *i-D* was a fad in the early 1990s. In style or total-look terms it could be argued that Grunge was an early 1990s fad. Adoption of a fad is based solely on the desire by the individual for a new experience that is not likely to become popular on a large scale. For this reason a fad tends to be viewed as non-viable in the commercial sense and usually eccentric in nature.

6.3.3 Product attributes

In designing and developing new products it is essential to understand what is being offered and therefore to appreciate the customer's perception of the

Figure 6.2 Four basics of fashion design.

product. As shown in Figure 6.2 there are four basics in terms of fashion design, namely, silhouette or form, colour, texture or pattern and style or total look. However, the fashion consumer will tend to view the garment as a series of attributes. Some of these will relate more closely to the social or psychological needs of the consumer and therefore will not always be recognized by the individual. However, it is essential that the fashion marketer is aware of both the subconscious and conscious aspects of the product to offer the best combination of need-satisfying benefits to the customer.

Thus the product offering can be analysed at three levels. First, the *core* product that satisfies the most fundamental needs. Secondly, the *tangible* product can be seen as the physical interpretation and presentation of the four design basics to create the most appropriate fashion for the market in question. Thirdly there is the *intangible* product, i.e. the additional services and benefits that supplement the previous two levels and create the total product offering.

Core attributes

The core of the product's attributes will revolve around the three basic tenets of clothing: protection, modesty and adornment. Since every garment will offer combinations of these functions to a greater or lesser degree the consumer must decide how well the combination matches his or her basic criteria for purchase. Buyers will always look for those products that satisfy the maximum set of needs simultaneously. In practice offerings will seldom satisfy all of them simultaneously and so each purchase decision will result in a compromise. The extent to which the customer has to make these compromises indicates the extent to which there are apparent gaps in the marketplace and therefore the need for more differentiation. This in turn helps perpetuate fashion change.

Tangible attributes

Tangible product attributes, or the interpretation and presentation of the 4 design basics to provide an overall style, will revolve around in the first place the set of design features which make up the actual product. For example, a basic ladies' blouse may offer variety in terms of shape (loose, fitted, etc.), sleeve type (set-in, raglan, dolman, etc.), type of collar and shape (one piece, two piece, pointed, round, etc.), and any decoration or trimmings etc. Secondly the designer must have regard to the appropriate use of fabric, texture, pattern and colour for any given season. These are both set in the context of overall style, and, for instance, coordination with other garments and accessories to form a 'total look'.

For example, it could be claimed that a hypothetical range of garments designed for the executive working woman offered high performance (durability, washability, etc.), an acceptable level of fashion for the given season, suitable styling for the executive role and versatility in wear. However, although the consumer may purchase specific items in the range at different times, it is highly likely that she would still expect coordination within the range to provide a suitable total look with whatever combination of garments she had purchased.

A designer and manufacturer should also strive to maintain standards of quality appropriate to the market which they have chosen to target. Quality control is becoming more and more important, although garment manufacturing does not have to comply with any British Standard in the way that product and engineering designs do. Therefore there is a variety of qualities of make and sizing specifications in clothing. Many consumers are quick to point out that a size 12 from one manufacturer or retailer may vary considerably from that of another.

However, retail dominance in the 1980s has resulted in the introduction of more stringent quality control procedures in recent years. More discerning consumers of the 1990s now require quality of service and choice as well as product and there are significant marketing implications in this.

Most retailers now employ teams of garment technologists whose remit is to work with in-house buyers and manufacturers and establish and maintain standards of make in line with given company policy. Quality manuals are used to provide guidelines on general standards such as fabric performance and size specification through to specifics such as the number of stitches per inch on seams which suppliers to use for component parts of the garment, such as trimmings.

The quality procedure in one large UK retail organization is as follows: retailers will require that buying samples (sample garments made to relevant quality standards) are approved before volume production. Once they have been checked by technologist and buyer against established standards, two sample garments will be 'sealed', one to be kept by the manufacturer and one by the retailer. These samples will become the yardstick against which the quality of volume production will be measured. When volume garments begin to come off the production line a technologist will usually approve and seal a further three

Figure 6.3   Branding strategies: a continuum of approaches.

samples, confirming that quality standards are being met and that the goods can be delivered into a central warehouse or direct to the store.

A further tangible attribute is seen in use of suitable packaging and branding. This is important in image creation, leading to differentiation in the marketplace which can be achieved very effectively through the use of labelling. Branding can be in the form of brand names, logos, trade marks etc. Certain brand names have become so powerful that they are synonymous with the product. Consumers may talk of their Levi's instead of their jeans, or of a Burberry instead of a raincoat. In the same way suitable packaging is as important in the fashion industry as any other.

Brand names are a very important vehicle for providing the customer with assurances regarding quality and consistency of standard, the St Michael brand name of Marks and Spencer is a case in point. They also can provide assurances as to the suitability of fashion content for the season in question. Strong brand names can be very advantageous when establishing overseas markets. Young Japanese consumers with very high levels of disposable income are dedicated followers of British fashion. Traditional labels such as Burberry have established strong links in Japan, as have designers such as Paul Smith, Katharine Hamnett and Margaret Howell. Paul Smith began trading in Japan in 1982 under licence; by 1990 he had around 47 shops selling approximately 70 000 suits per annum.

As shown in Figure 6.3, companies can employ various strategies as regards the use of brand names, such as:

- A variety of names can be used with no obvious link, the caveat here being that substantial promotional budgets will be needed to establish each one in the mind of the consumer;

- Specific ranges may be given individual brand names, in this way some common link can be emphasized such as range coordination across several garment categories, or ranges that have been designed with a specific theme or purpose in mind;

- Use of only one brand name across the entire organization and its offerings to create a powerful image in the mind of the consumer. In time, use of well-established brand names can be stretched to introduce new products into different markets. This policy of brand stretching goes beyond brand extension, where new products are introduced into the same category. Use of this approach can increase the survival chances of new products and reduce launch costs. Avon, the American cosmetics and toiletries retailer has in recent years stretched the company's name by introducing ranges of children's clothing and personal security equipment.

The role that packaging plays within the tangible product offering will depend very much upon the nature of the product's image and the importance of branding and packaging within that. Although the main function of packaging is that of protection, it has often become intrinsic to the overall offering and its status, as exemplified by labels such as Racing Green and Monsoon, where the brand name and corporate colour scheme or fashion stories and colours for the season in question are reflected in the packaging design. The packaging may even have a functional use in its own right; continued use will help reinforce brand and image with the customer.

Intangible attributes

Intangible attributes, the additional services and benefits that supplement the core and tangible attributes include services intrinsic to the purchase such as credit facilities, delivery arrangements, and after sales service such as alterations and money back guarantees. Certain UK fashion retailers are beginning to follow the example of their American counterparts in providing customers with consultation as to personal image. This may include advice on the most appropriate garment styles for different body shapes and height, as well as colours most suited to the individual's complexion and hair colour.

Image and reputation of the seller, possibly because of an effective promotional campaign constitute further intangible attributes. However, word-of-mouth recommendation, appealing shop interiors and exteriors and even satisfaction with previous purchases can all be contributory factors to the build up of longer-term loyalty. Lastly, there are consumers' quality and value perceptions, which are closely related to image and reputation but more often linked to customers' attitude towards price levels.

6.3.4 Licensing

The 1980s spending boom encouraged many big name fashion houses to expand their commercial activities through retailing and licensing. For many large investors, the appeal of high fashion lies not so much in their collections, but rather in the lucrative licences for perfumes and other products bearing the designer's name. Under a licensing agreement the designer will lend his or her name to products made by mainstream manufacturers. Ralph Lauren now licenses products ranging from bags and belts to sunglasses. Such is the extent of the operation that his company now has only one factory for tailored menswear and two flagship stores in New York and London; everything else is licensed. In 1990 there were 125 Polo/Ralph Lauren shops worldwide.

In licensing, fashion houses such as Lauren and Dior must maintain a delicate balance between profiting from the prestige of their name without simultaneously jeopardizing their exclusivity and high fashion image and reputation. Ralph Lauren concerns himself with every detail, from the quality of the product to how it is delivered and presented in the shops.

Cardin, on the other hand, has more than 800 licences for items ranging from scuba diving equipment to sunglasses and while it is now one of the highest turnover fashion companies it is reputed to have foregone its status as a high fashion house to become so.

6.4 The fashion industry and new product development

6.4.1 The role of the designer

The role of designer in the fashion industry is crucial to its success. The task is specifically one of interpreting society's current and anticipated mood into desirable, wearable, garments for every type and level of market. To do this effectively, designers must be in tune with the wider social, cultural, economic and political environment within which human beings conduct their daily lives; only then will their ideas truly reflect current prevailing conditions and the impact they are likely to have on future consumer needs. Thus the designer will draw on a wealth of ideas; the media and entertainment, other cultures, social attitudes and mores, historical and contemporary events all provide important sources of inspiration.

The skill in any good design really lies in maximizing the value that can be added to a set of basic raw materials. It is therefore dependent on the quality of the original design, its suitability for the market and the way it is made to meet customer requirements. Any designer should be skilled in striking the right balance between new product development and other marketing costs and the life expectancy and therefore anticipated sales and profit contribution of the product. However, serious concern is being expressed within the industry that the increased speed of the whole fashion cycle is beginning to stunt the growth of young designers and that the demand for new ideas and collections is so strong that the chance to develop ideas properly does not arise.

6.4.2 The influence of haute couture

In terms of influence the industry continues to operate in a hierarchical sense. The more renowned and internationally accepted designers (historically the haute couturiers, although this section of the industry is now in something of a downturn) continue to be a very significant source of new ideas regarding fashion direction. At the same time however, influences from elsewhere will pervade. Late in the 1980s the influence of 'street fashion' was felt throughout the industry. The skill for many designers, and particularly those who are trying to appeal to the wider, mass market, will be to interpret the wealth of ideas and sources of inspiration into garments that are appropriate for high street consumption.

The point should be made here that haute couture and mass production are quite different. The former evolved from the desire for luxury and conspicuous consumption from the elite strata of society; the latter developed in response to the growing post-war affluence of the majority and the desire for an improvement in living standard and lifestyle. Thus it has historically been the function of mass production to select and adapt appropriate couture design to meet the needs of the public at large. While the recognized leading designers in Europe, America, Japan and elsewhere continue to act as sources of inspiration, their supremacy and unattainability for the masses is maintained by employing the best in fabric, make, embellishment, etc. and producing fashions that can only be afforded and worn by a select, fashion conscious and extrovert few. However, even the leading designers are vulnerable; if their sense of direction and development is not consistently strong they will fail to develop a progressive adaptability. The stereotypical style that may result could leave the way open for new designers who have a better understanding of the way fashion develops.

6.4.3 Organization of the fashion industry

In recent years the haute couturiers have, along with established designers, tended to move towards greater brand differentiation to capitalize on their names and some have also decentralized their manufacturing operations to cut costs. Some manufacturers now produce and distribute designer collections, enabling haute couture or designer names to be made available to a larger market at more accessible prices through ready to wear ranges. The announcement by the French government in 1992 that it was planning to encourage new designers into haute couture indicated the fact that the couture market is in decline. Younger customers are being tempted away from the idea of luxury for its own sake and are now demanding clothes by the newer designers that are indisputably contemporary in their direction and approach.

Production capacity of the manufacturing sector in the industry will be split in different ways. Some will devote their entire production to retail own-label ranges, others may run own-label, (i.e. manufacturer) ranges alongside. The third possibility is to allocate certain capacity to manufacturing garments under license (see above). Similarly, retail strategies may be based on 100% own-label ranges in store, or mixing retail label with manufacturer- and/or licensee-labelled merchandise.

Thus within the industry chain the process of converting basic raw materials into finished marketable goods will involve teams of people working together at each level. Yarn and textile producers will employ designers and technologists and may employ the services of colour consultants and fabric forecasters in their work. Teams comprising in-house designers, pattern cutters and sample machinists, production and sales personnel will work together in manufacturing organizations on the development of own label and licensed ranges.

At the same time their designers and production personnel will be working with buyers and merchandisers in retail organizations on the development of retail own-label merchandise; retail buyers and merchandisers will, in turn, be working with teams of their own in-house designers, quality controllers, garment technologists and possibly even store personnel during their planning cycle. Retail dominance as described earlier has also led to retail buying and merchandising personnel working closely with yarn and textile producers in a bid to differentiate ranges at an even earlier stage in the chain. Fabric will be dyed or woven according to retail specification and subsequently ordered for the garment manufacturers.

6.4.4 The sequence of events

There are four major stages of influence in the new product development and fashion diffusion and adoption process. These are, chronologically:

- The colour meeting in Paris known as the *Concertation* where approximately forty leading fashion industrialists representing major yarn, textile and garment manufacturers, top designers, stylists, colour consultants and fashion forecasters gather. Together they will establish the major colour trends (based on around 30 colours) that will dominate the fashion scene two years from the time of their meeting. The trends will usually be based on themes of darks, brights, pastels and neutrals. Work will then begin by various sections of the industry on interpreting and adapting the basic story to suit their own particular requirements. For example, the International Wool Secretariat and Cotton Institute will work on appropriate interpretations for their respective yarn and textile industries.

- The biannual yarn and fabric fairs where the new colours, textures and patterns will be presented as trends for twelve months ahead. In France the major fair is *Première Vision*, in Germany it is called *Interstoff* and in the UK, Fabrex. *Première Vision* also features an audio visual presentation that details the sources of ideas and inspiration used by the Concertation team.

- The biannual international fashion fairs in Paris, Milan, New York and London where leading designers will present their latest collection ideas 6 months ahead of the season in question. Representation by the media is very strong at the international collections, showing the enormous influence the media now have on fashion awareness and acceptance.

- Reportage in the trade and commercial press of the designer collections is described above. The power and extent of modern day mass communication systems is such that the media are instrumental in shaping and influencing the fashions that are ultimately accepted. This process is shown in Figure 6.4 below. Simultaneously journalists now provide a two-way flow of information, reporting 'upwards' on street styles that have been a significant influence on top designers over the last few years, (and often creating their own fashions and fads in the process), as well as 'downwards' on developments in the collections to the public.

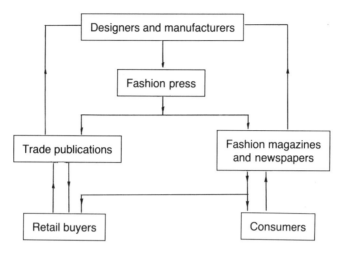

Figure 6.4   The two-way flow of fashion information.

6.4.5 The process for developing new products

Change in the form of new product development is an intrinsic part of the culture of all organizations associated with the fashion industry whether directly in manufacturing or retailing or indirectly in the media or public relations. While product strategies will invariably be linked closely to corporate objectives, continual new product development will also enhance and strengthen image, brand name, etc.

Traditional models used to describe the new product development process will describe many stages from concept through to actual launch. However, the time scale to which the fashion industry works is such that several of these stages will function simultaneously. To demonstrate this, the example chosen to work through is that of a high street multiple retailer. Whether textile or garment manufacturer or retailer the principles and procedures described are very much the same since all are involved in the process of buying, sampling and selling. Obviously the time scales will vary according to how far back in the chain they go.

6.5 Retail buying sequence: autumn and winter season

6.5.1 Early September

Analysis and development of new concepts take place, along with analysis of last year's range, to identify good and bad sellers based on performance and average weeks' cover. This is an indication of the rate at which a style is selling and the number of weeks it would take to sell out completely at the current rate. Lines which have averaged ten weeks' cover, or less, will be seen as good sellers, anything above this will not have been such a success and is not likely to be repeated. If a line has averaged over 20 it will be deleted. The analysis will be by style, fabric, colour and price point and will form the basis for the range going forward. Supplier performance also will be examined, by line (rate of sale, prices and profitability) and by quality and reliability, for instance, in delivery.

At the same time an analysis of forward trends is conducted (working here with in-house design studio staff and colour and fashion forecasters if relevant). This is to gather new ideas, colours, fabrics etc. that can be applied to the range.

The actual plan will be built up around improvements or revisions to existing products, additions to existing product lines and the incorporation of new products into the range.

6.5.2 Late September

First stage screening, further development of concepts, initial product development are all now able to proceed. Initial presentations of range plan ideas for basic approval take place and, the alteration cycle begins. Further research is now needed for concept development and is conducted by, among other ways, shopping trips to Europe and America. Initial buyer and supplier meetings take place to exchange ideas and give direction, while sampling and the alteration process also takes place at this time.

6.5.3 Early to mid October

Second stage screening is conducted, while product development continues. Visits are made to the fabric fairs. Supplier development continues. Once the concepts and styles have been approved by the controller, a presentation is made at director level.

6.5.4 November through to end of January

Product development is now finalized, and provision for test marketing within the proposed new ranges is planned. Sampling and negotiating with suppliers and agents is in full swing, culminating in agreement on prices. Range meetings take place with controller and directors at end of January for approval of final ranges. Sealed samples as described, are taken, and work now begins on accurate buying figures and phasing of deliveries.

Range plans at this stage will feature certain styles to be included as experiments or test lines at the beginning of the season. It may be that they have a higher element of fashion in them than the norm and are therefore seen as carrying more risk. However, flexibility will be built into the range to purchase more of the new ideas if they prove to be successful once launched.

6.5.5 Mid February

Marketers begin to develop the other mix variables, and prices are finalized. Other marketing tasks include liaison on contract preparation, and the development of in-store and other promotional ideas.

6.5.6 April to May

Chasing production, quality checks and monitoring progress are the main preoccupations now. Feedback from these is used in a continual review process.

6.5.7 July to August

The first phase of the range is launched in stores. Phasing of deliveries according to preplanning is set at approximately every 6–8 weeks.

6.6 The product mix and range planning

6.6.1 The nature of the product mix

The product mix or product range is the assortment of goods a company offers for sale at any time. Before each season the organization must not only consider how it might alter or modify its classic, (i.e. more basic) lines which are therefore less liable to radical change; it also must undertake careful planning of its fashion ranges in terms of width, depth and fashion content (and simultaneously anticipate and plan for the risk involved). Decisions concerning the mix of products also will relate to changes in broader company objectives. These may range from sales and profit growth, via emphasis on increasing market share or targeting new markets to return on investment targets, etc.

6.6.2 The planning cycle

The frequency of the planning cycle is probably greater in the fashion industry than any other because of its seasonal nature. Changing customer preferences ensure a perpetual drive for change. Volatility in terms of the seasonal variety of products offered and the speeds of change in fashions require skill, creativity, a propensity for risk-taking and in-depth knowledge of end-user requirements in order for companies to plan effectively, and implement and control what is being offered in any given season.

Traditionally companies have planned for two seasons, autumn/winter and spring/summer. However, many are now moving towards the incorporation of mid-season ranges. For some this will mean a totally new set of garments, accessories, etc. and for others it will merely involve adding top-up variety to the major lines that were introduced at the beginning of the season.

At every stage in the planning cycle the team, which may comprise any combination of textile and/or fashion designers, production managers, salespeople, buyers, merchandisers and store personnel, will focus on the permutation of fashions being offered. The following terms are used in the example below which highlights the two major stages:

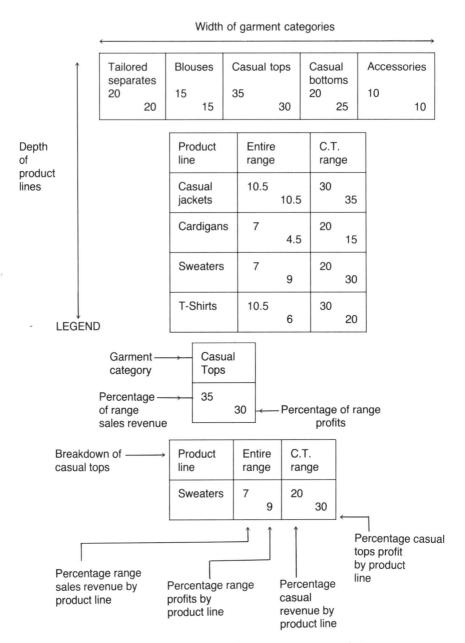

Figure 6.5 Stage 1 range planning: hypothetical womenswear range analysis.

Garment category

This refer to types of garments in a generic sense, i.e. as a whole class or group. This could be such terms as market being served, context of wear, fashion look or statement, etc. For example, a manufacturer of mens' and womens' jackets may offer ranges that appeal to the same target market in terms of age, income, interest in fashion and other segment characteristics. Alternatively the ranges may be functionally based on, for example, rugged outdoor use, and appeal to a wide age range.

As another possibility, the ranges may comprise a mixture of classic through to high fashion garments that have been manufactured using similar production methods and materials. However, due to their fashion content their appeal lies at either end of the fashion spectrum. In such a situation it is highly likely that the manufacturer would differentiate the ranges by distinct promotional, distribution and pricing strategies.

Product line

This is a breakdown of garment categories into fashions that are related in more specific, identifiable ways. Here an established variety of words or terms will probably be used to describe the breakdown into product types. Thus a casual jacket might be described as an anorak, a parka, blouson, boating, donkey, etc.

Style

Each product line can be broken down into a variety of specific designs appropriate for the given season.

Width and depth

The dimensions in terms of number and variety in each stage of the planning process are shown in Figures 6.5 and 6.6.

Figure 6.5 shows how a hypothetical range of womenswear might be broken down into the following garment categories: tailored separates, blouses, casual tops and bottoms and accessories. Casual tops have then been further broken down into specific product lines as follows: casual jackets, cardigans, sweaters and T-shirts. At the same time, the figure shows a possible percentage breakdown of total sales revenue and profits for the range by garment category. A further breakdown has been given within casual tops showing the percentage contributions of each to their own garment category and to the overall range.

Range plan detail for style 1:

Design detail:	Round neck, long sleeve single cotton jersey T-shirt. Single rib collar with top stitching, straight edge cuff.
Pattern:	Printed triple stripe
Colourways:	Navy with white stripe, Ivory with navy stripe
Size range:	S M L XL
Pack size:	2 4 4 2
Total quantity:	720 units
Qu. per size:	120 240 240 120 units

Additional comments:
If manufacturer: Own label, to all UK licensees
If retailer: Basic, all-store line

Analysis of percentage sales revenue and profit contribution:

Contribution to casual tops range:

	Percentage sales revenue	Percentage profit
Style 1	12.25	9.0
Style 2	12.25	9.0
Style 3	7.0	7.5
Style 4	3.5	4.5

Contribution to T-shirt range:

	Percentage sales revenue	Percentage profit
Style 1	35	30
Style 2	35	30
Style 3	20	25
Style 4	10	15

Figure 6.6 demonstrates how stage 2 in the planning cycle could be applied to one specific style within the line of womens' T-shirts. The figure also quantifies percentage sales revenue and profit of each style within the T-shirt range itself and as a contribution to the overall casual tops range.

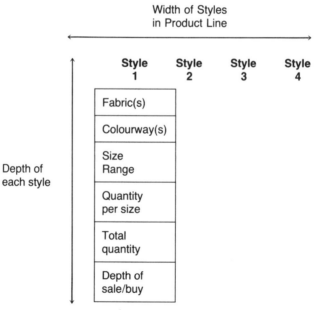

Figure 6.6 Stage 2 range planning: womens' T-shirts. Hypothetical breakdown of specific product line.

Thus in retail terms the T-shirt range would feature two basic styles that would go to all stores and amount to 70% of sales revenue. The more fashionable style 3 might be sent to specific branches, e.g. the top 50%. While style 4, the highest risk in terms of fashion content, might be featured in only 10% of stores and probably only at those stores most likely to sell high fashion garments. At the same time profit expectations would vary, *pro rata* style 4 has the highest profit potential.

As the organization grows, it may be strategically sensible and profitable for it to diversify its ranges into non-garment categories such as accessories, luggage, home furnishings, etc. However, these decisions will usually be taken at board level since they will relate fundamentally to the nature of the company's business.

The recent retail example of Next plc demonstrates how it is possible over time to move into broader clothing and non-clothing areas from an established base. From its original target group of 25–40 year old women the company established itself with appeal to a much wider age range. Success eventually led to the development of several differentiated womenswear ranges, menswear and childrenswear, home furnishings, jewellery, watches and clocks and finally horticultural products (although this range, offered via a mail order catalogue never actually reached a nationwide market).

6.6.3 Range planning checklists

Improved technology means that planning teams are now better informed regarding sales histories for previous seasons. At any one time there are many dimensions of historical information available, e.g., seasonal best and worst selling styles, colours and sizes; customer sales patterns; geographic variations; specific rates of sale for garment styles; most popular price levels, etc. The first essential stage in any planning cycle is to analyse what has happened in previous seasons to enable more informed decision making so the form can ultimately capitalize on previous success.

Pre-planning checklists

The following pre-planning checklist indicates where the analysis should focus:

- **Sales history:** Good and bad sellers; most popular designs and why? Best/worst customers in relation to best/worst stores. Specific styles and why? Rates of sale of styles offered, reasons for variations. Although certain styles may appear to be faster sellers there may have been problems regarding others, e.g., availability.
  Colour/fabric/pattern trends. For example were best sellers limited to only certain colours, fabrics, etc. and if so, which ones?

- **Emerging trends:** Are there any new trends emerging from sales of high fashion lines, e.g., colours, styles, fabrics? Which are applicable to the range in question – i.e. which will suit the intended target market? To what depth should risk be taken?

- **Pricing:** Were the price levels appropriate?
  Did the styles offered represent good value for money?
  Was the balance of price levels right?
  Was it similar to that of competitors?
  Were target profit margins achieved overall by various styles?
  If not, how can profit margins be improved?

- **Competitors:** How successful in the previous season in question? Regular analysis of competitors should have been carried out during the season via comparative shopping surveys, information from other manufacturers or retailers, trade press articles, publicly available financial information etc. Have there been instances of successful practice that can be followed?

Balance, cohesion and synchronisation

Once ranges have been determined the following will serve as a useful check list to ensure balance, cohesion and synchronisation:

- **Garment categories:** Is the percentage breakdown appropriate? Is the balance correct for customer requirements, and are there enough options to meet a variety of preferences and tastes?

- **Product lines:** Are the styles within each appropriate for the target market in terms of design content, style, fabric, colour, pattern, texture? The tension here will be between offering width or depth of range – where should the balance lie between offering safe lines and high fashions with more risk? Decisions regarding which new fashion directions should be incorporated are crucial; today's riskier lines could very easily become tomorrow's best sellers, as they become more widely accepted and therefore safer over time.

- Do the above two items fit the company image we are trying to portray? For example, the garment label or company name may be well established in a high fashion context.

- Is each range balanced? Is there cohesion in what is being offered or might there be too much emphasis on certain styles and not enough on others? If there seems to have been a tendency to favour one or two styles, might competitors be doing the same? If this is a possibility the market will be flooded when the ranges are launched. Are the proposed size ranges balanced?

- Is the range profile balanced over time? This is particularly important when styles are phased in over a season rather than launched simultaneously. Does the phasing ensure availability of interest in the range at all times?

- Are the design proportions synchronized? For example, when considering a range of mens' outerwear, if jacket lapels are narrow, are shirt collar point lengths also small? Are ties slim enough to provide a small enough knot? Are widths of trouser bottoms and other design features in proportion to those of the jackets?

● Is there balance across the pricing structure? Are the price levels right? Is there a relative balance of prices across lines and garment categories?

6.7 Fashion and related life cycles

6.7.1 The risks inherent in fashion

The cycle of marketing activity begins and ends with consumer needs; as the most urgent set of needs is satisfied in the form of appropriate products, others emerge. In turn these new needs become of prime importance and create the driving force leading to a desire for further new products. Nowhere is this process more apparent than in the fashion industry; the continual development and introduction of new products into the marketplace is axiomatic to its very existence.

Paradoxically, while an essential undertaking, no aspect of the marketing mix is as uncertain as the introduction and acceptance of new products, particularly when they have a fashion element in them. Implicit in the pluralist nature of today's fashions is the existence of several typical looks or styles in any given season, and the incorporation of many modifications and variations according to the market requirements. The result is that all levels of fashion conscious consumers are able to distinguish between styles that are currently popular and others that belong to previous seasons and are therefore deemed out-of-date. The ability of the individual to observe and react to these phenomena in a negative way ensures the perpetuation of the fashion cycle.

Implicit in the abbove is that at any moment in time a style considered unfashionable by some may yet be deemed fashionable by others. The net effect of this is that the product's profile will vary over time in terms of sales revenue, profits generated and the target market it appeals to as the fashion becomes more widely accepted and therefore less fashionable. To avoid or at least minimize the risk of failure of new fashions, a method of forecasting the onset of popularity with the rate and extent of possible adoption and diffusion patterns would be invaluable to marketers. Furthermore the ability to recognize symptoms of decline or failure at an early stage or perceive changes in the nature of the target market during the season could lead to appropriate changes being made to promotion, pricing and distribution policies to maximize sales and profit potential.

6.7.2 Limitations of theoretical models

Although it has been argued that fashion is the synthetic creation of the seller, particularly with the growth of retail concentration in the last decade, the existence in terms of diversity of direction offered in the marketplace at any one time and the numbers of 'dictated' designs that fail every season are evidence enough that fashions are decided by the majority. Taken collectively the public is closer to the *zeitgeist* or 'spirit of the age' than any individual designer, manufacturer or retailer; it is the consumer who has the last word in what will or will not become fashionable. At the same time the majority of tastes do not swing from one extreme to another every season; in the main changes are gradual and incremental. The implication here is that historical data relating to sales patterns of previous seasonal successes and failures can, to a certain extent, be used as the basis for planning anticipated success rates for new styles (or at least estimating the degree of risk involved). However the real skill lies in being able to identify the most appropriate seasonal fashion directions for the target market in question, while using historical data to plot the likely success rate of the new selections in an effective way.

While the concept of the product lifecycle described below provides a useful framework for analysing sales revenue and profit patterns over time, such analysis will always be retrospective. Thus the model is not able to answer important questions relating to the why and how of product acceptance or failure, nor of why different rates of acceptance and success exist. However, if the seasonal performances of incremental product changes are analysed in the context of variations in the rest of the mix during the cycle, and their performance compared over time, it is feasible that acceptance and diffusion trends can be identified on the basis of product attributes or bundles of utilities. The caveat here is that relying solely on this information and using it too literally can very quickly lead to boredom on part of the consumer, ultimately leading to purchase decisions being made elsewhere in the pursuit of fashion.

Therefore, the real value of the product lifecycle concept lies in its use as a tool for planning and controlling anticipated as opposed to actual rates of sale. At the same time understanding how varying the emphasis of other mix variables can impact on product performance at different stages in the cycle. In the longer term greater understanding of interrelationships will result in more effective planning for appropriate changes according to emerging sales and profit performance.

6.7.3 The fashion product lifecycle

The concept of the product lifecycle is based on the proposal that all products have a finite 'lifecycle' that can be plotted over a given period using the biological analogy of growth, development and decline. It proposes that all products will go through four major stages, namely introduction into the marketplace, growth, maturity and decline. However it has already been pointed out that the nature of products in the fashion industry varies according to the rate, extent and time scale of acceptance of any new offering. Thus while fashions and fads do make up successful new product introductions, garments that are more classic in nature will never actually go 'out of fashion', nor will they rarely be 'in fashion', rather they will continue to meet established target market requirements. Thus the concept should be modified when analysing various fashion product classifications.

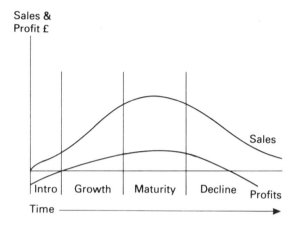

Figure 6.7   The fashion production life cycle.

The life cycle of a fashion garment, extending over one or several seasons, probably comes nearest to the bell-shaped curve normally used to depict the product lifecycle model (see Figure 6.7).

The sales and profitability patterns and marketing implications of the model are described below.

Introduction

New fashions take time to gain acceptance. Some consumers will be more innovative than the majority and, while they are willing to pay higher prices, unit costs could potentially still be high due to low sales. However, to counterbalance this the high fashion element (and therefore exclusive nature) of the style at this stage may mean that customers are willing to pay very high prices, leading to generation of high profits. Selected promotion will emphasize image and high fashion nature; the main aim will be to educate and inform the consumer as quickly as possible. Size of the market will however be limited. Distribution will tend to remain exclusive.

Growth

Competition increases as the fashion gains exposure and begins to have wider appeal. Products will be modified to reduce costs and be offered at lower price levels. Sales will begin to rise sharply; new price bands will be established quite quickly. Distribution, still selective at this stage, will be wider as the fashion is diffused. Promotional emphasis will be on broadening exposure to gain acceptance of the fashion by the opinion forming element of the mass market.

Maturity

At this stage the fashion will have mass appeal; this period will be the longest in its life cycle. Competition will be intense, and prices will begin to fall to appeal to a very large market. Products will be further modified to achieve the ensuing lower price levels and profit potential will be falling. Distribution will be wide; promotional emphasis will be on reinforcement of what has by now become an established fashion.

Decline

The style is rapidly going out of fashion. Competitors are gradually eliminated as sales and profits are falling drastically and the prospect of being left with obsolete stock is near. Those left in the market may try to extend the product's life by intensive advertising, extending distribution or searching for new segments. The alternative segments are likely to balance concerns about the likely success of the product against others such as price levels and the remaining life of the product.

6.7.4 The fad life cycle

The life cycle of the fad will tend to be very short, peaking quite sharply and declining almost as quickly as it rose in popualrity (see Figure 6.8).

The sales and profitability patterns and marketing inplications of the cycle are described below.

Introduction and growth

In the case of a fad there is no introductory period coupled with rapid growth; the objective will be to capitalize on popularity as quickly as possible. However the ability to do this will be restricted to a great extent by its 'fad-like' nature.

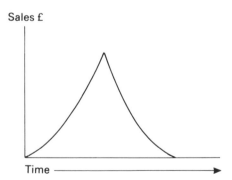

Figure 6.8 Sales of a fashion fad.

Thus sales are pitched at a price the market will bear, probably higher than the fashion item it has been derived from, if this is applicable. Pricing strategy will aim to maximize profits even at launch stage, and the general emphasis will be on offering the new and different to a very specific type of consumer.

Maturity and decline

As maturity is reached decline will begin very rapidly. Sales and profits will also decline, the emphasis here will be on getting rid of any remaining stocks as quickly as possible, either by reducing prices or varying distribution channels. Promotional costs may be incurred in persuading new segments of the fad's dying appeal.

6.7.5 The classic life cycle

The style will have established itself over a time and, once established, will maintain its popularity with its target markets. Periodically the style will become fashionable; the shape of its curve, therefore, will tend to undulate gently (see Figure 6.9).

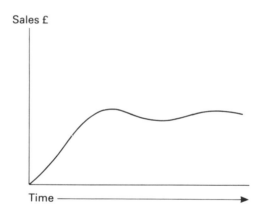

Figure 6.9   Sales of a fashion classic.

Sales and profitability patterns and marketing implications of the cycle

Classics will already be established in the mature stage of the cycle (although they will occasionally be revived as fashion). Distribution channels, price and profitability levels will rise relative to what the established market will bear. Promotional policies for classics will tend to be based on reinforcement of well established, accepted styles. Over time the market for classics could increase as demographic shifts in the population lead to larger numbers in mature age brackets (classics tend to be bought by older, more mature consumers). Earlier in

Figure 6.10 Hypothetical example of a three level analysis within the casual menswear sector.

this section the point was made that the life cycle concept would be most useful where analysis of decisions regarding product and other mix variables could be made regarding sales and profit patterns and where analyses could then be compared over time.

A second dimension in terms of the concept's utility as a planning tool is where comparison can be made over time between the performance of specific styles of brands in relation to broader market and sector trends. Analysis of life cycles here can be made at three related levels (as shown in Figure 6.10), from a general product classification or garment category through to specific product lines within each category and then to various garment styles or brand names (see the earlier section on product mix and range planning).

6.7.6 Fashion oscillations

Some empirical evidence exists to substantiate the proposition that fashions will oscillate over time from one extreme or opposite to the other. These extremes may be in the form of silhouette or shape, colour, fabric texture or pattern and overall style/total look; in other words the four basic design dimensions mentioned earlier.

The driving force behind these oscillatory trends is the continual search by the individual to satisfy a variety of needs, ideally within one purchase decision, and the inherent inability of any one garment to satisfy all of them simultaneously. The net result is that a compromise has to be made between the ideal set of satisfactions sought and the reality of the product's potential set of satisfactions. This will ultimately open up possibilities for many different offerings, the spread of which will depend upon the extent to which compromise has had to be made.

However, every satisfactory purchase made will initiate new drives, These drives will be based on the perpetual need to search for different offerings to satisfy new needs. Paradoxically, therefore, as one design satisfies a combination of needs it extinguishes the very needs that produced it, simultaneously encouraging those needs least well fulfilled by the design to come to the fore. The human drive for social approval results in the tendency for oscillations to reach extremes that are still universally adopted within market segments, for example miniskirts which are worn by a variety of body shapes and sizes within the youth market.

Neglect of some essential design element or embellishment over a long period also can lead to a vigorous revival. The sudden upsurge of many fashions can be explained from such frustrations, the classic example being Dior's post-war 'New Look'.

Sophisticated mass communications have resulted in consumers becoming more fashion conscious and fashion aware. The trend in the 1990s is towards the desire for considerably more diverse ranges of products in the marketplace and the need for more personalized, or customized, fashion. The general result of this is that fashion swings or oscillations are becoming shorter in a time-based sense, often leading to confusion in the marketplace. Here again, however, historical analysis of trends can help when trying to determine future developments.

6.8 Summary

At the end of this chapter readers should be able to:

- Understand the role and importance of the product element of the marketing mix in the fashion industry.
- Analyse and describe the perceived attributes of fashion items by the intended target market.
- Describe the fashion diffusion process within the industry and its bearing on the process of new product development.
- Understand how product mixes and ranges are planned and controlled.

Further reading

Adcock, D., Bradfield R., *et al.* (1993), *Marketing Principles and Practice*, Pitman, London.
Baker, M.J. and McTavish, R. (1976), *Product Policy and Management*. Macmillan, London.
Cannon, T. (1992), *Basic Marketing Principles And Practice*, 3rd edn., Cassell, London.
Kotler, P (1994), *Marketing Management; Analysis, Planning and Control*, 8th edn., Prentice Hall International, New Jersey.
Study Text (1993), *Marketing*, BPP Publishing, London.

UK, European and USA trade journals, fashion press and popular magazines all contain information regarding contemporary fashion developments.

Chapter 7
Pricing Garments and Fashion Services

7.1 Introduction

This chapter begins by considering price first as a concept and then in relation to other elements of the fashion marketing mix. External and internal factors affecting price are examined. The principal methods of setting prices used in the fashion industry are outlined and an explanation of discounts and the concept of break-even is given. The chapter concludes with a discussion of pricing strategies and the administration and nature of price changes.

7.2 Different views of price

According to economists, price is the point at which exchange between buyer and seller takes place, where supply and demand are equal. Anyone who has witnessed sales of out-of-season garments or clothing that have not enjoyed the popularity hoped for, will notice that reductions occur to a point at which the stock is bought. However, price as an element of the marketing mix involves much more than the perspective of the economist.

The accountant tends to concentrate on the relationship between costs of production and the need to provide a certain return on capital invested with the final price that is to be charged. Cash flow is a major concern of all accountants and as such, price decisions can influence the volume of an item that is sold over time. For example, pricing bikinis at £8.99 each may mean that the entire stock is sold within four weeks of launch within a retail outlet. A higher price of £10.99 may mean that the same goal of selling all the stock takes eight weeks. Admittedly, in the latter case an extra £2.00 profit per pair has been earned, but at the cost of holding the stock for a longer period. An additional risk of charging £10.99 is having to reduce prices to shift stock that is particularly susceptible to changes in the climate.

Marketing personnel are interested in price decisions for many reasons. Prices that are set can determine the rate and extent to which marketing objectives are achieved. A company with a goal of achieving a 10% increase in market share will conclude that lower prices may give a competitive advantage that encourages purchases. Similarly, the goal of building a reputation for good quality may well lead to higher prices that follow from the higher costs of using better quality fabrics and imposing more quality checks in manufacture. Marketing managers are also interested in the price perceptions of buyers. As noted in Chapter 3, perception flows from an inner reality that may not be an accurate representation of true price levels. A company's products may be the cheapest on the market, but the advertising or the stores that sell the product may contribute towards an image that contradicts one of low prices. In such a case, opportunities may be missed as consumers don't even bother to check the accuracy of their perceptions. At the level of organizational buyers, from the manufacturer selecting fabric to the retailer acquiring stock, then awareness of price levels is usually a professional imperative. On the other hand, consumers vary considerably in their levels of awareness of prices. With branded products it is easier for consumers to make judgements, therefore comparison shopping is likely to be a common practice for many shoppers. Products from different manufacturers, even if within the same product category like black denim jeans, present consumers with challenges to make direct comparisons due to differences in styling, quality of construction, quality of materials used and image.

The above perspectives and salience of pricing decisions for companies mean that many people within a company may have direct and legitimate interests in price decisions. The locus of influence and control will vary according to the organization of particular firms and to the relative importance given to financial and marketing matters. This is not an argument for the supremacy of marketing over other functional considerations, but a recognition that many disciplines should be involved in price decisions.

7.3 The role of price decisions within marketing strategy

The price levels for a product range selected by an organization can, along with other elements of the marketing mix, decide the success or otherwise in attracting certain target markets. Setting price levels too low may send confused messages and alienate some buyers who feel that the product may be poorly made. Excessive prices may inhibit other people who may feel other products, while not similar, offer better value for money. Others may feel that high prices are solely a premium for immediate ownership and that waiting a short period may yield price reductions. Therefore price decisions help determine who buys and how much they buy.

In relation to decisions about place matters, pricing decisions can secure access to certain outlets. To give retailers opportunities to achieve their profit margins, manufacturers must recognize the needs of the retailer's target market and the margins that are expected. If a retailer expects that an item will be a fast seller then a lower margin may be accepted. Similarly, higher margins are expected on slow moving items or risky new fashion products that may or may not be quickly accepted by the consumer.

Product matters are related to price decisions in many ways. The nature and extent of the product line may limit the flexibility possible in setting prices. For example, a coordinated range of skirts, jackets, blouses and accessories may be so priced as to encourage the purchase of several items by the consumer. Rigidly sticking to a fixed profit margin on each product in the range could undermine a policy that would otherwise lead to higher sales and profits by varying margins of items within and between the coordinated product lines. If the prices of products were left as a sum of their costs of manufacture plus a fixed markup, then variations in prices of different sizes of the same garment would be the obvious outcome. A size 16 overcoat may use nearly twice as much material as a size 8, yet few retailers would contemplate charging more for the larger one. In this sense, smaller customers subsidize larger customers, but in practice most manufacturers, retailers and consumers accept the notion of averaging costs and prices across different sizes.

Promotion and pricing decisions most closely relate with regard to the image that is being put forward to consumers. Most people perceive a relationship between price levels and quality, though not always a linear one. Usually the expectation is that high quality goes with high prices and low prices reflect low quality or possibly out-of-date or out-of-season clothing. The selection of a particular media to reach a certain target market may mean that prices are not even mentioned in promotional messages. Ready to wear merchandise from Hugo Boss, advertised in the Financial Times with no mention of price, is such an example. At the other extreme a store selling garments aimed at low-income groups may make price a prominent feature of its window displays and advertising. Marks and Spencer originally began promoting itself as a store where everything was priced at one penny, but strategic repositioning plus inflation have changed the company's practices since then.

The above discussion shows the interrelationship between price, target markets and other elements of the marketing mix. There is one particular area where pricing does differ from other elements of the marketing mix. All other elements of the marketing mix entail costs which it is hoped will lead to increased sales and profit. Pricing, while also affecting sales will be a direct determinant of revenue out of which marketing and other costs are met.

7.4 External factors influencing price decisions

7.4.1 The nature of competition in the particular market

At a broad level it should be noted that competition comes not just from other garments suppliers, but also from other products and services that compete for consumers' discretionary income. High prices for garments may encourage consumers to spend more money on other consumer durables like hi-fi systems or on leisure activities like holidays. The unattractiveness of the prices of garments in relation to other competing products and services should be kept in mind. The relative sales and trends of various sectors of industry, plus the inflation rates by sector, are indicators of how well or otherwise this inter-sector competition is being met.

The more homogeneous the product the greater the price competition. The fashion industry tries to encourage non-price competition by the branding and

Figure 7.1   External factors influencing price decisions.

creation of unique designs and images for ranges. At the designer level of the market, such garments are in limited supply through exclusive outlets and, the creators hope, for limited periods. The ability of competitors to produce similar products is restricted by some legislative protection of the design. Consumer confidence in garment quality and the ability to purchase an up-to-date design immediately enables higher prices to be charged. For other products such as socks the latitude to command exclusivity or any special design point that can be reflected in a higher price is more restricted.

7.4.2   Joint or related demand for products

This may arise where the increase in demand for one product is accompanied by an increase in demand for another. Good weather may well spur demand for swimwear, sun-hats and sunglasses. Retailers, well aware of these linkages, may design the layout of the store and adjust prices accordingly to make the most of complementary demand. Other examples include the purchase of a new tie that may stimulate the purchase of a new shirt. New colour themes for a season, if adopted, may stimulate a whole range of purchases. Thus a new evening dress may be accompanied by the purchase of new hosiery, underwear, coat, cosmetics, hairstyling, shoes and handbag. Such outcomes are the aspiration of many department stores. It is the relative pricing, besides the selection and coordination of appropriate items in the above list that is crucial in deciding the successful sale. Manufacturers who produce such complementary items independently need to anticipate the needs of intermediaries and the ultimate customer when setting prices.

7.4.3 The nature of the product

Whether the product is seen as an essential or not is a factor that influences the power of the seller in setting prices. Target markets differ considerably in what is seen as essential. A dinner jacket may be seen as a luxury by some, but as an essential item by a manager who has to attend many formal functions.

Some items of clothing and footwear are essential for protection and warmth. The rate of replacement of garments and the ability of consumers to defer purchase, obtain repairs, make clothes themselves or buy second hand goods, remains within the consumers' discretion. One related factor that influences the pricing of fashion products is the perceived life of the product. If a garment is seen as a 'classic' that will last for many seasons or years, such as a Barbour jacket or Burberry raincoat, then premium prices are more easily tolerated. In relation to other markets such as power supply, the fashion industry does not enjoy the privilege of producing items whose demand is insensitive to price changes. The nearest that the fashion industry comes to such demand is when there is only a limited supply of a unique design that is eagerly sought by buyers.

The speed with which some firms in the industry are able to produce garments that are similarly styled and made from comparable fabrics or fibres, means such uniqueness does not go unchallenged for long. The issue here is not one of counterfeits, although that is a serious problem for some firms. The intrinsic difficulty of ensuring full protection for fashion designs is where the slightest difference in styling can be used as a basis for contesting a claim for breach of copyright. Inelasticity of demand is therefore limited in the fashion industry by the ease with which comparable alternatives can be quickly supplied.

7.4.4 Other members of the distribution channel

If one member of the distribution channel is able to charge higher prices this may tempt those earlier in the chain of distribution to increase prices and share in the profit potential. The ability of manufacturers to change retail outlets and the willingness of other outlets to stock a profitable product range is a key variable that influences the setting of prices at the retail level.

Within certain sections of the retail clothing sector there are traditional margins that must be accounted for when setting prices. One large retail group, for instance, is known to have a company policy of multiplying supplier prices by 2.3 to arrive at a retail price. Such practices must be anticipated by manufacturers as, depending on the balance of power with the retailer, these traditional margins may be used as a mechanism to force down the manufacturer's selling price.

Changes in the costs of raw materials, labour or manufacturing at earlier stages in the distribution chain are factors that can influence the ultimate price to the consumer. With the growing internationalization of the clothing industry, the ability of retailers to procure stock from sources in different countries is greater than ever before. The power of suppliers to pass on price increases unchallenged is diminished except where the supply of a fabric or design is either unique or very well known such as Gore-Tex or Lycra.

7.4.5 Government policy and legislation

As has been noted in an earlier chapter on the market environment, governments can influence the readiness of consumers to pay particular prices via policy related to inflation, investment and employment.

Government policy on taxation, in particular value added tax (VAT) and corporation tax, might be said to provide extra 'costs' that must be borne by the fashion consumer. The change of emphasis of taxation from earnings to expenditure in recent years has, at the macro level, influenced demand for fashion products. The Office of Fair Trading, the Monopolies and Mergers Commission and the European Commission are all charged to defend the public and business against various price fixing methods as described later in this chapter.

7.5 Internal factors influencing price decisions

7.5.1 The ability to control costs

The ability of the company to minimize costs is a major determinant on the price levels that can be set. As costs can be decreased so either profitability can be enhanced or the ability to compete at low prices can be strengthened.

7.5.2 Other elements of the marketing mix

The relative importance of other elements of the marketing mix of the company is a factor influencing pricing decisions. The company competing directly on price to achieve high volume distribution at low margins is in a very different position from the company setting out to create an image of high quality at premium prices.

7.5.3 The product range

The breadth and depth of product lines and the price relationships between items in those lines are factors that must be considered when setting prices. A warm lining for a raincoat sold separately will need to be assessed not only in terms of individual cost, but also for the impact it has upon the total demand and profitability of the raincoat and lining together.

7.6 Main methods of setting prices

There are many ways of setting prices, but most are variants of the two principal methods, namely cost-plus pricing and market-based pricing. Cost-plus pricing is simply calculating the cost of raw materials, labour and overheads such as administration and adding an amount to cover profit to arrive at the selling price. Market-based pricing is founded on market research to find the optimum selling price which then acts as the main driving force on cost containment via design and quality control effort.

7.6.1 Cost-plus pricing methods

A cost based method aims to ensure that no product is sold at a loss. The practice is common where the product is non-standard, such as designer wedding gowns, or where there are many small independent retailers supplying the market. Cost-plus pricing is also used with tender proposals, for instance, when a clothing manufacturer makes a proposal to supply uniforms to a large corporate client. A simple example is given below based upon a manufacturer supplying a retailer with zip-up tops made of cotton jersey.

The concept of the markup is explained in more detail below. In the example in Table 7.1, the profit margin per item is fairly low, but this may be deemed appropriate for an item that faces much competition and is expected to sell in very large quantities. The markups for the manufacturer and retailer have been set at 25% and 65% respectively as the minimum rates of return needed to service the capital required for each business namely, shareholder dividends or the cost of loans.

The above example assumes that all of the zip-up tops will be sold at the full price. If the retailer is determined to clear stock, but not to sell below the cost of any item, then the lowest 'sale' price will be £5.15 plus VAT. If the retailer sells at VAT exclusive prices of between £5.15 and below £8.50 then the technique of contribution analysis is being applied. Contribution analysis is a variant of cost-plus pricing and works on the idea that any excess of price over cost enables a contribution to be made to the cost of capital to run the business—

Table 7.1 An example of cost plus pricing.

Item	Details	Quantity	Unit cost	Total cost
Cotton	Jersey	1.5 metres	£1.80/metre	£2.70
Trim	Polyfil thread	1	£0.08	£0.08
	Metal zip	1 @ 20 cm	£0.24	£0.24
	Knitted collar	1	£0.16	£0.16
Label	With logo and			
	care instructions	1	£0.04	£0.04
Labour to cut, make and trim @ 15 minutes				£0.90
Cost of production				£4.12
Manufacturer's markup @ 25%				£1.03
Manufacturer's selling price (excluding VAT)				£5.15
Retailer's markup @ 65%				£3.35
Retail Price excluding VAT				£8.50
Value Added Tax @ 17.5%				£1.49
Retail Price including VAT				
				£9.99

simply put, some profit is better than no profit. Clearly the whole of a company's pricing cannot be based on covering costs alone, as fashion companies need to do more in order to survive and grow. More sophisticated variants of contribution analysis can be used to link price setting to several financial ratios.

7.6.2 Market-based pricing methods

These methods rely on a good knowledge of consumer price sensitivity and awareness levels. For example, market research may indicate that buyers in a certain target market may respond very favourably to a hooded top made of cotton jersey, if the item is priced at £12.99 (including VAT). If the retailer enjoys considerable purchasing power then the retail price of £12.99 can be used as a base to determine target buying prices for the retailer. The example in Table 7.2 shows how with a starting price of £12.99 the target retailer buying price or manufacturer selling price is determined.

Table 7.2 Calculation of target buying prices.

Cotton jersey hooded top including	
VAT at 17.5%	£12.99
Less VAT at 17.5%	£1.93
Retail price excluding VAT	£11.06
Less retailer's markup at 65% of buying price	£7.19
Retailer buying price or manufacturer selling price	£3.87

Similarly, the manufacturer may then use the selling price of £3.87 as a target to challenge designers, pattern cutters and production staff to achieve certain economies. In practice, many large UK retailers work very closely with manufacturers to decide prices that attempt to match consumer expectations.

7.6.3 A comparison of markups and markdowns

A markup is where profit is expressed as a percentage of costs and it is shown by the following formula:

$$\frac{(\text{Price} - \text{Cost})}{\text{Cost}} \times 100$$

Thus a selling price of £30 with a cost of £20 gives a markup of 50%.

A markdown is where profit is expressed as a percentage of the sale price and it is shown by the following formula:

$$\frac{(\text{Price} - \text{Cost})}{\text{Price}} \times 100$$

Thus a selling price of £60 with a cost of £24 gives a markdown of 60%.

$$\% \text{ markdown on selling price} = \frac{\% \text{ markup on cost}}{100\% + \text{markup on cost}} \times 100$$

$$\% \text{ markup on cost} = \frac{\% \text{ markdown on selling price}}{100\% - \% \text{ markdown on selling price}} \times 100$$

Figure 7.2 Markup and markdown formulae.

Different firms use different approaches to calculate profit and selling price. However, all are variants of either a markup or a markdown. Indeed, knowing one it is easy to express profit in terms of the other. The formulae showing the interrelationship of the two main measures of profit margin are shown in Figure 7.2.

Using the above formulae we can see that, for example, a markup on cost of 25% is the same as a markdown on selling price of 20%. Similarly a markdown on selling price of 66.7% is equivalent to a markup on cost of 200%.

Sometimes fashion retailers use a simple formula to calculate a retail selling price, including VAT, given a particular quotation from a manufacturer. The retailer wanting a markup of 120% and knowing that VAT is charged at 17.5%, may simply multiply the quoted cost price, excluding VAT, by 1.375 to arrive at a tax inclusive retail selling price.

7.6.4 Discounts

The issue of margins leads naturally into a discussion of the purpose and types of discounts that are offered. The principle of economies of scale applies by which both buyer and seller recognize that larger quantities enjoy larger discounts. For the manufacturer, selling large quantities to fewer buyers means lower delivery and other overhead costs. Retailers naturally appreciate such advantages for both manufacturers and wholesalers and will press within negotiations for the largest quantity discounts possible.

Variations on the simple quantity discount are the cumulative and non-cumulative discounts available. Some negotiations may result in extra discounts becoming available should the buyer purchase certain minimum quantities over a fixed period, say one year. This extra discount may then become available as a rebate or credit against future purchases. The main aim of cumulative discounts is for the seller to encourage loyalty to the supplier and to induce small buyers to purchase more.

At the consumer level the retailer may encourage a customer to buy a jacket and a skirt, for example, by offering 10% off one item if both are purchased simultaneously. This type of discounting at the retail level operates erratically and is usually offered by the small outlets to tempt those potential consumers who are vacillating about a purchase.

Another common form of discount is the cash discount. Business to business discounts of this form usually take the form of a percentage reduction if payment is made within a fixed, usually short period. For example, 1.5% discount may be offered if payment is received within thirty days. Recent changes in legislation in the UK now allow retailers to charge different prices to consumers depending on the method of payment, be it cash or cheque versus a credit card payment. The obvious benefit for the retailer of a cash payment is improved cash flow and the avoidance of a payment of between 2% and 5% to the credit card company. The incidence of differential prices has yet to become widespread and, due to the different charges levied by the credit card companies, is most likely only to be favoured by the small retailers.

7.6.5 Break-even calculations

A central concern of marketing personnel in the fashion industry is balancing the relationship between price and volume. For example, a clothing manufacturer may manufacture 40 000 pairs of jeans and wish to know how many must be sold to cover costs. In other words, at what point will the manufacturer break even and begin to earn profits. The first example assumes the manufacturer is in a relationship where prices are fixed by fierce competitive pressures and tough negotiating from retail buyers.

Alternatively, a designer who owns a retail outlet may have considerable discretion over price levels, but wonder about the profitability of the different volumes that could be sold at different prices. Break-even analysis is a technique that can help decision making needs in the two examples just given.

Break-even analysis is an aid that can show the relationship between fixed costs, variable or marginal costs, total costs, sales revenue and output or volume. Fixed costs are those costs incurred by the fashion company that do not change as the volume of purchases or production changes. Some examples of fixed costs include business rates, purchase of a computer for wages and salaries for security staff. In practice, many fixed costs are variable in the long term, such as costs of plant for manufacturing. If these variations can be set aside, then a simple technique that can give a fairly sound guide to setting price level can be found in break-even analysis.

Variable costs are those costs that are directly affected by the level of output, some examples are the amount of material used, the direct labour costs in pattern cutting, making up and tailoring and packaging costs. Total costs are the sum of fixed costs plus variable cost per unit multiplied by the output or volume. Sales revenue is simply price multiplied by volume sold. In practice, the price taken for the calculations is one that is exclusive of VAT.

The formula that shows the relationship between the above variables is as follows:

$$\text{Revenue} = \text{Price} \times \text{Volume} = \text{Total Costs} + \text{Profit} \qquad (1)$$

When revenue is less than total costs, a loss (or negative profit) will result.

Where:

$$\text{Total Costs} = \text{Fixed Costs} + (\text{Variable Cost per unit} \times \text{Volume})$$

and

$$\text{Profit} = \text{Profit per unit} \times \text{Volume}$$

At the break-even point, no profit is earned and all costs are covered by sales revenue. Hence:

$$\text{Revenue} = \text{Fixed Costs} + (\text{Variable Cost per unit} \times \text{Volume})$$

Or:

$$\text{Price} \times \text{Volume} = \text{Fixed Costs} + (\text{Variable Cost per unit} \times \text{Volume})$$

To determine the break-even point we can do some simple simultaneous equations where:

$$
\begin{aligned}
\text{FC} &= \text{Fixed costs} \\
\text{VC} &= \text{Variable cost per unit} \\
\text{V} \ \ &= \text{Volume} \\
\text{P} \ \ &= \text{Price}
\end{aligned}
$$

Thus we know that at the break-even point:

$$(P \times V) = FC + (VC \times V)$$

By taking ($VC \times V$) from each side of the equation we get:

$$(P \times V) - (VC \times V) = FC$$

Which, when simplified is:

$$V \times (P - VC) = FC$$

Next divide both sides of the equation by ($P - VC$)

$$V = \frac{FC}{(P - VC)} \tag{2}$$

Of course ($P - VC$) is really the gross profit per unit.

To calculate the break-even volume, we divide the fixed costs by the difference between the price and the variable cost per unit.

If we wished to know the minimum price at which all the output was sold and covered all costs, i.e. the break-even price point, the formula is calculated as follows:

We know that at the break even point:

$$(P \times V) = FC + (VC \times V)$$

If we divide each side by V we get:

$$P = \frac{FC}{V} + VC \tag{3}$$

The value given here for price is the minimum that must be charged if the entire volume is sold and no profit is earned. In practice, a seller would wish to charge higher prices and earn some profit. The formula does at least help establish a baseline for making pricing decisions.

7.6.6 Break-even analysis – an example

A small retailer of knitwear in a franchise operation may have rental and other fixed costs amounting to £45 000 per annum. If 3000 items of stock for resale are purchased per year at say £16 each (excluding VAT), then the total variable cost is £48 000. Assume here that the sales assistants are paid a fixed wage of £45 000 that is included in the fixed costs. If sales assistants were paid a commission for each item of knitwear sold, then this would be a variable cost and would have to be added to the purchase cost per item. Thus the total costs for the knitwear retailer are £45 000 fixed costs plus £48 000 variable costs, giving £93 000 per annum.

If the knitwear retailer wishes to calculate the minimum price that must be charged to cover costs and sell all the garments then formula (3) must be used:

$$P = \frac{FC}{V} + VC$$

Substituting we get:

$$P = \frac{45\,000}{3000} + 16$$

Therefore, if a price of £31 (plus VAT) per unit was charged the business would break even.

If the retailer, after undertaking market research into competitors' prices, wishes to charge £39.95 (including VAT) per item, the question is now to determine the minimum number that must be sold to break even. A price of £39.95, including VAT at 17.5%, gives a VAT exclusive price of £34.00.

Formula (2) is used to calculate the break even volume thus:

$$V = \frac{FC}{(P - VC)}$$

Substituting values we get:

$$V = \frac{45\,000}{34 - 16}$$

which gives a volume of 2500 units to break even.

If the retailer sells all 3000 garments then if the original formula (1) is used:

$$\text{Revenue} = \text{Price} \times \text{Volume} = \text{Total Costs} + \text{Profit} \tag{1}$$

$$34 \times 3000 = 45\,000 + (16 \times 3000) + \text{Profit}$$

$$102\,000 = 45\,000 + 48\,000 + \text{Profit}$$

Thus the profit earned is £9000 or 8.82% of sales revenue.

7.7 Pricing strategies in relation to new products

The pricing objectives derived from a marketing strategy in relation to new products are to achieve growth, maximize profitability, or generate cash flow. The crucial decisions to be made prior to selecting a pricing strategy are the identification of the target market(s) and careful consideration of the other elements of the marketing mix.

7.7.1 Market skimming

This strategy is to charge high initial prices and then only reduce them gradually, if at all. A skimming price policy is a form of price discrimination over time and for it to be effective several conditions must be met.

First, the demand for the garments must be relatively inelastic. Inelastic demand only really exists for essential items that are in short supply or items that have a degree of exclusivity and a significant number of buyers who are relatively unconcerned about price. For the supplier the unit costs of producing a small volume must not be too high. Finally, the high profit margins on each item in a skimming policy will attract competitors unless the seller can protect the garments from being copied. Such a situation usually applies to haute couture and to a lesser degree to designer ready to wear ranges.

7.7.2 Market penetration

This strategy is the opposite of market skimming and aims to try to capture a large market share by charging low prices. The low prices charged stimulate purchases and can discourage competitors from entering the market as the profit margins per item are low. To be effective this policy relies upon considerable economies of scale in either manufacture, retailing or both. It also depends upon potential customers being price sensitive about the particular item and perhaps not perceiving much difference between brands. An example of this sort of policy may be seen in the plain 15 denier tights sold in supermarkets.

7.8 Pricing strategies to match the competition

Pricing objectives in relation to the competition include, as both active and reactive positions, an attempt to maintain price leadership, to stabilize prices or to discourage others from entering the particular market. Such strategies may also be linked to objectives concerned with building and maintaining the loyalty of other parts of the distribution chain. Aiming for stable prices while recognizing the traditional margins in the channels of distribution are characteristics of the marketing activities of many fashion marketing companies.

7.8.1 Price leaders and followers

In the case of the follower, the firm identifies a target market and sets prices in line with competitors who are serving the same market. A firm with limited marketing resources may simply shadow a competitor. Within fashion retailing it is quite common for sales assistants to visit other stores to monitor the price points for garments and accessories. Monitoring the competition is an essential part of any market research, but slavishly aping one's rivals' actions without a clear long-term goal is another matter. The leader in such a situation is usually the firm with the lowest costs and best profit margins. Followers hope to avoid a price war by stressing non-price aspects of competition like a higher customer service level.

Market research may indicate, for example, that a certain income group targeted by the firm is willing to pay between £25 and £35 for a blouse. The same research also may find that the main competitor is pricing similar garments at £29.95. The conclusion may be to charge at the same price or marginally lower, say £29.50. Such a policy of price matching can avoid a price war while maintaining profit margins. The policy of matching the competition is particularly vulnerable to enterprizing newcomers to the market who may be able to upset the cosy reassurance that sometimes emerges in some sectors. An economic downturn with pressures on margins or the slow sales on some product lines can easily render this policy susceptible to change.

The large retail groups may incorporate an element of matching the competition within an overall pricing strategy, by allowing local managers some discretion in meeting local competition by adjusting prices where necessary.

7.8.2 Price fixing

Overt or covert price fixing by sellers is illegal in the European Union and most western nations unless a defence can be made that such action is not against the public interest. Manufacturers are in the main prohibited from imposing retail prices upon retailers in the United Kingdom, and this is known as retail price maintenance. Manufacturers are sometimes able to use pressure relating to the supply or witholding of products or financial incentives to exert influence over retail prices and effectively inhibit competition. The European Union has an aim of free movement of goods within and between the member states and the intense competition within the fashion market works strongly against price fixing tendencies. However, in 1993 the French perfume industry was able to claim a victory in the European Court by winning the right to exclusive distribution of perfumes, thereby protecting the margins of outlets against so called 'grey' imports.

7.9 Price changes

Prices for clothing may need to change for a variety of reasons, but the administration and communication of those changes are important matters that can

Figure 7.3   Price changes.

affect profits greatly. An overview of price changes is given in Figure 7.3. Prices can increase because of higher costs, rising inflation, excess demand for the product or simply a misjudgment of prior price levels.

Decreases in price can be attempts to drive out or meet competitors, to take advantage of lower costs or to generate more demand. As fashion is about change, garment prices usually fall over time. The only exceptions seem to be rare items previously owned by celebrities or clothing in short supply that is identified with a fast emerging cult.

Whatever the cause of the price change it will affect customers, competitors and other members of the distribution channel. The uncertainty that accompanies the potential effect of any price change means that research and planning are essential. Buyer responses to price changes can be varied. For reductions, many may perceive the items to be end-of-season, unpopular, faulty or of lower quality. It also may be that buyers resist initial price reductions in anticipation of further falls. Price increases are only popular with those who bought at a lower price. Increases can signal that the product may soon be unavailable or that it represented good value for money with very low margins at the old price.

All price changes, when clearly marked, can attract attention and raise buyers' price awareness levels so that purchase values may then be reconsidered. As noted in the chapter on buyer behaviour, the concept of learning is important as price changes 'teach' consumers what to expect. Thus, if a store always marks items down by 20% after eight weeks, then a further 20% after another two weeks, some consumers will learn not to pay higher prices. The cycle of price reductions can therefore become reinforced as more people in the target market learn to avoid paying the premium prices.

The communication to consumers of price changes requires particular consideration. Changes promoted as 'massive reductions' can alienate those customers who paid higher initial prices, while simultaneously attracting the bargain hunters the supplier is seeking. How price changes are communicated depends upon the marketing objectives of the firm and the target markets being served. Announcing large clearance discounts in a sale in an outlet catering for higher income groups may be inconsistent with other aspects of the image. However, when the change is announced it is imperative that the sales staff and customers are in no doubt what price is to be charged and when the change takes effect. Much damage to customer goodwill can be done by lack of care in announcing price changes. Given the practices of a minority of unscrupulous retailers, many consumers approach sales with a healthy degree of scepticism. Thus care is needed to avoid a small oversight being construed as a deliberate attempt to mislead.

7.10 Summary

This chapter has considered price, both as a concept and in the context of the marketplace in relation to the other elements of the fashion marketing mix.
Pricing decisions are:

- subject to a wide variety of influencing factors, internal and external
- a strategic matter, and not to be approached in a short-term reactive way
- to be made within the wider framework of a clear understanding of the target market, the firm's overall marketing strategy and the competition.

Further reading

Livesey, F. (1976), *Pricing*, MacMillan, London.
Morden, A. (1993), *Elements of Marketing*, 3rd edn., DP Publications, London.
Piercy, N. (1991), *Market-led Strategic Change*, Butterworth-Heinemann, Oxford.
Walters, D. and White, D. (1987), *Retail Marketing Management*, MacMillan, Basingstoke.
Winkler, J. (1987), Pricing, in *The Marketing Book* by Baker, M. (ed) (1987), Butterworth-Heinemann, Oxford.

Chapter 8
Fashion Distribution

8.1 Introduction

This chapter examines the retail sector that for many people is the 'face of fashion', describing the structure of the industry and its constituent parts and includes an outline of recent developments. It concludes with a brief examination of criteria against which retail marketing effectiveness can be judged. The large-scale retailers are all involved in marketing activities and most have specialist marketing departments.

8.2 The importance of fashion retailing

The retail industry is important to the marketing of fashion clothing in a number of ways. First, and most obviously, it is the mechanism through which the clothes reach the consumer.

Secondly, with the growth in applying information technology it is able to provide, within hours at most, detailed feedback of what the consumer is buying. This allows changes in the marketplace to be quickly assessed, thus helping range renewal, particularly in such areas as replacement sizes and colours. Benetton has the tills of all its shops linked directly to its marketing and design departments as well as to its dyeing facilities so that changes in demand can be quickly observed and production changed accordingly.

Thirdly, it facilitates the application of target marketing (see Chapter 5).

Fourthly, it has been active in the promotion of design awareness to the shopping public, two well known examples being Habitat and Next, in terms of product design and store layout and equipment. Design also serves to promote market segmentation and improve sales and productivity ratios in relation to increasingly expensive selling space.

Fifthly, manufacturers and designers can achieve stability by owning their own retail units. As Paul Smith has said of his retail side 'it is a regular earner for us' (*Independent*, 9 August 1993 p 19).

Finally, the retail outlet through its store image can create loyal customers who may provide a measure of stability in sales income and profits. *Where Britain Shops 1993*, a report by Verdict Research showed that 37% of those questioned habitually shopped at one or two chains and 46% were loyal to independents.

What goes into creating a store image? Various writers have offered sugges-

Figure 8.1   Components of store image.

tions, Lindquist reviewed many studies and synthesized the following from them –
merchandise, service, store atmosphere, promotion, clientèle, physical facilities,
institutional factors and post-purchase satisfaction. Physical environment is an
important influence on image as Mary Jo Bitner (1992) outlines in a journal
article. The main components of store image are shown in Figure 8.1.

Another factor in building store loyalty has been the introduction of store-
based credit cards, which in addition to encouraging sales also afford opportunities for database marketing. The BhS Choice Card is one example.

Such is the importance of store image that some manufacturers and designers
actively strive to be represented in certain stores. This alongside other issues
such as reliability, cost, stockholding capabilities and coverage of the market
sought is a major consideration in channel management.

8.3 Structural issues

8.3.1 Basic structure

The industry has traditionally been divided into three distinct segments, which
have over the years performed differently.

Womenswear, the largest segment, has traditionally shown most growth, and
was worth an estimated £9bn in 1990.

Menswear has shown greater growth than womenswear in recent years as men
have become more fashion conscious, and grew by 73% between 1983 and
1988. In 1990 it was worth an estimated £7bn. However, just as it seems to do
relatively better than womenswear when the economy is booming, so it seems
to suffer greater decline in recessionary times.

Childrenswear is the smallest of the three retail markets, approximately a quarter that of menswear at an estimated £2bn in 1990. In retail fashion terms it is a difficult market to cater for, but in recent years it has seen a growth in specialist retail chains such as Adams and the introduction of continental retail brands such as Chipie and Oilily. Boots is aiming to break into this market through its subsidiary Childrens World.

8.3.2 Concentration

In common with other sectors of the retail trade, concentration in the fashion retail market has increased over the years. All three market segments described above are dominated by variety chains and multiples except at the designer level. Clothing retailing in the UK according to analysis by the TMS Partnership, is the most concentrated in the world with the four largest retailers Marks and Spencer, the Burton Group, Storehouse and Littlewoods accounting for 30% of total sales in 1990. Marks and Spencer alone accounts for some 16% of United Kingdom clothing sales. This has been achieved through economies of scale e.g. buying-power, promotional spending and managerial expertise.

It has been suggested that customers who want something other than the mass produced and marketed clothes provided by the major retailers will enable a considerable independent sector to thrive. Others point to entrepreneurial flair and ability to cater to local needs as reasons for their continued survival.

In this context those retailers who try to combine an element of exclusivity and the benefits of scale by trading from a limited number of outlets, such as Jigsaw, seem to have done relatively well in recent years.

The trade sector shares of the market in 1988 are shown in Table 8.1.

Table 8.1 Market shares.

Multiple clothing retailers	24.9%
Independent clothing retailers	18.6%
Variety chains	21.1%
Department stores	8.5%
Other retailers	11.4%
Other sources	15.5%

Source: The TMS Partnership 1988.

8.3.3 Numbers of outlets

The Department of Trade and Industry's (DTI) biannual retail inquiry shows a gradual decline in the number of outlets, although the 1980s retail boom reversed this trend. Though most closures are small retailers, they nonetheless continue to make up the bulk of the 40 000 or more outlets. This to some extent is offset by an influx of European and American clothing companies setting up retail outlets in the United Kingdom, two examples of which would be Ouiset and The Gap.

The 1990 retail inquiry figures, the latest available, put the number of outlets specialising in one or other of the three markets at 36 000 with some 9400 classed as in the general clothing business.

The retail boom of the 1980s also resulted in a large increase in the amount of selling space, particularly in out-of-town locations. It also created greater demand for sites in town centres with Next, for example, taking over Combined English Stores so as to acquire additional prime selling space. There is now an argument for saying that the nation has too many shops, and some reduction in numbers is necessary.

8.3.4 Outlet size

To the extent that clothing retailers and particularly those who serve the upper market levels continue to trade from established city centre sites, there is limited scope for increasing the size of outlet, though Marks and Spencer did build a fifth floor onto its Marble Arch store.

Moving to out-of-town locations offers the potential for increasing store size but can affect the image of the store.

8.3.5 Import and export

In common with other United Kingdom industries there is a considerable amount of overseas trade and as in sectors of United Kingdom industry the degree of import penetration is high and rising. Imports that were some £1.2bn in 1980, were double that figure in 1986 and some £4bn in 1992. Exports over the same timescale increased but only managed to grow from £0.8bn in 1980 to £1.6bn.

The reasons for this state of affairs are many and complex and often apply equally to other sectors such as the exchange rate, comparative labour and other costs together with tariffs and other barriers to trade such as subsidies and quotas. Free trade, that is countries being allowed to buy and sell goods and services world-wide without any restrictions is theoretically desirable but the international textiles trade like others is regulated.

8.3.6 Exports

Exports are mainly restricted to high value and traditional sectors such as knitwear where cost is less important as retail customers appreciate and are willing to pay for quality and style.

Much of the UK trade in textiles is with the other members of the EU, though the US and the Far East are important markets. As British retailers expand overseas these can provide useful export markets for the manufacturers who supply their UK stores. Marks and Spencer is one example of this happening. In 1992 they exported to twenty countries, with franchise and export sales in excess of £100m at retail prices.

8.3.7 Multi Fibre Agreement

This regulation takes place through the Multi Fibre Agreement (MFA) which came into existence in 1974 as a temporary expedient and is basically a framework for regulating trade in fibres, fabrics and clothing between developing low cost countries and the industrialized countries. Trade in textiles is regulated by means of bilaterally agreed quotas that can be changed to meet changing circumstances.

In December 1991 as part of the Uruguay Round of GATT (General Agreement on Tariffs and Trade) it was agreed that subject to agreement on other issues the MFA would be phased out over ten years from 1993, subsequently extended to 1994. The Uruguay Round negotiated in 1993 will encourage more clothing and textile imports from low-cost countries by liberalizing international trade even further.

8.3.8 The future for United Kingdom clothing firms

Under increased pressure from low-cost producers the British textile industry has steadily declined over the years as retailers have increasingly sought to import their merchandise from low-cost countries, originally in the Far East but now increasingly from former eastern bloc countries such as Romania.

However, there is some hope; improvements in technology and manufacturing techniques hold out the possibility of UK manufacturers being able to meet the demands for small-scale production runs. Retailers' increasing reluctance to hold large stocks and consumer pressure towards more diversity and exclusivity encourage the need for small runs and put a premium on a fast flexible response that will tend to help United Kingdom based manufacturers. Just in time (JIT) inventory control and a reluctance to commit budgets early in the season also offer the possibility of top-up orders even if the main order is initially placed overseas.

Pressure from the dominant retailers has resulted in United Kingdom manufacturers increasingly making use of subcontractors, many of which are overseas. An increased emphasis on design is also being placed on the manufacturers, many of whom now have an in-house design capability, though in recessionary times these may be cut back.

8.3.9 Relationships with manufacturers

One option for clothing firms is to operate as both a retailer and manufacturer, though this is becoming increasingly less attractive. The major disadvantage of this form of vertically structured form of organization is that considerable capital is tied up in manufacturing assets that, because of changing market conditions and increased overseas competition, provide progressively lower rates of return.

The major advantage for retailers with their own manufacturing concern was total control of the manufacturing process and security of supply. Perhaps the main exponent of this approach was Burtons which, in addition to its nationwide chain of stores, had extensive manufacturing facilities in the Leeds area, employing at one time over 10 000 production workers.

These advantages have been retained by the major retailers in their dealings with their suppliers because of their dominant role in the marketplace. Often suppliers are almost totally dependent on a particular retailer, who can in return for regular and substantial orders, demand total control over the manufacturing process and enforce narrow profit margins on the manufacturer.

Many retailers are cutting the number of suppliers they deal with; BhS is reducing this figure from some 750 in the early 1990s to about half that number. Those that remain must meet strict terms on price, quality, delivery times etc.

At the same time the reverse is occurring with some manufacturers who believe that the time taken to service small retailers would be better spent forging closer links with their major customers. An example of a supplier adopting this policy is Hardcore, the denim company.

8.3.10   Retail buying and selling

In all large scale fashion clothing retailers central buying is now the norm. Experienced buyers visit trade and fashion shows, overseas and United Kingdom suppliers and use prediction services to make decisions on what to buy for the coming seasons. Often the initial order will be for only part of the expected sales, the rest being confirmed later in the season as actual sales figures allow management to estimate likely demand more accurately.

Specification buying is becoming increasingly prevalent, whereby buyers place orders against rigorous predetermined standards of fabric quality, trim etc. Many leading high street fashion retailers have extensive laboratory facilities to monitor the quality of the clothes they sell. Some retailers also employ staff to allocate stock to their various outlets to maximize likely sales — these staff apportion new stock to the outlets by using past sales figures to estimate potential demand for new lines. Getting the allocations right maximizes sales and minimizes the likelihood of having excess stock in some branches which might, without a system of branch transfers to reduce it, result in this stock having to be cleared at a cost of heavy reductions. The biggest cost for all retailers is stock, so intelligent buying, good stock control and effective merchandising (see Chapter 6) are of paramount importance.

In this context several fashion retailers have adopted a concept known as 'edited retailing' whereby the customer is offered a limited though changing choice of merchandise that is highly coordinated, offering a high degree of product range compatibility. The concept of edited retailing is shown in Figure 8.2 below.

Next is a good example of this approach. As well as reducing risk, stock holding etc., it offers great scope for cross selling, in effect buying the whole 'look'. Though as George Davies states in his book, *What Next?*, 'The exercise taught me one of the keys to success in retailing . . . the trick is to give the illusion of choice.'

Figure 8.2 The edited retailing concept.

8.4 The industry's components

The retail fashion industry consists of many parts, the most important of which are outlined below.

8.4.1 Wholesalers

Market size and trends

The size of the United Kingdom market in the late 1980s was some £500m, the major companies having very small turnover figures in comparison to the large retailers. In 1987–8 only two had sales over £50m a year and the tenth largest a turnover of just £10m. Set against retail clothing sales in the same period of £15bn, this represents a small share of the total market.

The reasons for this small and diminishing share of the market are increased retail concentration and a more volatile fashion driven clothing market. Jaeger, perhaps anticipating these trends, withdrew in 1987.

The large multiples and department store groups deal directly with their suppliers, often overseas companies, through central buying departments. They are therefore able to avoid using wholesalers and the associated costs. Indeed Marks and Spencer, the market leader in many areas of the retail market, was one of the first, if not the first to deal directly with a manufacturer (Corah) and so break the grip of the wholesalers. Besides financial savings and better control over product quality, dealing directly with suppliers allows retailers to satisfy their, or more correctly, their customers' needs. A measure of exclusivity in terms of fabric, design content etc., enables them to differentiate themselves from their competitors.

The extent to which customers see the retailer's own label as better value than other brands improves sales especially in recessionary times when customers are even more value-conscious.

Although they carry fewer overheads and staff than manufacturers or retailers, the number of wholesalers and their market share will continue to decline. No longer needed by the large retailers they find themselves catering to a diminishing number of small firms, many of whom find their services of little or no use.

Some, like their counterparts in the grocery trade, have formed strategic alliances with retailers. One example of this is S. Casket and the mail order company Grattan.

Functions

The traditional functions of wholesalers are to:

- provide finance
- break bulk
- transport goods to the retailer
- provide information or advice.

These may be attractive to small scale retailers but are irrelevant to major retailers or small chains. Within the ranks of small retailers, those serving upper market levels will tend not to use them either.

Why is this the case? Each function will be examined in turn.

- **Provision of finance:** financing stock is attractive, but even if this is less costly than other forms of finance it could be counterbalanced by possibly paying higher prices and being restricted in one's choice of stock.

- **Break bulk:** this is an attractive proposition if applied to large volume, homogeneous goods in constant demand. This to some extent applies to 'basics' such as T-shirts but for short-life fashionable clothing it is not appropriate.

- **Distribute goods:** numerous distribution companies exist that offer a high quality, reliable and comparatively inexpensive service to suppliers and retailers alike.

- **Provide information or advice:** a knowledgeable wholesaler may be able to offer this, but other arguably more relevant sources exist e.g. trade shows, the trade press, prediction services and agents.

8.4.2 Mail order

Since the 1970s the mainstream mail order sector, providing large catalogues running to over 1000 pages, has declined in importance. Its two main advantages, easily available credit and a generous returns policy are now offered by the high street stores. Additionally the agents who operated the catalogue were servicing on average fewer customers each year, and many catalogues are now promoted on the basis that no agency is necessary. The sector still tends to suffer from a residual downmarket image, though its image is improving.

In recent years the more successful mail order operations have tended to be the smaller specialist newcomers catering to a specific target market; often with a higher socio-economic profile than the mainstream catalogues. These offer the convenience that is attractive to many with limited time to shop as well as an element of exclusivity and a more positive image. These specialist catalogues offer the opportunity to service niche markets profitably, sometimes where a store based retail system would be much less successful.

8.4.3 Discount clothing retailers

As with other sectors of retailing, there exists a significant discount presence that caters almost exclusively for the lower end of the market. Sited in low-cost premises and offering keen prices on clothing of a lower quality than that available in many major multiples, they operate on very high levels of stock turnover. A second variety of discount store are the outlets run by the major retailers to dispose of excess stock from their normal branches.

Thirdly, the introduction of factory outlet centres such as the one in the Hornsea Freeport shopping village may affect sales in full price outlets. Though it could be argued that they benefit both retailers and manufacturers since they provide outlets for out-of-date and substandard products that, if sold through normal retailers, could damage the brand's image. Additionally it allows the retailers to dispose of surplus stock so helping them to offer new lines to their customers.

A fourth variety, over whose impact the trade is divided, is the warehouse club. Very successful in the USA, they operate by charging a membership fee which entitles their members to buy goods at a substantial discount. Their clothing range tends to be limited though they may serve to reinforce the bargain psychology built up during the recession and so act as a restraint on some retailers' efforts to improve their margins by raising prices.

8.4.4 Multiples and variety chain stores

The former are businesses with at least ten outlets selling predominantly one merchandise group such as clothing or shoes. The latter, as the name suggests, sell a variety of merchandise, the four major variety chain stores with a significant clothing turnover being BhS, Marks and Spencer, Littlewoods and to a lesser extent Woolworths.

Having a place in most of the nation's high streets and out of town developments, these shops represent the success story of British clothing retailing. Their sales and market share have increased year after year at the expense of other retailers. For many years the fashion element in their ranges was minimal, as mass market tastes were only gradually influenced by fashion and good profits could be earned by large volume orders placed with suppliers. Adopting a more fashion oriented range increased the degree of risk through entering a more volatile market that was difficult to monitor.

With a growing fashion awareness amongst their customers and increased competition from smaller, more fashion oriented retailers, they have moved to provide more fashionable ranges. In this they have been helped by advances in information technology such as Electronic Point of Sale (EPoS), and manufacturing techniques that make the supply and retailing of smaller quantities profitable. The adoption of segmentation policies, most notably by the Burton group, (see Chapter 5) has also allowed them to provide a more fashion focused offering to their customers. Over-emphasis on segmentation, though, has caused at least one failure, La Mama, where there were insufficient pregnant career women of means to justify its existence. One prerequisite of segmentation is that the market should be sufficiently large to justify catering to it.

These shops tend to have prime sites which guarantee high levels of customer exposure to their merchandise. Location is of prime importance to retailers perhaps best summed up in the universal saying 'There are three things of importance in retailing—location, location and location.' Fosters Menswear take location analysis seriously, because they see it as fundamental to effective retailing. Fosters believe that at least 85% of variation in branch sales and financial performance is explained by measurable and largely external factors that can be examined before the chain commits itself to a new location.

One charge levelled at these chains is that they have succeeded in creating a dreary uniformity in the high street, each one having its BhS, Next, C & A, Miss Selfridge etc. with the same corporate fascias and colour schemes and, more importantly, the same merchandise catering to the same middle market needs. This is a view the retailers naturally take issue with though are nonetheless trying to offer a more individualistic service, in which they are aided by systems such as ACORN, MOSAIC and Townprint (operated by Burton), which allows them to build up a picture of the market in their immediate catchment area.

8.4.5 Department stores

Though small in number, only a few hundred, with virtually a static 3% to 4% of the overall retail market and rather unkindly described as the dinosaurs of the high street, department stores have an important role to play in retailing fashion clothing. Whilst catering to a wide market they are particularly attractive in terms of their strong AB customer profile and appeal to older customers. For mid- to upper-market labels they often provide the only suitable outlet, other than the designer opening his or her own store. This would demand not only a considerable capital investment but also would entail obtaining a suitable location for which, because of their relative scarcity, there is often great competition.

As those involved in purchasing fashion clothing are involved in an exercise in comparative shopping, department stores have the advantage that they have under one roof a wide variety of clothing from expensive designer labels to comparatively inexpensive basics.

Having a variety of concessions enables them to offer in addition to own label and bought-in manufacturers' brands a range of other labels.

Many department stores have reduced the number of their departmental product groups but remain strongly committed to clothing. Indeed Dickens & Jones has moved over the years from being a traditional department store to one offering a wide range of fashionable clothing and related merchandise and no other products. It dispensed with the last vestiges of non-fashion items such as glassware as recently as 1993.

Department stores often attract high concentrations of overseas visitors, many of whom spend considerable sums because of sterling's relative weakness and comparatively low UK rate of VAT.

8.4.6 The independent sector

Independents have over a number of years been losing out to the multiples and variety chains, who have economies of scale. In addition many have succumbed to large increases in rents as leases came up for renewal, which has less of an effect on those others who often own the freehold of the site from which they trade. The introduction of a uniform business rate has also proved disadvantageous to many, resulting in massive increases in rates in areas until now favoured as low rate areas. Some of these pressures are shown in Figure 8.3 below.

However, at the upper market levels independents are still strong and are positively encouraged in some locations such as Covent Garden and the Lace Market area in Nottingham. However, owners and developers tend to favour large retailers as they are better able to afford high rents and are more reliable in terms of meeting long lease commitments. Nonetheless in the late 1980s and early 1990s when most major chains were registering declines in sales and or profits, as a category independents fared relatively better.

Figure 8.3 Pressures on the small fashion retailer.

8.4.7 Supermarket involvement

Historically the supermarket groups have not seen the fashion clothing market as particularly attractive, preferring to concentrate their expertise and other resources on food, though competitive pressures may change this.

Sainsburys are involved through the Savacentre operation that was originally a joint venture with BhS. ASDA has the highest profile involvement through George, its in-store clothing operation set up by George Davies, the ex-Next chief executive. Tesco is involved in the childrenswear market.

8.5 Trends in retailing

The retail fashion market has seen considerable changes in recent years as have other sectors of the retail trades. Some of the more important are outlined below.

8.5.1 Franchising

From an estimated £400 m in 1980, franchising has grown to over £9000 m in 1993 though obviously only a small percentage is in the area of fashion clothing.

Franchising is defined by the International Franchise Association as a contractual relationship between franchiser and franchisee in which the franchiser offers or is obliged to maintain a continuing interest in the business of the franchisee in such areas as knowledge and training; wherein the franchisee operates under a common trade name, format or procedure owned by or controlled by the franchiser, and in which the franchisee has made or will make a considerable capital investment in his business from his own resources. The reason for its success as a retail format are the advantages offered to both franchiser and franchisee as outlined below.

Advantages to franchisee

- Obtains the benefits of the name, reputation, brand image etc, already established with the public.

- Less need for own capital as franchiser helps obtain capital, banks tend to be more sympathetic to requests for loans to the more established franchises than to those without the backing of a franchiser.

- Help in a number of areas, e.g. staff training, site selection (Dash, the leisurewear retailer is a specialist in this aspect) and purchase of equipment and stock.

- Benefits of any national advertising e.g. Benetton spends a multi-million pound budget to run the Benetton racing team.

- Exclusive sales territory granted for the duration of the franchise agreement.

- Less risk of business failure. A survey in 1986 undertaken for the *Financial Times* showed that after five years 80% of small businesses had ceased trading, whilst less than 20% of franchised businesses had failed – an example of the Pareto (80/20) rule.

Advantages to franchiser

- Rapid expansion is possible without causing cashflow problems.

- 'Tied' outlets for products/service.

- Initial fee plus regular royalty payments.

- Less risk. The franchisee puts up the capital and as his or her own boss has a direct incentive to make a success of the venture.

Many niche retailers, so popular in the 1980s, were franchises. One of the earliest and most successful for many years was Tie Rack.

According to the British Franchise Association, any company offering a franchise to set ethical standards must have run its own outlets successfully for a minimum of one year.

8.5.2 Concessions

Also known as shops-within-shops, they can be defined as space leased by the host retailer to another retailer, wholesaler or manufacturer from which to sell its merchandise. Sales through fashion concessions in the early 1990s exceeded £600 m of which some two thirds were womenswear.

One of the earliest examples was Jaeger as concessionaire and Selfridges on Oxford street as the host retailer. This concept expanded greatly in the 1970s and 1980s. Debenhams, before its takeover by Burton in 1985, had over a third of its selling space and income from concessions. Since then Debenhams and many other retailers have reduced their dependency on this type of operation.

Examples of concessions are Moss Bros, which is both a host retailer and concessionaire, Country Casuals, Liz Claiborne and Jacques Vert. Many fashion clothing concessions operate in department stores, sometimes trading from a sales area of only $20\,m^2$ or less.

Possible advantages to the host retailer provided by concessions include:

- Flexibility through short-term contracts
- Benefit of specialist expertise in buying and merchandizing
- Additional interest to customers
- Reduction of certain costs, such as fixtures and fittings, training and wages
- Reduced stockholding costs and risk
- Guaranteed income for the store.

Possible advantages to the concessionaire include:

- No high start-up costs for their own retail outlet
- Good exposure to host shop's high volume of customers
- Concessionaires can test market at a relatively low cost new ideas that, if successful, could result in expansion and ultimately opening their own stores and, if not, still enable them to relinquish the concession.

There are of course disadvantages. In respect of the host retailer these revolve around the possibly adverse effect poor concessions have on the store's image and the competitive threat to its own sales by the concession. A Mintel Retail Intelligence Report in 1985 quotes an acceptable industry figure of 8:2, eight sales to be generated from people attracted to the store by the concessions for every two lost by the store to their concessions. The major disadvantage to the concessionaire is the high cost of the space leased, whether charged as rent per square foot or as a percentage of sales, which can be well over 25% of turnover.

8.5.3 Physical distribution

There are several transport companies who specialize in the clothing sector. This involves considerable investment in warehousing and equipment. In addition to moving and storing clothing, many customers are demanding additional services such as pressing garments.

Like others involved in the fashion industry the specialist carriers are having to change to meet new demands. Increasingly, their clients are looking for a complete supply chain with JIT (just in time) supply at the end of it to allow better stock management. This situation is well developed in other parts of the retail industry, notably in the food sector. Deliveries of new seasonal lines are also taking place later and later, so allowing less response time. Some fashion retailers have already contracted out the distribution side of the business.

The physical delivery of goods is also important to the mail order sector. Next employed as one of its selling points a better system of getting clothing to its mail order customers, Empire Stores now promises a 24 hour delivery service.

8.5.4 Service provision

Many retailers in a variety of sectors now see the provision of a high level of service as a way of establishing a competitive advantage.

In the retail fashion sector high levels of personal service together with good product knowledge and knowing customers' likes and dislikes have traditionally been seen as a strength of the independent sector. Provision of a high level of service is likely to be seen as increasingly important in the more mature age market, which demographically and economically will become more important in the future. The growing tendency to promote shopping, and particularly clothes shopping, as a leisure activity is another reason for offering high levels of customer service.

Common areas of service include late night shopping, free parking (for out-of-town sites only), a liberal returns policy, pleasant decor, helpful staff and a variety of payment methods. For clothing retailers another important area is that of changing facilities, which in some stores are non-existent and in others range from poor to luxurious. Those retailers who cater to the teenage market have a tendency to provide communal facilities while those who target a more mature market offer individual cubicles.

However, such provision is expensive and refurbishment costs are high, particularly so at higher market levels. The provision of high levels of personal service can conflict with a need to reduce operating costs in the form of staff levels, with many larger retailers moving towards employing part-time rather than full-time staff.

8.5.5 Internationalization

United Kingdom fashion retailers have been slow to expand overseas. Early examples such as M&S venturing into Canada met with limited success, though the chain is now establishing a strong and growing international presence. Other United Kingdom fashion retailers with an overseas presence include the Burton Group and Laura Ashley.

The successful retailers in this context tend to be those who establish their operation with a local partner, at least in the initial stages. Examples of such ventures are Burton entering the Spanish market through concessions in department stores, as has Laura Ashley in Japan. Marks and Spencer has an international franchise operation that enables it to recruit suitable local partners in markets where it feels the need to have one. The perceived high risk in relation to relatively low rates of return has in the past tended to discourage such expansion.

The retailers' overseas competitors have in the last few years been attracted to the United Kingdom in increasing numbers, particularly from continental Europe, some building up a considerable branch network.

Two of the major British mail order concerns, Grattan and Empire, are owned by Otto Versace, the German mail order house, and the French company La Redoute respectively, and Renown (Japan) bought Aquascutum in 1990.

8.5.6 Teleshopping

Electronic ordering through the medium of a domestic television set and telephone can take place via a computer terminal such as the Minitel system in France. In America, the department store group Saks became the first upmarket retailer to enter the market in 1993. Its first one hour show brought sales of $575 000 of its own label casualwear range.

Teleshopping has the potential to effect major changes in shopping patterns. Its impact on the retail fashion market in the United Kingdom, in such areas as mail order, will develop over the coming years influenced by consumer acceptance and its own cost effectiveness.

8.5.7 Retail branding

Branding as in other areas of retailing now plays a crucial role. It helps differentiate one retailer from another and is both a consequence of retail concentration and a factor in its continued growth.

The attractiveness of brands or labels in terms of product has encouraged some manufacturers to diversify into the clothing market and *vice versa*, often through the licensing of the brand name. (See Chapter 6) Its importance to consumers is greater in the north than the south. Younger consumers also attach more importance to branding than do older age groups as peer pressure to be seen with the 'right' label is not an issue with the latter.

Advertising (see Chapter 9) plays an important part in building brand awareness and loyalty, and many major retailers spend heavily in this area as Table 8.2 indicates.

In the late 1980s and early 1990s advertising for clothing was about £50 m per annum.

Table 8.2 Major retailer advertising.

(£000s)	**1989**	**1990**	**1991**	**1992**
Benetton	655	345	228	763
Burton	503	929	1993	1300
C & A	7437	4238	4724	6600
Jaeger	135	211	228	329
Jigsaw	209	–	106	–
Laura Ashley	1715	1141	590	202

Source Register: Media and Expenditure Advertising Limited.

Table 8.3 Entrant to buyer conversion.

Segment	% of entrants	% of buyers	% conversion from entrant to buyer
Fashion	7	4	16
Fashion-aware	23	18	21
Classic	9	14	42
Mainstream	42	51	37
Downstream	19	13	28

8.6 Retail marketing effectiveness

Obviously the overall measure of success is long-term profitability. A sub-goal of this is usually to increase sales in relative terms on an annual or seasonal basis. Other indicators are sales per square foot and sales per employee.

Another indicator is the conversion rate, or the number of customers who buy as a proportion of the total number who enter the store. The conversion varies by consumer segment as shown in the example of a menswear retailer (see Table 8.3), taken from *Drapers Record* (18 July 1987).

A low conversion rate may be due to a variety of factors such as inappropriate price points, unattractive merchandise, staff lacking product knowledge of selling skills.

As much of the marketing effort in the industry comes from the retail sector, the large retailers invest considerable money and effort in market research (see Chapter 4) to measure its effectiveness.

8.7 Summary

At the conclusion of this chapter you should be able to:

* Understand the importance of the UK fashion retailing business;
* Describe the retailer's relationship with the manufacturing sector;

- Explain the importance of imports and exports to the United Kingdom fashion retail industry;
- Outline the structure of the industry;
- Indicate how retail marketing effectiveness can be assessed.

Further reading

Bitner, M.J. Servicescapes: the impact of physical surroundings on customers and employers. *Journal of Marketing*, Volume 5, April, 1992.

Cox, R. and Brittain, P. (1993), *Retail Management*, 2nd edn., Pitman, London.

Davies, G. (1991) *What Next?*, Arrow Books, London.

Gardner, C. and Sheppard, J. (1989), *Consuming Passion*, Unwin Hyman, London.

Harris, D. and Walters, D. (1992), *Retail Operations Management*, Prentice Hall, London.

McGoldrick, P.J. (1990), *Retail Marketing*. McGraw Hill, Maidenhead.

Retail Intelligence Report (1985) Mintel Ltd, London.

Special Report (1993), *Where Britain Shops 1993*, Verdict Research Ltd, London.

Chapter 9
Fashion Promotion

9.1 Introduction

Effective communication is as important to channel members as it is to consumers, and it is the promotion mix that provides the necessary tools and techniques, like advertising, sales promotion, public relations and personal selling, to achieve this.

This chapter is about the types of promotion methods that make up the fashion promotion mix, their characteristics and use by the fashion industry and the factors which influence their effectiveness. It will go on to consider how to plan promotion campaigns to meet the needs of those involved in the fashion industry and its many different customers.

In terms of the practice of fashion marketing, important trends have determined the increasing emphasis on the development of sophisticated fashion communication systems. Such trends include: changing cost structures can make reliance on advertising too expensive; advances in customer database management; greater use of direct mail and response marketing; recognition of the importance of quality customer service to gain a competitive edge and co-operative efforts between retailers, intermediaries and manufacturers in communicating with customers. All parties can benefit from cooperative promotion, as a brand name as well as store and manufacturer corporate identity can be developed economically. Partnerships also develop between organizations with totally different products who may be targeting the same customers, for example Whitbread and Red or Dead. This type of partnership reinforces the image associated with the designer and brand name and, the partners hope, will result in more sales as well as customer loyalty.

A proliferation of different media has emerged, fragmenting the market even more. Customers will have a wider choice of channels with the rapid expansion of cable television and as it grows their channel switching power increases. The development of integrated communication media efforts is more important than ever before and inevitable. This integration is most apparent with regard to advertising and sales promotion activity.

Before looking at the main methods of promotion in detail it is first important to consider the implications of a theoretical communication model for achieving marketing objectives and the factors that influence the effectiveness of the promotion mix.

9.2 Fashion communication theory

Whether the objective is to persuade more customers to buy a company's product, to improve customers' perception of a brand image or to increase store loyalty, any communication directly involves customers or potential customers in the process as the diagram below shows. Understanding of the basic concepts behind the theory of communication can help determine some ground rules for devising effective promotion campaigns.

Figure 9.1 shows that in any communication to customers, from face-to-face selling to a consumer reading an advertisement in a magazine, the process involves a sender (the encoder), a message (the symbols), a means of sending the message (channel) and an audience (the decoder). The feedback loops show that the fashion marketer should monitor the process at all stages to ensure that the message is received and acted upon as intended.

Fashion promotion, unfortunately, is not quite as simple as Figure 9.1 shows channel noise or various distractions such as other advertisements, children shouting in a store or a telephone ringing, can interfere with the message. Such distractions, coupled with the sender and receiver's perceptions based on their own set of values and attitudes, means that a promotion must always be based on a system designed to enhance communication if objectives are to be achieved.

If the following framework is adopted, the risks of poor fashion marketing communications will be minimized:

- Define fashion communication objectives clearly
- Specify the target market for the message in terms of intended audience characteristics
- Define the information needed to help consumers receiving the message make a decision to buy or consider buying

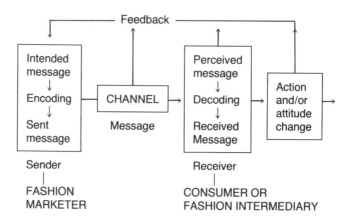

Figure 9.1   A communications model.

- Calculate the costs of various activities needed to achieve these objectives
- Determine how the budget should be tioned between various activities
- Identify who will be responsible for carrying out the activities
- Detail how the fashion promotion activities will be evaluated and controlled.

9.3 The fashion promotion mix

The promotion mix is the particular combination of promotional methods and media used by an organization to achieve its marketing communication goals. An overview of the fashion promotion mix is shown below:

Figure 9.2   The fashion promotion mix.

9.3.1 Factors influencing the fashion promotion mix

The planning of the right promotion mix can be influenced by several factors, the main categories being strategic, distribution, consumer, product, price and promotional methods.

Strategic considerations

Consideration must be given to the company's strategic goals. If the organization is pursuing new markets or actively trying to increase its market share then promotional policies may assume greater importance. The activities of direct competitors must be tracked, for the weight of advertising spending by a major competitor can place constraints upon the nature and type of response that is necessary.

Distribution policies

Distribution and service plans must also be considered. Should there be emphasis on 'push' or 'pull' promotion? Push refers to creating enthusiasm and support among channel members. The relationship between retailer and supplier may determine a need to win support by offering point of sale material or contribution towards an advertising campaign. Some powerful retailers will only stock some product lines if they are assured that an adequate amount of promotion will be directed at the consumer. Pull strategies concentrate on encouraging consumer demand for the product. Pull approaches are perhaps most appropriate for well known brands.

Product and price factors

The very nature of the product along with its lifecycle position will also have a great influence on the nature of promotion plans. For example, a confused image could emerge if an upmarket expensive range was heavily advertised in a young mass market weekly magazine reinforced by a widespread poster campaign. The launch of a new product obviously requires different treatment to a basic, well established line with market dominance and relatively low marketing costs.

The announcement of price reductions clearly involves promotional considerations, as does the decision whether to make price information a key component of the promotional message. These matters are covered in Chapters 6 and 7 on product development and pricing.

Consumer factors

The desired consumer response to a promotional campaign is an important factor. Does the organization wish to raise customer awareness of a new range of garments or does it wish significantly to increase sales of specific products in the short term?

The customer characteristics e.g. age, socio-economic group, sex, lifestyle etc; along with the size of the market and location of customers will significantly influence promotional plans. A married professional couple aged between 40 and 50 with no children are more likely to read quality press and specialist magazines and journals rather than the *Sun*, *Daily Mail* or *Woman's Realm*. Different groups of customers will respond differently to various types of communication as shown in the Chapters 3 and 5 on Consumer Behaviour and Market Segmentation. The same message, for example, presented in the *Sunday Times* and the *Sun* will be perceived differently because of the differences in readership and the image these newspapers present.

As noted in Chapter 3, consumer expectations, as influenced by the promotional message, must be matched by the products at the retail level. A mismatch between the image and the reality, be it in different quality levels or colourways, can lead to dissatisfaction and negative word of mouth communications about the firm.

9.3.2 A comparison of promotional methods

The relative capabilities, costs and effectiveness of each type of promotion method must be considered. Figure 9.3 below shows a broad comparison of each main type of promotion.

Source credibility refers to the general esteem with which the source is regarded, for instance an editorial article in *Marie Claire* praising a new line of knitwear is generally more believable than an paid advertisement in the same magazine. Message character simply describes the extent to which each consumer receives a message that addresses specific needs or is standardized. Message control is the extent to which the fashion firm can specify the exact message to be delivered to the customer. Obviously a press release may be subject to major editing or even be ignored by the media. The target audience refers to the size of audience reached, and with a sales promotion activity like a preview fashion show for regular customers some degree of specialized targeting is possible. Cost per target customer is included as the prime way of making cost comparisons. Thus if a one page advertisement in a glossy fashion magazine costs £8000 and it reaches 480 000 readers in the target market then the cost per target customer would be £0.0167 each.

Expenditure figures for fashion promotions are difficult to disaggregate due to the activities of retailers who promote other goods alongside clothing items.

Factor	Advertising	Sales promotion	Public relations	Personal selling
Source credibility	Fair	Fair and variable	Good	Fair to low
Message character	Standard	Standard	Standard	Specific to buyer
Message control	Total	Total	Limited, by media controls	Total
Target audience	Mass	Mass, but can be limited	Mass	Small
Cost per target buyer	Low	Low	Low	High

Figure 9.3 Characteristics of promotional methods.

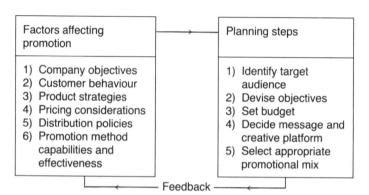

Figure 9.4   Planning fashion promotion.

Over half of all advertising expenditure relates to press and magazine advertising, and this therefore exceeds television advertising which accounts for less than 30% of all advertising expenditure. Direct marketing includes promotional efforts by post and telephone. Figure 9.4 shows the considerations to be borne in mind when planning a fashion promotion.

9.4   Fashion advertising

9.4.1   The nature of fashion advertising

Kotler (1994) defines advertising as 'Non-personal communication paid for by an identified sponsor.'

Advertising is becoming more prominent as companies recognize the need to develop strong brand or corporate images not just directed at consumers, but at the trade as well. A strong brand or corporate image can put companies in a powerful position in negotiating contracts with retailers. The use of branding and corporate image by fashion companies was in the notion of the 'complete look' and was first introduced to extend not just to clothes and cosmetics, but to whole lifestyles. Brands can have 'personalities' of their own and by targeting well defined segments can offer benefits beyond their functional value and so make the role of advertising much easier.

Cooperative advertising has increased not just between manufacturers and retailers. The use of generic advertising is often used in the fashion industry where wool, for example, is being promoted by manufacturer or retail sponsorship. A clothing manufacturer may advertise a new range of clothing, emphasizing the use of Lycra or Gore-Tex as a major feature.

Institutional advertising is used to promote a corporate image. It can be a valuable tool, fostering goodwill with a company's publics, through stationery, packaging, transport liveries, reception area, publicity materials and sales publications etc. A consistent, strong corporate image can be developed by a company as long as it is matched with the perceptions and needs of customers and potential customers.

Nevertheless the proportion of budgets spent on advertising in the fashion industry remains small compared to many others, though key retailers are increasing their expenditure. Within fashion, some product sectors enjoy more advertising than others, for example, hosiery, lingerie, footwear, jeans and sportswear. The most popular advertising medium is the magazine. The popularity of the magazine in the United Kingdom as the principal medium for fashion advertising stems largely from its visual nature coupled with the enormous specialist range available to facilitate the selection of target markets. Although advertising costs are high, the ability to target specific groups through new channels via cable and satellite television is increasing. Many more magazines are being developed each year and the recognition of the power of the rejuvenated cinema market as a vehicle for targeting 15 to 24 year olds, means the use of fashion advertising may very well increase during the 1990s, but in new ways. The use of direct mail advertising has increased largely due to greater use of computerized databases linked to psychographic and geodemographic profiles as described in Chapter 3.

As with any promotion method there is little point in pursuing an advertising activity unless it is an integral part of the fashion marketing function. This means the communications effort must be coordinated with all other marketing activities. There is little point in taking a two page advertisement in Vogue when retailers do not have sufficient stock to meet demand.

9.4.2 Advertising planning

As already mentioned effective planning of promotion should consider particular factors. The following steps take these into account.

Setting objectives

Whenever possible these objectives should be quantifiable, should specify a time scale and should be designed to help consumers move through the buying stages.

Examples of typical advertising objectives:

- To increase market share
- To increase expenditure by existing customers
- To increase store traffic
- To increase sales of specific products
- To create brand awareness
- To reassure customers
- To launch a new product
- To generate enthusiasm from channel members

- To encourage customers to trade up from one garment or service to a more expensive one
- To reinforce the corporate identity.

The above are general statements. If they are to become effective they must be clearly defined – for example, to ensure that 45% of customers in the target market have heard of a new range of run-resist hosiery within 2 months of the product launch.

Establishing an advertising budget

No one formula can be adopted for this aspect of planning which always causes much controversy and conflict within the fashion organization. Since fashion marketers are increasingly being asked to justify expenditure the promotion budget has become a very important issue.

The following are the main methods used for determining the advertising budget:

- **What can be afforded:** a self-explanatory title for this method used because some organizations do not have enough cash flow to justify using other methods. This is the weakest method and is usually adopted by smaller fashion firms.

- **Incremental:** the new budget is based on previous expenditure. For example, an increase of 5% over last year's allocation.

- **Percentage of sales:** is probably the most commonly adopted method. The percentage used can vary, but there is a norm for most that can be determined from trade associations and other sources. The fashion industry has a low percentage, around 2% of sales. This method however can result in budgets sometimes being inappropriate for particular trading conditions.

- **Match the competition:** provides a good reference point but means the organization is following rather than leading. As with all the other methods discussed so far this does not take notice of changes in the marketplace or opportunities which may arise.

- **Objective and task method:** the firm outlines its promotional objectives, determines the tasks needed to satisfy those objectives and then establishes the appropriate budget. However, it is difficult to set goals and specific tasks. Research indicates that larger organizations are more likely to adopt this method.

No matter how scientific the methodology used, ultimately budget determination is often arbitrary and in practice a pragmatic approach is needed. This means all of the above methods should be considered and an appropriate solution should be sought. It may, for example, be sensible to consider the percentage of sales method as a starting point. More importantly, the following factors should be considered:

- **What market is the firm competing in?** The broader the market the higher the level of advertising required.
- **What is the current market position?** Improving share necessitates spending proportionally more than higher placed brands.
- **Where will the firm advertise?** The same rate of spending in every city or region will not produce the same results.
- **How important is the role of advertising?** Poor market share may be attributed to distribution deficiency, pricing or a weak salesforce rather than inadequate advertising.

Using an agency

The decision to use an advertising agency is an important one. Some agencies offer a full service covering creative work, media planning, marketing research, sales promotion and public relations while others offer a particular specialism. A useful checklist is provided by KDA Communications Group Limited:

- Define what you want from an agency
- Draw up a shortlist
- Check the calibre of senior management
- Ensure an agency has marketing expertise
- Make sure an agency is well structured, financially stable and not over-committed
- Discover if an agency is an IPA (Institute of Pracitioners in Advertising) member and if it is recognized by other industry organizations
- Look for an agency with a good mix of clients
- Ask questions about staff turnover, organization and training
- Check the creative staff have proven skills in creating campaigns that are memorable and work
- Ensure that an agency's production department is up-to-date with the latest printing and reproduction techniques
- Discover if an agency uses modern media-buying methods and can justify media selections
- Look for an agency that can provide detailed, relevant research and can evaluate it intelligently
- Test the credentials of agencies that claim to be 'full service'
- Find out how an agency intends to charge production costs
- Ask to see work completed for other clients. This is often more effective than the usual agency presentation process.

Determine message and creative platform

This has a crucial impact on the success or failure of an advertising campaign, but it is not easy to make decisions about the message content and how this is to be conveyed. Guidelines for the message and creative platform are given below.

- **What to say.** It is understood that the first considerations must be the advertising objectives and the target customer, but the focal point of an advertising message is the advertising appeal. The appeal should tell potential buyers what the product offers and what it can do for them. Themes are often developed to provide continuity to an advertising campaign, but are also commonly used to reinforce a brand image, thereby helping to maintain distinctive competitive positions. Themes also help ease the introduction of new fashion products and services.

- **How to convey the message.** Several formats have been developed as guidelines, some of which are set out below. There are many more.

    Stressing the product's unique selling points (USPs), e.g., clothing to protect against the sun.

    Telling a story or the history of a fashion product.

    Reflecting the lifestyle or desired lifestyle by careful selection of situations showing people wearing the garments.

    Real life situations can be used for instance where someone has a problem and the advertisement shows the solution.

    Demonstrations can be used to prove the product's claim which may be, for example, to withstand 100 washes and still retain its shape and colour.

    Comparative formats directly contrast one brand with another to show superiority over the competition. Although usually the competitor's brand is referred to as a leading brand from a competitor or Brand X, it is usually obvious which brand is being referred to. Blatant reference to a competitor's brand has been increasingly used by certain sports footwear manufacturers recently.

    Testimonials may be made by celebrities, television or sports personalities whom the target customers will identify with. They endorse the product either by using it or making a statement supporting the brand.

    The association format uses analogies to convey the message by creating an emotional mood and communicating the psychological benefits through exciting associations such as sporting events and/or showing beautiful scenery.

    Fantasy appeals seek to associate the product with the target market's wildest dreams and hopes. Cosmetics producers often feature fantasy as a theme.

    Montage formats present the audience with a number of different situations, scenes and visual effects to create excitement and demonstrate the various situations for wearing garments.

Media selection

The main advertising media are press, television, radio, cinema, posters and direct mail. There are many other minor advertising media, for example hot air balloons, matchboxes, taxis, buses, on golf tees and in holes on the putting green, to name a few. Many have considerable potential use in fashion advertising because of their novelty value and visual impact which many reinforce the desired product image. However, most of these other media lack the detailed, and independent, assessment of audience size that can be reliably delivered by use of the main media.

Selecting the medium that most effectively reaches the target market is no simple task. The following criteria have to be taken into account when devising media plans.

- **OTS (Opportunity to see).** This is the number of opportunities which a particular audience has to see a specific advertisement. A high OTS can be achieved by a large number of people being exposed once or a small number being exposed several times.

- **Reach.** It is important to state the required reach, i.e. the number or proportion of an audience group or segment exposed to an advertisement at least once.

- **Frequency.** This is the average number of exposures per individual reached in a particular period of time and advertisers will have to decide how many advertisements should be shown and seen. An advertising frequency of 60, for example, could be achieved either by showing an advertisement three times daily on five specific days of the week before, during and after a particular news programme over four weeks, or one advertisement every six days throughout the year.

- **(CPT) Cost per thousand.** This calculates the average cost of reaching 1000 of the population. If, for example, it costs £30 000 for a 30 second television spot with an audience of 15 million then the cost per 1000 is calculated by dividing 30 000 by 15 million and multiplying by 1000. This gives a cost of £2 per thousand.

- **Media Weights.** Different media vehicles have different target audiences and different characteristics which may affect the perception of an advertisement. When this is combined with the fact that the type of copy and artwork used can also affect perception of the advertisement then it is sensible for advertisers to apply media weightings to the various choices to help make the most important selection.

- **Target population weights.** This concept recognises that members of the target population have differing worth to the advertiser and therefore differing weights of importance. Television companies, for example, sell packages of guaranteed TVRs (television rating points). One television rating point is one percent of the target audience. A target or 120 TVRs means that 30% of the target audience will have on average four OTSs. It also could mean that 20% have seen it six times.

- **Media vehicle appropriateness weights.** The same advertisement in different newspapers can have a different impact in, for instance the quality and tabloid press. A distinctive mood is created by different vehicles which may affect reception of advertisements. Consider, for example, the impact of the same Next dress advertised in *Woman's Own* compared to *Harpers and Queen.*

- **Advertising exposure weights.** These try to establish the difference between vehicle OTS and advertising OTS. A particular magazine for example may have an 80% readership and only 40% will read a specified page. Therefore the OTS at most can only be 40% of total readership. The front, back and inside cover pages will have a greater readership than others while the position on the page can also have an impact.

- **Advertising perception weights.** These are used to bridge the gap between advertisement OTS and perception of the advertisement. Page size, colour, quality of reproduction are all important. The use of full, or process colour for example may attract a 50% greater weight than black and white.

Creation of the advertisement

The creation of a successful advertisement requires the copy (the words) and the art (pictures, graphs, charts, layout, white space) to work together and complement each other. Most advertisers follow a hierarchy of effects such as AIDA. This stands for attention, interest, desire and action.

This model is useful in helping to remind advertisers of the need to create advertisements that will, from the very first glance or hearing, grab the attention of the target audience and move them from being interested through to wanting to go out and buy garments, or make enquiries about them. An adapted version of the model is shown in Figure 9.5.

Timing and scheduling

The scheduling of advertising depends very much on all of the above factors. There are however three main patterns of timing

- **Concentrated pattern** is normally used for new brand launches to swamp competitive advertising and is also relevant to products that have seasonal demand such as those sold in January sales.

- **Continuous pattern** is commonly used for brand leaders that have a high advertising to sales ratio.

Source: AIDA model as adapted by the Direct Marketing Centre

Figure 9.5   Steps for successful creative work.

- **Intermittent pattern** is the most widely used because of the high expenditure involved with the continuous pattern. Bursts of advertising are planned to achieve more concentrated impact periodically.

The media schedule must show the size or length of insertion, insertion dates and times, the anticipated costs, and the projected reach.

Media research can help media buying and scheduling as it shows which publications are read by what type of people, how many and what type of people are likely to watch a particular television programme, who listens to what on the radio and when, etc.

Advertising evaluation and control

This is still very much an area neglected by many companies. Although research cannot identify precisely what will and will not work, it can help to reduce risk and facilitate the identification of good features of the campaign.

If carried out effectively, research can help in a number of ways:

- to assist problem definition
- to guide creative strategy development and the type and level of effort required
- to evaluate strategy achievements post exposure.

Advertising objectives set in communication terms, such as raising brand awareness, will enable more effective evaluation than if based purely on achieving particular sales or profit targets. Research before, during and after campaigns using the main techniques as outlined below will as a result be more relevant. Standards, as a base for comparison, also should be specified if an effective evaluation procedure is to be adopted.

Advertising research methods can be categorized into two main types; namely copy research and media research. The former measures matters such as the effectiveness of the messages and recall rates and uses such techniques as laboratory and Hall tests, projective techniques, coupons and telephone response rates using 0800 numbers. Sales measurement before, during and after advertising should be considered, though not relied on in isolation. Consumer audits can ask a random group of customers about their buying behaviour of specific products and then again after advertising has been carried out.

For media research, the main secondary sources are as follows:

- Newspaper and magazine readership is measured by National Readership Surveys sponsored by JICNARS (Joint Industry Committee for National Readership Surveys). ABC (Audit Bureau of Circulation) audits the sales or circulation of over 2000 different publications.

- Radio audiences are measured by RAJAR (Radio Joint Audience Research).

- Television audiences are measured by BARB (Broadcasters' Audience Research Board).

- Cinema audiences are researched by CAVIAR (Cinema and Video Industry Audience Research).

- BRAD (British Rate and Data) and MEAL (Media and Expenditure Advertising Ltd) provide a good reference for media planning because they detail circulation and audience figures as well as costs.

9.5 Fashion sales promotion

Sales promotion involves promotional activities that add value to fashion products or induce consumers or intermediaries to buy or provide an incentive for channel effectiveness. It differs from advertising insofar as the company may own, rather than rent, the media that are used, for example, a brochure compared to a poster advertisement.

9.5.1 The advantages and limitations of sales promotion

The main advantages of sales promotion are that it:

- Helps attract customer traffic and maintains brand or store loyalty
- Enables quick results to be achieved

- Serves as a reminder function
- can increase impulse buys
- Can create excitement
- May motivate other channel members.

However there are limitations, the main ones being:

- The image of a firm may be devalued if there are too many promotions
- Consumers may view it as a decline in quality
- Customers may wait for promotions rather than buy at regular times and prices
- Customers may focus on the incentive rather than the garments.

9.5.2 Developing a sales promotion plan

As with advertising planning key steps can be followed:

Setting objectives

These are usually demand oriented and can relate to channel members or consumers. Channel member related objectives are concerned with such aspects as:

- Obtaining distribution
- Receiving adequate store display and shelf space
- Increasing retail or wholesale enthusiasm
- Increasing sales
- Gaining cooperation in promotional expenditure.

Consumer related objectives are concerned with such aspects as:

- Increasing brand awareness
- Increasing trial of a product or service
- Stimulating repurchases
- Obtaining impulse sales
- Supplementing other promotional tools.

Assigning responsibility

This can be shared by the company's advertising or sales manager, if such roles exist, and/or an advertising or specialist sales promotion agency. The advertising manager normally coordinates activities relating to mass promotion and the sales manager likewise in relation to trade shows, exhibitions, special events and demonstrations.

Outlining the sales promotion plan

The following areas must be described:

- Creative platform. (See advertising section)
- Conditions, e.g. is proof of purchase required?
- Media selected
- A schedule of events
- Duration
- Cooperative effort required of other channel members
- Budget and costs of different types of sales promotion methods.

Selecting a sales promotion vehicle

Before discussing the main types used the following factors must be considered:

- Company image. Sometimes sales promotion activity can devalue the image if it does not reflect customer aspirations normally associated with the product or brand;
- Company objectives;
- Costs of different sales promotion methods;
- Participation requirements of customers;
- Channel or customer enthusiasm for particular methods.

There are many different types of sales promotion activity some more relevant than others to the fashion industry. As stated earlier, sales promotion can be divided into the trade oriented and the consumer directed, these are described in detail later and are shown in Figure 9.6. The characteristics of various types of activities will be described, and there will be more discussion of the importance of trade shows and exhibitions as a vital fashion promotion tool.

Coordinating the sales promotion plan

Increasingly advertising and sales promotion plans are being integrated. Fashion marketing staff should be informed of any publicity for special events and any

TRADE PROMOTIONS	CONSUMER PROMOTIONS
Exhibitions	Coupons
Trade fairs	Competitions
Sales competitions	Multipacks
Fashion shows	Special offers
Point of sale	Tie-ins
Special discounts	Gifts

Figure 9.6   Some examples of fashion sales promotions.

activity that will support them, so that the impact can be optimized. Coordination should extend beyond the promotional mix to include all components of the fashion marketing mix.

Evaluation and control

Sales levels should be analysed before, during and after a sales promotion campaign as should customer perceptions of the products, brand, store etc. being promoted. If customers delay in purchasing products in anticipation of sales promotion activities, as sometimes happens with fashion merchandise, then the evaluation will not give a true picture, but nevertheless should still be carried out to identify trends. Too often insufficient analysis is carried out. As with advertising evaluation, attention should not be solely confined to sales performance.

9.5.3 Sales promotion directed at channel members

Conferences, trade fairs and exhibitions

Trade fairs, exhibitions and conferences are very important as they provide face-to-face contact with specifically targeted customers or potential customers and a high proportion of those attending have buying authority. They also have the ability to generate high quality leads for conversion to sales.

The exhibition sector was worth £1320 million in 1991, 9.3% of total media expenditure, and according to research by Taylor Nelson is set to expand steadily. (Source: *Exhibiting The Facts*, Exhibition Industry Federation). This expansion is a reflection of changing cost structures within marketing along with more emphasis on customer care. Single European events, such as in Paris at Porte de Versailles, are valuable to the fashion sector because they traditionally attract international buyers and designers alike.

Cotterell (1992) stated that 84% of exhibition visitors have a buying influence of some kind. An important part of exerting influence upon buyers is getting the right location within the exhibition space, and decisions on the size and shape of stand, the stand content and staffing levels. These are the major considerations when setting up a stand and are discussed more fully below.

As most fashion exhibitions are often very large, visitors tend to plan their routes carefully. Ensuring they visit particular stands is a priority and makes location so important. A site that gives good visibility and is likely to gain customer traffic because of its position is obviously better. A position near an entrance, at an end of an aisle, or the bottom of the stairs is often good for attracting passing traffic.

Competitive compatibility and exhibitors who sell products that may be complementary should be considered when deciding where to locate as they will help to build the right type of traffic. The activities being carried out by neighbouring stands should be considered also. Loud music, loud staff and heavy wine consumption on one stand may not be conducive to customer attraction and retention for the stand next to it.

In estimating the size of space needed exhibitors should consider estimating how many visitors the company is aiming to talk to and for how long. The expected total number of visitors to the whole exhibition will be known and usually many will have identified their interests before attending or will have been specifically invited. The length of time the exhibition is open and the number of anticipated visitors to the stand will determine the number of staff required allowing for breaks. The amount of space required for standing or sitting with visitors as well as any displays or presentation material should indicate how much space is necessary in total. Space obviously costs money that has to be accounted for as part of the promotional budget, so these estimates are important.

Stand frontage is very important as this determines how much of it is made visible to passers by and similarly how much visibility the exhibitors have of potential customers. Space is bought by the square metre and the ideal shape is that which offers a wide front with shallow depth. Often a stand will be presenting new garments, services or ideas. The benefits of these new concepts need to be made clear. Appropriate headlines for the stand that reflect what is being offered should also be produced aiming to capture interest.

Promotional material and displays are often creatively used to create a particular ambience or theme symbolic of the exhibiting company or its products or services. Replication of the office environment should be avoided as this presents a barrier to good communication. Low voltage rather than bright lights will also help towards creating the right ambience. Use of artwork can attract attention and promote interest in the stand. The most commonly used types of promotional material at fashion exhibitions are postcards, leaflets, brochures, business cards, bags, small posters and videos.

Fashion shows

Fashion shows can be targeted at both consumers and the trade. Designer fashion shows are attended predominantly by trade and fashion journalists and photographers who are invited to preview the latest season's collections. The major international shows take place in Paris, London, Milan and New York and are excellent vehicles for gaining designer publicity. Approval by the fashion media is often crucial to the survival of some designers. Being able to create winning designs is not enough. Designers need to promote themselves. Fashion shows can create a desirable designer name that retail buyers may then wish to be associated with. As well as the major designer shows, there are charity shows and retail sponsored shows that the public can attend and through which publicity can be gained for designer, manufacturer and retailer.

Training for fashion retail staff

Manufacturers will often provide training for retailers' sales staff especially if specialized selling skills are required, as for example in selling lingerie where measuring and fitting are important.

Trade allowance and special offers

Discounts may be given for prompt payment, buying certain volumes or purchasing during specific periods for example. Further details about discounts are given in Chapter 7. Sometimes merchandise is given free instead of discounts. Channel members may be given gifts, very often hospitality, for buying new lines etc. Most major fashion retailers have strict company policies on the receipt of gifts.

Point-of-sale material

The manufacturer or wholesaler may give the retailer a display stand for its products and actually set it up. Material in the form of leaflets or other literature, such as promotional postcards or brochures, also may be provided to help retailers inform or sell to the customer.

A free item may be given to the wholesaler or retailer for demonstration purchases, such as an outfit to be worn by some sales staff.

Sales competitions

Sales personnel may be offered prizes, a bonus or incentives and gifts for sales achievement.

Cooperative promotions

This is where two or more channel members share the cost of a promotion, they are also called 'tie ins'. These promotions, if successful, can reinforce brand image, increase awareness, expand the customer base and cut costs.

9.5.4 Sales promotion directed at consumers

Coupons

Manufacturers may give a price reduction on specific merchandise when a coupon is redeemed by the customer. Coupons can be delivered through newspapers, magazines, post, or on and in packages. Care must be taken to avoid customer dissatisfaction with the effort required to achieve a discount.

Competitions or sweepstakes

These can attract attention to a product range or store and generate excitement. They generally require little effort from the customer.

types of merchandise are appropriate for multipacks such as hosiery, low value undergarments, T-shirts etc. They enable the customer to receive a discount for buying in quantity.

Special offers

These offer customers merchandise at a reduced price and the objective is to create immediate purchases.

Special events

Manufacturers or retailers sponsor celebrity appearances, fashion shows and other activities. (See the section on conferences and exhibitions earlier.)

Gifts

Customers may be given a gift for making a purchase or opening a new account or referring friends or relatives to the company. This is very common practice in the fashion mail order industry and in the party plan system of distribution. Customers who spend over a certain amount may be offered gifts such as a travel bag or tie when buying a suit.

Demonstrations

Although not very common, sometimes demonstrations are used to show customers the performance capabilities of products. A common practice, especially with sportswear, is the use of in-store videos to show the garments being worn or to create an image or develop certain associations with the brand.

9.6 Public relations

The main objective of public relations is to foster goodwill. It strives to establish and maintain a favourable image through a pre-planned, long-range programme by communicating with its publics who are consumers, suppliers, shareholders, trade customers, employees, unions, government, pressure groups and the local community.

As a marketing tool for the fashion industry this is particularly relevant especially in relation to communicating with the trade as well as consumers. The total income of the top 150 public relations consultancies was £216 million in 1992. (Source: *PR Week*)

The importance of the fashion media and journalists was outlined in Chapter 3 in relation to opinion leadership. The comments of fashion journalists after a fashion show or trade fair can greatly influence trade buyers as well as consumers. It is therefore important to foster good relations with the press. Often, fashion journalists are celebrities in their own right.

The impact, for example, of the television programme *The Clothes Show Live*, *The Clothes Show* magazine and The Clothes Show Exhibition on the promotion of fashion is substantial. There is an emphasis on British fashion in the content, but the main characteristic of it as a promotion tool is in its ability to stimulate word of mouth communication. The *Clothes Show Live* programme is involved in activities such as sponsoring fashion shows, reporting on Student Fashion Week, fashion awards, hosting competitions to become a model, bride of the year and finding new design talent. *The Clothes Show Magazine* with its target market of ABC1's aged between 15 and 34 provides a ready-made market for companies to promote their products. Endorsement by the *Clothes Show* vehicles may be very beneficial.

The British Fashion Council was created in 1983 to promote the fashion industry, and wins much publicity by sponsoring fashion awards and developing links between designer and retail names.

Designer affiliations are becoming increasingly prevalent. Retailers in particular rather than manufacturers are supporting and promoting new and young designers as well as highly successful names. Examples are Vivienne Westwood and Littlewoods Mail Order Group; Red or Dead and Miss Selfridge; Joe Casely-Hayford and the Burton Group's Top Shop. These collaborations can provide several benefits for all involved.

Designer affiliations need not be between organizations in the same sector. Partnerships between companies whose target markets aspire to or identify with particular designer names can reinforce brand images by such affiliations and endorsements and can make interesting news. Various brands of drinks, for example, support certain designer names.

Some examples of public relations activities are:

- An editorial on a fashion company showing the growth of an organization and how it is successful in protecting the environment by controlling pollution;
- A talk at a local college by a retail buyer about career opportunities in fashion;
- A fashion show, sponsored by a local retailer, the proceeds of which go to a charity;
- A sponsored tour for an up and coming rock group.

9.6.1 Publicity

The important and diverse elements of this area of public relations are shown in Figure 9.7. Publicity is media coverage that is not paid for, has a mass audience and a high level of credibility. As publicity includes non-paid-for media coverage, it is tempting to view it as free advertising. It is not 'free', as to be effective considerable skill must be exercised by the publicity staff to ensure the right coverage in the right media, and such skill has to be paid for.

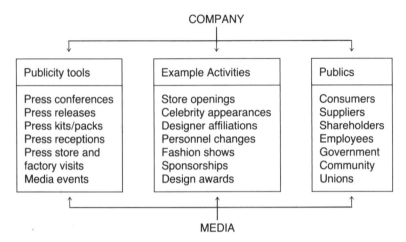

COMPANY

Publicity tools	Example Activities	Publics
Press conferences Press releases Press kits/packs Press receptions Press store and factory visits Media events	Store openings Celebrity appearances Designer affiliations Personnel changes Fashion shows Sponsorships Design awards	Consumers Suppliers Shareholders Employees Government Community Unions

MEDIA

Figure 9.7 The Scope of Fashion Public Relations.

Publicity is sometimes difficult to plan as newsworthy happenings can occur so quickly. Winning an award such as the British Designer of the Year can catapult a designer to stardom overnight. A snowball of events will take place because the fashion press will request interviews, give editorial coverage and make the designer name a desirable one to be associated with or emulated.

However, most publicity gained is achieved through careful planning and targeting the right media. It involves the following types of activities:

- Holding press conferences;
- Discussing and promoting fashion items with editors of newspapers and magazines;
- Building good relations with key contacts and journalists;
- Researching and writing about the organization, such as its history and development, exports, awards for industry, designer associations etc.;
- Gathering data and maintaining a detailed source list of files (e.g., contacts, editors, trade organizations, buyers);
- Writing press releases and preparing press kits;
- Planning publicity campaigns;
- Planning and organizing photosessions.

Some examples of activities to report are:

- Major store renovations
- Store openings
- New designer affiliations
- Celebrity appearances or affiliation
- Personnel changes
- New product ranges
- New trading concepts

- New credit policies
- Fashion shows.

The interaction provided by such events is illustrated in Figure 9.7.

9.6.2 Preparing press information

It is so important to get this right the first time. A vigorous, simple, direct, short and succinct approach in writing style is best. A simple example is given below in Figure 9.8. Given a specific magazine or newspaper to target, the message could be developed further to tailor the content to the interests of the readership.

The first paragraph is the most important. The information should be well laid out and include the company name, contact persons and telephone numbers on every page. It is usual to include 10×8 black and white photographs charging for colour if required. If the release runs to more than one page, the words 'more follows' should appear at the foot of each page except the last, and the headline should be repeated at the head of every page.

9.7 Personal selling

Personal selling is inter-personal promotion carried out by retail sales staff or company sales personnel. It is the process of learning the needs and wants of a prospective buyer and of presenting a product, service or idea so that the buyer is motivated to buy it.

PUBLICATION EMBARGOED   DATE
UNTIL (DATE)/FOR   COMPANY LOGO
IMMEDIATE RELEASE

PATRICK MURRAY WINS

THE QUEENS AWARD FOR EXPORT AND TECHNOLOGICAL ACHIEVEMENT

Patrick Murray Limited has won the Queen's Award for export and technological achievement. This newly established company situated in the Scottish Borders, has earned a world-wide reputation for producing quality knitwear which combines traditional craft and fibres with modern design and colour.

Of the company's total output 50% is exported to countries as far away as the USA and the Far East as well as those within Europe.

Ends

Please contact Sue Siddle at Sue Siddle PR. Tel:xxx xxx xxxx for further information

---

Figure 9.8   A sample press release.

This implies a focus on needs and wants rather than product features. It also suggests that salespeople must perform in a number of different ways:

- Provide a service
- Use persuasion
- Communicate effectively
- Solve problems
- Educate potential buyers.

Developments in fashion marketing such as the changing role of direct marketing, technological innovations and growth in telesales techniques have influenced the role of the salesperson. The main implications of such changes have been a reduction in sales force numbers, fewer calls by representatives per client are needed and more support is available in processing orders, following up queries and providing after sales service.

The above changes do not imply that the role of the salesperson is less important. In fact the reverse is true. In the fashion industry expertise in selling is crucial to initiating interest by the trade and winning orders in a fiercely competitive environment. The selling function may be carried out at the customer's premises or the manufacturer's or at trade shows.

Two main advantages of this form of communication over other forms of fashion promotion are:

- The whole buying process can be carried out so that feedback can be obtained, and objections dealt with;
- The flexibility of selling allows communication to be tailored to suit the requirements of individual customers.

9.7.1 The selling process

The process detailed below concentrates on the manufacturer or wholesaler selling to the fashion retail sector. However, the process and principles identified in Figure 9.9 can, with little modification, be applied to fashion consumers.

Identifying sources of customers

Potential sales come from people or organizations who might buy the firm's products or services. They are those who can definitely benefit from the product, qualify financially to purchase it, and have the authority to influence or make buying decisions. Once they have been identified the next stage of the selling process can begin. There are many sources of potential customers and some are shown below:

- Leads from advertising, newspapers, magazines, trade journals, directories, trade fairs, exhibitions and conferences;
- Enquiries by post or telephone;

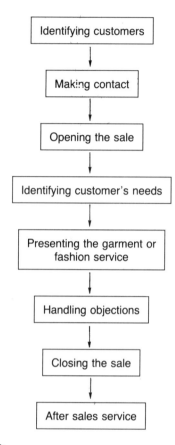

Figure 9.9 The fashion selling process.

- Referrals;
- Non-competing, complementary sales people;
- Former work colleagues and old school friends (networking).

In the fashion sector there are key events in the fashion calendar that are ideal for locating leads and these should be identified well in advance to enable effective targeting of customers. For example, the London Menswear Exhibition is held during late August in Earl's Court.

Making contact

To get to see the prospective customer and deliver a planned sales presentation requires information on whom to call and the best ways to make an appointment with the potential client company. Cold calling is usually not a good idea.

First impressions are very important in establishing rapport with a prospect. A professional approach includes a thorough product knowledge, detailed understanding of the customer's needs and social skills.

Opening the sale

Respect for the fact the buyer must be very busy has to be shown by not wasting time on irrelevant remarks in the first meeting. Once the salesperson and buyer have built up a relationship more small-talk can be engaged in, but opening remarks must be business related at initial meetings.

Identifying customer needs

One method is the SPIN technique that makes use of effective questioning to determine the customer's needs.

- **Situational** questions ask for background information such as 'Do you price your garments on the sales floor?'. The answers will indicate areas to probe with problem questions.

- **Problem** questions ask about difficulties with a buyer's present purchasing situation, for example, 'How does unpacking and pricing your garments on the sales floor affect your staff and customers?'

- **Implication** questions ask about the effects of stated problem areas, for example, 'Are you happy with the implications of unpacking and pricing your garments on the sales floor?'

- **Need/solution** questions ask for a customer statement of need and desire for a solution to the need, for example, 'Would you be interested in a way to avoid unpacking and pricing garments on the sales floor?'

Once the right questions have been asked the buyer will begin to state needs that should be followed up by the seller with more questions to encourage the buyer to make statements about explicit needs.

An implied need is a non-specific statement indicating wants or needs, for example, 'The department looks untidy when my sales staff are unpacking and pricing garments on the sales floor.' An explicit need is an unambiguous statement of wants or desires, for example, 'I need a way to avoid my sales staff taking selling time to unpack and price merchandise on the sales floor.'

The salesperson in the above situation could offer to supply merchandise already priced and ready to hang straight on the rails.

Presenting the product

The purpose of the presentation is to gain attention and/or arouse interest and a feeling of need for the product or service. The presentation can also show how the garment can satisfy the customer's recognized needs. In addition, there can be demonstrations, questions addressed and any objections raised may be countered. Lastly, but most important, the customer can be persuaded to buy.

The buyer's interest can be captured in a number of ways such as complimenting the customer, appealing to their curiosity or making use of questions. Letting the customer handle the garment is particularly important as many buyers can quickly gauge the quality of the product and find out the properties and 'handle' of the fabric. It also helps to build trust between buyer and seller. Offering to provide a free service, for example, assistance with display, pricing or stock management can also help to capture interest.

A model that could be used for presenting the product is FAB (features, advantages and benefits). The concept of converting features to benefits was mentioned in Chapter 3 in connection with consumer motivation.

A feature is a neutral characteristic of a product or service. An example of a feature statement is, 'All our garments contain 50% Lycra'. An advantage is a product characteristic that may help some buyers. An example of an advantage statements is, 'Our range of garments stretch to fit comfortably and do not lose shape after repeated washing'. A benefit is a product characteristic that meets an explicit need. Examples of benefit statements are, 'You said your busy customers were concerned about feeling comfortable as well as looking good at work' or 'Our range of garments with their stretch and easy to launder qualities would be ideal for the working woman'.

Handling objections

Handling objections is fundamental to the success of selling. If objections are raised they tend to be concerned with the following aspects: price, product, waiting for newer products or the latest technology, service, the salesperson, a poor time to buy, or inherent suspicion. Objections from customers can be seen as signals that they are unaware of all the benefits or that they are uncertain. In accordance with the fashion marketing concept, it is no part of ethical fashion marketing to pester a customer into buying a product that does not meet their needs.

Since there is always the likelihood that some objection will be raised, the salesperson should be prepared by thinking about possible responses before the presentation. There are several ways of dealing with objections, including active listening and careful questioning. It is important to remember that overcoming objections could provide an opportunity to close the sale.

Closing the sale

The following items must be covered before closing the sale with a fashion business client:

- Have objectives been achieved?
- Check there are no misunderstandings between the parties
- Check all the statistical and technical data are correct
- Record and feedback agreements

- Examine all documentation
- Review and summarize the benefits to the buyer.

Some of the above actually provide an opportunity to bring the negotiation to a close. There are several closing techniques that can be used, three examples are given below.

- **Assumptive close:** the salesperson assumes the sale is definite, for example, 'How do you wish to pay for the coat?'
- **Critical time close:** this can be used when there is a limited supply, for example, 'I can't guarantee the discount unless an order is placed today.'
- **Contingency close:** this is based on making a promise, for example, 'If I can get you the colours you want by Thursday, can we agree to an order?'

After-sales service

It is important to follow up a sale either with a telephone call or visit to confirm that the order has arrived and ensure there are no problems. If there are, they must be dealt with immediately as this can influence future orders from the customer. A satisfied customer will also increase the likelihood of positive word-of-mouth recommendations.

The nature of the products, target market, power relationship between supplier and buyer, and the buying culture will all influence the level of after-sales service. The salesperson must understand what the expectations are of both the buying and selling company and ensure agreement on this is achieved in any sales negotiation.

The job of a sales manager is difficult as most of the sales force will be working in the field and spend little time in the office. Communication problems, motivation and control of the sales force render the sales manager's task particularly difficult compared to other marketing management positions.

9.8 Summary

This chapter has dealt with the various aspects of fashion promotion that make up the promotional mix:

- Advertising
- Sales promotion
- Public relations
- Personal selling.

The details of any proposed promotion have been briefly covered as follows:

- Target customers
- Objectives

- Campaign planning and coordination
- Cost
- Allocation of responsibility
- Execution
- Feedback and review.

Further reading

Advertising Association (1993), *The Marketing Pocket Book*, NTC, Henley-on-Thames.

Bird, D. (1993), *Commonsense Direct Marketing*, 3rd edn., Kogan Page, London.

Cotterell, P. (1992), *Exhibitions: an exhibitor's guide*, Hodder and Stoughton, Sevenoaks.

Davies, M. (1992), *The Effective Use of Advertising Media*, 4th edn., Business Books, London.

Donaldson, B. (1990), *Sales Managment: Theory and Practice*, Macmillan, Basingstoke.

KDA Communications Group Limited (1993), *How to Choose the Right Advertising Agency*, Newcastle-Upon-Tyne.

Kotler, P. (1994), *Marketing Management: analysis, planning and control*, 8th edn., Prentice Hall International, New Jersey.

Lancaster, G. and Jobber, D. (1990), *Sales Technique and Management*, Pitman, London.

McCorkell, G. (1990), *Advertising that Pulls Response*, McGraw-Hill, Maidenhead.

Northover, J. (1990), *The Exhibitor's Handbook*, Kogan Page, London.

Smith, P.R. (1993), *Marketing Communications, An Integrated Approach*, Kogan Page, London.

Chapter 10
Fashion Marketing Planning

10.1 Introduction

Putting all aspects of a marketing mix together to achieve the goals of the organization is the most important fashion marketing task. Activities must be planned, coordinated, effectively implemented and the results monitored. This chapter deals with the fashion marketing planning process, beginning with a broad overview of the process of planning fashion marketing continuing with the central role of the mission statement and marketing objectives.

The analysis of marketing activities and the marketing environment by a marketing audit is described. A synopsis is given of SWOT (Strengths, weaknesses, opportunities and threats) analysis, a crucial underpinning to the development of a fashion marketing strategy. Consideration of strategic alternatives follows with reference to earlier material on segmentation and competitor analysis.

The chapter concludes by presenting a framework for producing a fashion marketing plan and examines some important issues concerned with the implementation of plans.

10.2 The planning process and objectives

10.2.1 The planning process

A marketing strategy is a specification of those markets the firm wishes to target with marketing activities and how competitive advantages are to be created and achieved. A marketing strategy is developed within the broader framework of corporate strategy and goals. The focus of this chapter will naturally be upon fashion marketing plans, but the whole context of the fashion marketing planning process should be kept in mind. Figure 10.1 shows the broader view of the process.

Fashion marketing planning has been described as a process. It is a continuous activity and if undertaken correctly should be self-improving. The process requires the setting and communication of standards, effective implementation or corrective action and timely feedback on performance. The starting point in the process is taken from the marketing objectives, although, as noted above, these are subject to wider corporate decisions.

10.2.2 The mission statement

The mission statement should begin by asking what business is the firm in and what kind of business would it like to be in? Normally this should be defined sufficiently broadly to allow flexibility but still be specific, for example, providing fashionable eveningwear and accessories rather than selling dresses. It also should be defined in terms of customer need, bearing in mind the firm's strengths in relation to the competition. Mission statements should be short and inspiring for company employees; they provide reasons for the firm's survival and growth and are a touchstone for judging corporate behaviour and development. Mission statements should be communicated to all interested stakeholders in the firm, employees, suppliers, customers and shareholders.

For example, Marks and Spencer has the aim of providing 'Quality, value and service in clothing' as part of its mission statement. The company also has a full range of operating principles that derive from the broad mission statement and these are communicated in the annual report and are used in advertising copy and personnel communication initiatives.

10.2.3 Marketing objectives

These will be more specific than the broad mission statement and will include quantified data such as profit levels, number of new business customers, market share, etc. As shown in Figure 10.1, marketing objectives derive from corporate objectives. The latter are broader and include all aspects of the company's operations like production, personnel and safety, as well as marketing objectives.

Marketing objectives should be clear, written, measurable and attainable, but still challenging. They also should be specific and stated in relation to time constraints. Two examples of marketing objectives are 'Our aim is to increase sales turnover from £9 500 000 to £10 500 000 in the next financial year, and

Figure 10.1 The fashion marketing planning process.

se the profit margin by 5%', and 'To increase the number of distribution
is from 16 to 21 within the next six months.'

keting audits and SWOT analysis

10.3.1 A marketing audit

To achieve marketing objectives the current situation must be analysed. Periodic
reviews of the marketing goals, operations and performance of fashion companies are known as marketing audits. The concept is very similar to financial
audit, unfortunately the former are carried out less frequently than the latter. The
marketing audit involves sets of detailed questions that are asked to determine
the status of the firm in relation to its objectives, customers, competition and
marketing environment. One of the main reasons for a marketing audit is to
identify areas where corrective action may be needed. The marketing audit is
usually organized into two main categories covering the firm's internal and
external environment.

The audit of the external marketing environment covers the items identified in
Chapter 2. Common frameworks adopted for the external marketing audit include
PEST or STEP analyses, both of which cover social, technological, economic
and political aspects of the environment. The framework in Chapter 2 elaborates
on the above factors and distinguishes between controllable and partially controllable variables that require monitoring and analysis. The external audit should
examine current activity and projected trends in both macro and micro marketing
environments. It is imperative that all assumptions are made explicit in the audit,
so that later modifications can be made to facts about developing events. For
example, an assumption about forecast inflation rates for the next twelve months
will have an impact upon the company's pricing policy. Thus data from the
Retail Price Indices can be used later, if necessary, to revise plans.

The scope of an internal marketing audit would cover detailed analysis of
sales, profits and market share data by product line and product range. As with
the external audit a series of questions are asked about objectives, activities and
achievement. For example, the adequacy of the size of the sales force may be
assessed in relation to changing distribution trends or the frequency of product
line deletions may be examined. The audit also may question how prices are set,
the sufficiency of data about competitors' prices or the effectiveness of dealing
with customer complaints. The whole range of marketing activities are subject to
audit and are judged against customers' perceptions and marketing objectives.

10.3.2 SWOT or situational analysis

The outcome of a marketing audit is usually a detailed document specifying
achievements and suggesting, where necessary, corrective action. Another use of
the audit is the construction of a SWOT analysis, which is also known as a
situational assessment of the firm. The SWOT, in essence, is the key issues
emerging from the audit.

Internal	Strengths	Weaknesses
	e.g. Functional areas Design expertise Location Facilities/Size	
External	Opportunities	Threats
	e.g. Competitor promotions Market trends in fabrics, etc. Customer attitudes to 'green' issues Intermediary activity Regulatory changes, etc	

Figure 10.2 Strengths, weaknesses, opportunities and threats.

SWOT analysis considers both internal and external factors about either the whole company or a particular fashion product line or range in relation to customers, competitors and trends in the marketing environment. Strengths and weaknesses concern internal factors and opportunities and threats concern external factors. Figure 10.2 shows some components of a SWOT analysis.

Obviously the marketing audit is a good starting point to prepare a SWOT analysis, however not all companies undertake regular marketing audits. The first marketing audit is invariably the most difficult for most companies as benchmarks or experience may be unavailable. Subsequent audits can begin with the preceding audit and marketing plan.

A few guidelines are given below to enable the preparation of a simple SWOT analysis. The SWOT should be concise, specific and communicate the key issues facing the firm. The items identified should be related to each other and not simply an *ad hoc* collection that doesn't point to future action. A clearly written analysis is helpful when it points to solutions or direct consequences. For example, 'A new outlet of a large competitor threatens our childrenswear department. Allow for a potential slow-down in sales turnover of 8–10% in next 12 months.' The alternative for the above childrenswear department may be to change the marketing mix to meet the threat more directly.

An important dimension of the SWOT analysis is the need for objectivity. This argument equally applies to the marketing audit. Fashion marketers charged with producing a marketing plan can sometimes be too close to the firm to be objective, as identifying certain weaknesses can be construed as admitting past failures. Outsiders, like marketing consultants, can bring a broader and more objective perspective, but they are expensive and they do take time to get to know the operations and procedures of the particular firm. At times, it can be most useful to employ a manager from another department or branch of the same company or a retired senior executive to bring objectivity coupled with company knowledge to help with the SWOT analysis.

10.4 Marketing strategy

10.4.1 Strategic choice and marketing tactics

If the marketing objective describes 'What' has to be achieved, then the marketing strategy details 'How' the objectives are to be achieved.

Marketing strategy consists of important long-term decisions to which the competition cannot react quickly. It is the relationship of the firm with its environment. As marketing is an activity that is closely concerned with that environment, there is often considerable similarity between the corporate and marketing strategies within a firm.

The terms strategy and tactics need to be distinguished. Strategy is doing the right thing and is ultimately the search for effectiveness. Tactics, on the other hand are doing things right, they lead to efficiency. Unfortunately, some firms who apparently don't believe in planning have allowed short-term tactics to override strategy as shown in the discussion of promotional pricing in Chapter 7. Therefore, deciding upon the correct strategy and moving in the right direction are important for firms and require considerable effort.

The SWOT analysis shows how the fashion firm will fare in the future and this should be compared with the marketing objectives that were established earlier. Often there will be a gap between objectives and the current situation and the larger the gap the more risky or adventurous the marketing plan must be.

From the SWOT analysis the firm should be able to make detailed assessment of the competition, its own distinctive strengths and which market segments to aim for.

10.4.2 Assessment of the competition

A framework for assessing the competition is the same as the one used for the SWOT analysis, and some sample questions are shown below:

- Employment statistics and levels of expertise
- Organizational structure
- Number and location of distribution outlets
- Manufacturing capacity and flexibility
- Links with intermediaries
- Market share statistics
- Key products and services offered
- Promotional expenditure and impact
- Customer service levels
- Market segments targeted and trends
- Price levels
- Growth status – whether contracting, stable or growing
- Particular challenges to the firm
- Areas of vulnerability from the firm.

10.4.3 Selecting marketing segments

Market segmentation involves identifying separate market entities, with different needs and characteristics, so that the firm may specialize the product offering or marketing programme by segment or target.

Market segmentation was discussed in detail in Chapter 5 along with consideration of a positioning statement for the firm. Segmentation strategies, such as concentration and multi-segment strategies were also described. Examination of the company's resources and the assessment of the competition, as determined in the sections above, should help to decide the precise strategy. Segment size, identification, profitability, access and stability also should be considered at this stage.

10.4.4 Determining a marketing strategy

The Ansoff matrix can be a useful tool to aid in the development of marketing strategy. A version of the matrix applied to fashion marketing is shown in Figure 10.3 below.

In the main, strategies are considered that offer new products or services to existing customers as in quadrant 2 or the same products or services to new market segments as in quadrant 3. High risk options should only be considered if the planning gap, identified above, is achievable given company resources. The higher the quadrant number in the above figure, the riskier the option.

Consolidation can be seen as a risk aversive strategy, however, under certain circumstances it can be a shrewd move. When the market is in recession or the company is facing restructuring, for example, a consolidation strategy may be the best option. Market penetration is simply achieving a greater share of existing markets and may be gained by offering comparative advantages in pricing or services or by more effective advertising.

Market development concerns the marketing of existing products in new markets. Thus a small fashion retailer may open another store in a new city or a

Fashion product or service

	Existing	New
Existing	1 Consolidation or market penetration	2 Fashion product or service development
New	3 Fashion market development	4 Diversification

FASHION MARKETS

Figure 10.3 The Ansoff matrix applied to fashion.

clothing manufacturer may start exporting to Japan. Sometimes market development may be evident when a new use for an existing product is found. For example, Harris Tweed may be used as trim in braces and belts as well as for outerwear and all items may be offered to the same market.

Fashion product or service development is the mainstay of most fashion marketing firms, although the rate of introduction of new market offerings varies considerably. This strategic option has been extensively discussed in Chapters 5 and 6.

Diversification is where new products are developed for new markets. The degree of difference from existing markets and products can range from marginal to massive, and the greater the difference the larger the risk. A minor form of diversification for fashion firms is vertical integration where, for instance, a manufacturer sets up or buys some retail outlets or *vice versa*. A company manufacturing mens' suits that enters the formal womenswear market would be making a relatively small change of direction and some expertise in design, manufacture and marketing may be transferable.

The most common move for fashion companies is into fragrance markets, Laura Ashley No 1 and Hugo Boss are two such examples. Where there are totally unrelated products and markets in a diversification move, then the organization is called a conglomerate. The licensing arrangements of some larger French fashion houses make them appear like conglomerates with home furnishing, sunglasses, cutlery, shampoo, cigarette lighters, and dozens of other non-clothing items all sold under the same brand name. The main benefit of diversification is to spread the risk of trading across more than one market.

Having selected the correct marketing strategy to pursue attention must be paid to more detailed planning. A marketing plan must be devised with specific marketing mix(es) for the selected target market(s).

10.5 The fashion marketing plan

The fashion marketing plan is a document that details marketing action for a specified period. It states what has to be done when, how and with what effect. The plan gives details of the marketing strategy and how the firm will achieve its marketing objectives. The plan also allocates responsibilities and resources, schedules major activities and enables senior management to monitor the implementation of the fashion marketing strategy.

There are variations in how a plan should be structured, these variations are minor and usually just reflect the house style of the fashion firm. The following sections cover the main components of a marketing plan.

10.5.1 Summary for senior management

This is self evident and usually centres on profits, sales and resources.

10.5.2 Marketing objectives

These should be stated concisely and be related to the mission statement.

10.5.3 Situational analysis or SWOT

As noted above the SWOT should be related to the competition and produce a coherent and related set of recommendations.

10.5.4 Marketing analysis

This is an assessment of market segment options, the competition, the marketing environment and major trends.

10.5.5 Marketing strategy

A statement of how objectives will be met by reference to segmentation and positioning of the product.

10.5.6 Marketing mix programmes

This section should detail product, price, distribution and promotional activities. This is probably the most detailed part of the plan as it states what is to happen along with the scheduling and coordination of activities. The plan should also show the allocation of tasks, accountability for implementation and costs of the activities.

10.5.7 Forecast results and budgeting

The forecast sales and profits from the plan should be given along with market share data and other relevant quantifiable criteria. Some firms place the expected results in the marketing objectives section. To facilitate calculations and comparisons, it is helpful to place revenue and profit data with information on costs and budgets. Some approaches to budget setting were described in Chapter 9. The total budget is derived from the marketing mix programme costs mentioned above.

10.5.8 Resourcing and implementation issues

This item is to outline any staffing or physical resources that may be needed to enable the plan to be effected. For example, the introduction of a marketing database, for direct mail activities aimed at regular customers, may have major implications for staff training in information technology and the purchase and maintenance of computer equipment. Possible resistance from staff or fashion intermediaries to certain strategic changes should also be identified along with recommended action to overcome or minimize negative effects. For example, the importation of garments made in a country that generates polarized political opinion may meet opposition from sections of the workforce or certain active consumer groups.

10.5.9 Marketing control and evaluation

Measurement of the plan is essential so that corrective action can be taken if necessary. Given the objectives and expected results specified above, this section of the plan details the frequency and nature of measurements to be taken. Mechanisms for comparing actual with planned results and the reporting procedures must be shown. Some plans incorporate contingency corrective action in the event of deviations from the plan.

10.6 Implementation and organizational issues

10.6.1 Planning horizons

The timescales for fashion marketing plans vary considerably. All plans are related to the fashion calendar, usually two seasons as noted in Chapter 6. They are also linked to the target market and the nature of the product lifecycle. Chapter 6 also described product lifecycles from the high fashion fad to the fashion classic and these are major factors in the timescales adopted in the fashion marketing plan. All planning may be carried out for a variety of purposes, but one should strive never to forget its most basic function which is demonstrated in Figure 10.4.

Planning helps in anticipating and avoiding proble

Figure 10.4   The value of planning – an irony.

Most fashion firms will have long-range plans lasting from three to five years or longer, medium-term plans for one to three years and short-term plans that may cover one season or up to a year.

All three types of plan need to be coordinated, therefore short-term plans become part of medium-term plans and so on. The more complex and changeable the marketing environment that the firm faces, the greater the tendency to need long-range plans and to review fully and update those plans regularly. Except for a very small minority of firms supplying stable items of clothing, possibly functional classic items like uniforms, most fashion firms are confronted by a volatile and competitive marketing environment.

10.6.2 Organizational culture

Another factor influencing marketing planning is the organizational culture of the firm. As noted in Chapter 1, fashion is about change and many managers, in coping with the demands of immediacy, adopt a short-term perspective. Large parts of the fashion industry do appear to lurch from one deadline to another, with the consequence that many managers concentrate on dealing with daily matters and short-term issues. Given the high failure rate of fashion firms and the constant uncertainty in the market, many managers feel that long-term planning is of limited value compared to concentrating on doing immediate tasks well. Another factor inhibiting long-range planning is the mobility of staff within the fashion sector. High labour turnover and head-hunting (staff poaching) activities can mean that staffing changes can jeopardize the planning process and the security of marketing plans from the competition.

The establishment of a marketing plan, particularly in a rapidly changing environment can mean a substantial change of resources within the marketing department of a fashion firm. For example, the decision to place more emphasis on support for retailers via in-store promotion and merchandising may mean a reduction in the advertising and publicity budgets. These changes also may mean staff redeployment or redundancies that can demoralize staff and lead to reduced enthusiasm for implementation of the plan. The lesson to be learned is that encouraging participation in the marketing planning process and concern for, and communication with, those involved in implementation is crucial for success.

10.6.3 Management styles

The previous sections argue that planning for the long term, within the fashion sector, is difficult. It is important to note that long-term plans are essential for survival and growth, and that means commitment from senior management to long-term planning. The approaches adopted by some fashion executives can be summarized by the management styles shown below:

- **Management by conjecture:** i.e., Why worry about the future?
- **Management by crisis:** i.e., Let's deal with problems when they arise
- **Management by subordinates:** i.e., Each fashion marketer does their own thing
- **Management by prayer:** i.e., Things will get better, we hope!

The flaws in each style above are easily spotted, the approach advocated in this text is management by objectives, as described in an earlier section.

All fashion firms should plan for the long term. The resources and energy they allocate to that process are a function of the target market, organizational culture, product life cycles, the particular marketing environment and the commitment from senior management. A prudent approach for many fashion firms seems to be to plan on a rolling principle so that short-term plans always exist and they are reviewed and modified appropriately to meet new circumstances and challenges.

10.7 Summary

This chapter has dealt with further marketing planning, covering:

- the organizational mission
- marketing objectives
- marketing strategy.

Strategic alternatives were further examined in relation to:

- marketing audits
- SWOT analysis.

Strategic marketing plans can be constructed more easily in the light of the information thus obtained. The chapter concluded by emphasizing the importance of adequate long-range planning in the context of organizational culture and management styles.

Further reading

Dibb, S., Simkin, L., Pride, W.M. and Ferrell, O.C. (1994), *Marketing: Concepts and Strategies*, 2nd European edn., Houghton Mifflin, Boston.

Lancaster, G. and Massingham, L. (1993), *Marketing Management*, McGraw-Hill, Maidenhead.

McDonald, M. (1989), *Marketing Plans: How to prepare them: How to use them*, 2nd edn., Heinemann, London.

Piercy, N. (1992), *Market-Led Strategic Change*, Butterworth-Heinemann, Oxford.

Walker, O.C., Boyd, H.W. and Larreche J.-C., (1992), *Marketing Strategy: Planning and Implementation*, Irwin, Boston.

Glossary of Fashion Marketing Terms

Advertising is persuasive and/or informative non-personal communications paid for by a clearly identifiable sponsor.

Break-even analysis shows the relationship between fixed costs, variable or marginal costs, total costs, sales revenue and output or volume.

Causal research is used to determine the relationship between variables, e.g. the relationship between advertising and repeat purchases.

Concessions, also known as *shops-within-shops*, can be defined as space leased by the host retailer to another retailer, wholesaler or manufacturer from which to sell its merchandise.

Consumer behaviour provides a framework for identifying consumer needs and target markets, and enables the anticipation of consumer responses to marketing action.

Cooperative promotions are where two or more channel members share the cost of a promotion.

Cost plus pricing is simply calculating the cost of raw materials, labour and overheads, and adding an amount to cover profit in order to arrive at the selling price.

Demographics is the study of changes in the size and make up of the population.

Descriptive research provides an accurate description of the variables uncovered by the exploratory research.

Exploratory research is an attempt to uncover any variables that may be relevant to the research project as well as an investigation of the environment in which the research will take place.

Family life cycle is an attempt to classify people according to the age of head of household, marital status, and the age and number of children.

Fashion is about continuous change, clothing and related products and services, and the exercise of creative design skills. *Fashion* is a current mode of consumption behaviour applied specifically to clothing products and related services.

Fashion classics can usually be seen as the midpoint compromise of any style, i.e. total look or composite effect. Colour and pattern may vary, but the classic customer does not seek the satisfaction of a new seasonal experience in the way that the fashion and fad counterparts do.

Fashion fads will meteorically rise in popularity only to suffer an abrupt decline as they become adopted. As a fad becomes fashionable it also becomes unfashionable.

Fashion marketing is the application of a range of techniques and a business philosophy that centres upon the customer and potential customer of clothing and clothing related products and services in order to meet the long term goals of the organization.

Fashion marketing concept attempts to embrace the positive aspects of high concern for design, customers and profit by recognizing the interdependence of marketing and fashion design personnel.

Fashion marketing plan is a document that details marketing action for a specified period. The plan gives implementation details of the marketing strategy and states how the firm will achieve its marketing objectives.

Fashions usually have a slower rise to popularity, plateau with continuing popularity and then decline gradually; often this cycle relates to a season, whether autumn/winter or spring/summer.

Franchising is a contractual relationship between franchiser and franchisee in which the franchiser offers, or is obliged to maintain, a continuing interest in the business of the franchisee in which areas as knowledge and training; wherein the franchisee operates under a common trade name, format or procedure owned by or controlled by the franchiser, and in which the franchisee has made or will make a considerable capital investment in his business from his own resources.

Geodemographics are systems derived from statistical analysis of census variables to discover residential areas, usually census emuneration districts, that are linked to purchasing behaviour and media usage.

Innovation is anything the consumer perceives to be new, and could include an 'old' product introduced into a new market.

Lifestyle or **psychographics** is a classification of consumers based on activities, interests and opinions (AIOs).

Markdown is where profit is expressed as a percentage of the sale price.

Market-based pricing is founded on market research to find the optimum selling price which then acts as the main driving force upon cost containment via design and quality control effort.

Market penetration pricing tries to capture a large market share by charging low prices. The low prices charged stimulate purchases and can discourage competitors from entering the market as the profit margins per item are low.

Market research is used to refer to research into a specific market, investigating such aspects as market size, market trends, competitor analysis, and so on.

Market segmentation is where the larger market is heterogeneous and can be broken down into smaller units that are similar in character.

Market skimming pricing charges high initial prices and then only reduces prices gradually, if at all. A skimming price policy is a form of price discrimination over time.

Marketing is both a way of thinking about the firm from the perspective of the customer or potential customer, and a management process concerned with anticipating, identifying and satisfying customer needs to meet the long term goals of the organization.

Marketing analysis is an assessment of market segment options, the competition, the marketing environment and major trends.

Marketing audits involve sets of detailed questions that are asked to determine the status of a firm in relation to its objectives, customers, competition and marketing environment.

Marketing environment is all the influences beyond the control of fashion companies that affect marketing action. It includes consideration of the social, cultural, technological, economic and political contexts within which fashion marketing occurs.

Marketing intermediaries are the main channels that help to get fashion products and services from the manufacturer to the consumer.

Marketing mix describes the specific combination of marketing variables used by a fashion marketer to meet the needs of specific groups of customers known as target markets. It comprises decisions made about products, prices, promotion, services and distribution that are assembled in a coherent and profitable way to represent what the firm is offering to the consumer.

Marketing research covers investigation into all aspects of the marketing of goods or services, such as product research and development, pricing research, advertising research, distribution research, as well as all the aspects of market analysis covered by market research.

Marketing strategy is a specification of those markets the firm wishes to target with marketing activities and how competitive advantages are to be created and achieved.

Markets are places for buying and selling, for exchanging goods and services, usually for money. To constitute a market there should be a genuine need, the customer(s) should be willing and able to buy the fashion product and the aggregate demand should be sufficient to enable a supplier to operate profitably.

Markup is where profit is expressed as a percentage of costs.

Mass marketing assumes all customers in a market are the same. It is based on the idea that customer needs do not vary and that the company can offer a standardized marketing mix that meets the needs of everyone.

Multi Fibre Agreement (MFA) came into existence in 1974 as a temporary expedient and is basically a framework for regulating trade in fibres, fabrics and clothing between developing low cost countries and the industrialized countries.

Multiples are businesses with at least ten outlets selling predominantly one merchandise group, i.e., clothing or shoes.

Niche marketing is where a clearly defined segment is targeted with a narrow product range.

Opinion leadership refers to the degree of influence exerted in a given choice situation.

Perception is the process whereby buyers select, organize and interpret simple stimuli into a meaningful and coherent picture of the world.

Personal selling is interpersonal promotion carried out by the sales staff of a retailer, wholesaler or a manufacturer.

Positioning is to do with the perception by the target market of the firm and its marketing mix. Positioning is how customers see the market, although that perception may have been influenced by marketing action.

Price is the point at which exchange between buyer and seller takes place, where supply and demand are equal. Price is the amount of money that is exchanged for fashion products and/or services.

Product can be defined as anything that can be offered in the marketplace that might satisfy a need. Products may be classified as convenience, shopping or speciality goods.

Product life cycle is based on the proposal that all products have a finite 'life cycle' that can be plotted over a given period using the biological analogy of growth, development and decline.

Product mix or **product range** is the assortment of fashion products a company offers for sale at any point in time.

Promotional mix is the particular combination of promotional methods and media used by an organization to achieve its marketing communication goals. It includes advertising, sales promotions, public relations and selling.

Publicity is media coverage that is not paid for and has a mass audience and a high level of credibility.

Public relations aims to establish and maintain a favourable image through a pre-planned, long range programme by communicating with its publics including consumers, suppliers, shareholders, trade customers, employees, unions, Government, pressure groups and the local community.

Sales promotion involves promotional activities that add value to fashion products or induce consumers or intermediaries to buy or provide an incentive for channel effectiveness.

Sampling involves selecting a small number of people from the larger survey population whose characteristics, attitudes and behaviour are representative of the larger group.

Social class refers to divisions of people according to their economic position in society, whether they are aware of that position or not.

SWOT (*strengths, weaknesses, opportunities and threats*) analysis considers both internal and external factors about either the whole company or a particular fashion product line or range in relation to customers, competitors and trends in the marketing environment.

Variety chain stores sell a variety of merchandise. The four major variety chain stores with a significant clothing turnover are BhS, Marks and Spencer, Littlewoods and, to a lesser extent, Woolworths.

Index